LEGENDARY LOCALS

OF

METAIRIE

LOUISIANA

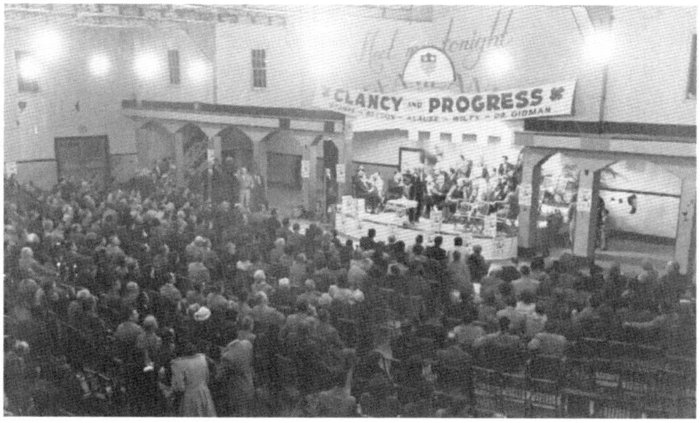

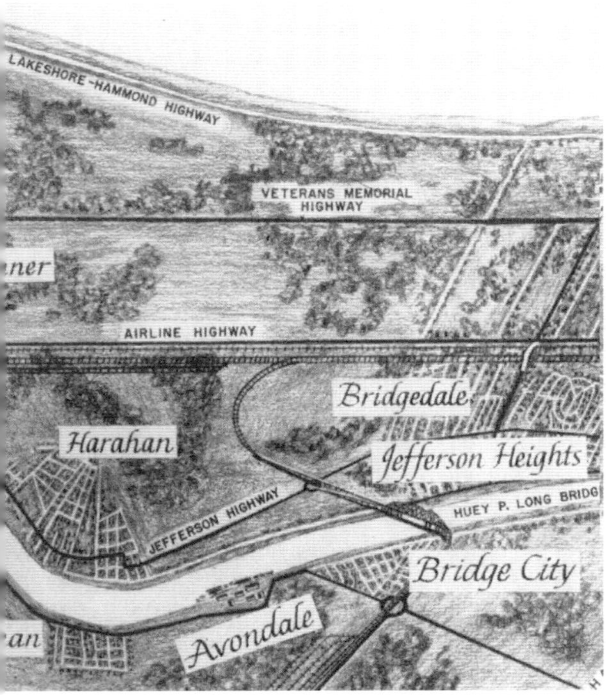

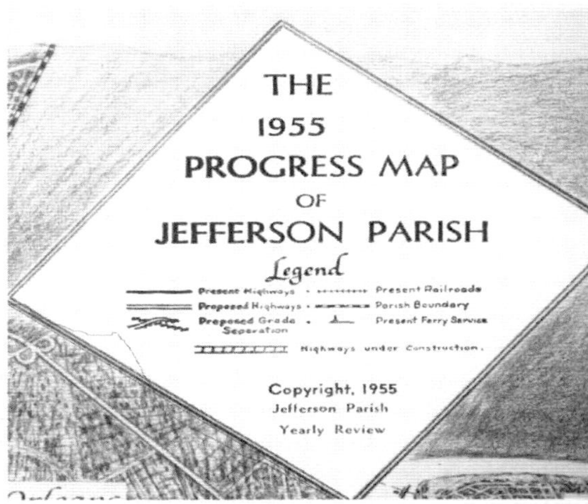

Progress, 1955
On February 18, 1954, ground was broken for Veterans Highway by parish president John J. Holtgreve. There were few homes or businesses in sight. Although Old Metairie and Bucktown near the lakeshore were well populated, the majority of Metairie was still unsettled. From the late 1950s to the 1970s, many suburbs would spring up from this boggy land. (*Jefferson Parish Yearly Review.*)

Page 1: Dreamland
In 1952, Sheriff Frank Clancy held a political rally at a large hall just off Metairie Road near Causeway Boulevard. "Clancy and Progress," read the banner that barely concealed the hall's slogan: "Meet me tonight in Dreamland." The building is long gone, as is the sheriff, but folks continue to attempt to make their dreams come true in Metairie. (Time-Warner.)

LEGENDARY LOCALS

OF

METAIRIE

LOUISIANA

CATHERINE CAMPANELLA

LEGENDARY LOCALS

ISBN 978-1-4671-0060-1

Legendary Locals is an imprint of Arcadia Publishing
Charleston, South Carolina

Printed in the United States of America

Library of Congress Control Number: 2012950062

For all general information, please contact Arcadia Publishing:
Telephone 843-853-2070
Fax 843-853-0044
E-mail sales@arcadiapublishing.com
For customer service and orders:
Toll-Free 1-888-313-2665

Visit us on the Internet at www.arcadiapublishing.com

Dedication
To Lily

On the Cover: From left to right:
(TOP ROW) Rufus Cressend, Rummel mascot namesake (Courtesy of Rufus Cressend; see page 106); Norma Latino, musician (Courtesy of Henry and Anne Harmison; see page 46); David Ferrie, alleged Kennedy conspirator (Courtesy of United Press International, see page 82); Ellen Degeneres, entertainer (Courtesy of Alan Light; see page 114); Eddie Krass and Vince Campanella, friends and community volunteers (Courtesy of Julie Krass Kroper; see page 125).
(MIDDLE ROW) Carlos Marcello, racketeer and G. Wray Gill, attorney (Courtesy of United Press International; see page 81); Dave Treen, governor (Courtesy of John Andrew Prime; see page 92); Leigh "Li'l Queenie" Harris, singer (Courtesy of Eliot Kamenitz; see page 111); Mike Azzarello, community volunteer (Courtesy of Roxanne Varnelle; see page 115); Peter Gennaro, dancer and choreographer (Author's collection; see page 78).
(BOTTOM ROW) Tom Dempsey, NFL kicker (Author's collection; see page 85); Shirley Ann Grau, writer (Courtesy of the Louisiana Digital Collection; see page 61); Scott Walker, broadcaster (Courtesy of Scott Walker; see page 103); Mahalia Jackson, gospel singer (Courtesy of the Associated Press; see page 86): Becky Allen and Rickey Graham, entertainers (Courtesy of Mid City Theater; see page 116).

CONTENTS

ACKNOWLEDGMENTS

Thanks to Antonio Deano Assunto, Mike Azzarello, Meredith Azzarello Brayden, Harry and Dolly Breaux, Angela Burise, Nathan Burise, Meredith and Vincent Campanella, Rufus and Yvette Cressend, Matthew Dillon, Charles B. Dupre, Henry and Anne Harmison, Leigh Harris, Jerry Hendrick, Paula Hoefeld, Julie Krass Kroper, D.C. "Infrogmation" May, Joan Bonnabel Fasterling Meyers, Linda Ohrabka, Dawn Romano, Hazel Romano, Denise Broussard Sassone, John "Jack" Schott, Chef Frank Sclafani Sr., Roxanne Varnell, Bob Walker, and Carlyle Dana Vann for their generous help.

The following abbreviations are used throughout the book to attribute image sources:

(AP)	Associated Press
(HNOC)	Historic New Orleans Collection
(JPYR)	*Jefferson Parish Yearly Review*
(LDL)	Louisiana Digital Library
(LOC)	Library of Congress
(TP)	*Times-Picayune*
(UPI)	United Press International

Unless otherwise noted, all other images appear courtesy of the author.

INTRODUCTION

There are few American cities so richly endowed with the blended spirit of as many nationalities as New Orleans. And so it goes that Metairie, an entity of itself but also an offspring of the city, would be comprised of the same rich mixture and become every bit as colorful. It just took Metairie longer to grow up, for various reasonable reasons that will be discussed here.

Large swatches of land were granted—from Lake Pontchartrain to the Mississippi River—by the French government during the early 1700s. Plantations were established by the Du Breuil, Chartier, Chauvin, and Labarre families, but large-scale agrarian development proved impossible. While New Orleans, the bustling Queen of the South, was booming with industry, financial institutions, and one of the greatest of America's ports during the mid-1800s, Metairie was still mostly undeveloped, with only the high ground along the ridges of the river, the lake, and Bayou Metairie (which ran alongside Metairie Road) used for farming, pasturing, and nurseries. The Bonnabel, Betz, Fagot, Bertucci, Maggiore, Barousse, Rolling, Persigo, DeLimon, Vincent, Marrero, Masset, Eastman, Friedrichs, Arnoult, Riviere, and Papworth families moved in around the turn of the 20th century.

The word "Metairie" first appeared in the *Daily Picayune* in an advertisement on May 10, 1827, alerting readers that a stray mule had been found on Mr. Hazeur's property and would be sold by the Fourth of July if not claimed. A June 16, 1883, advertisement offered "FOR SALE – 25 GOOD MILCH [dairy] COWS with young Calves. Apply to ALFRED BONNABEL, Metairie Ridge, 1 1/2 miles from Halfway House." Even into the middle of the 20th century, Metairie was largely rural. Advertisements in 1945 offered "four fresh cows with calves and farm equipment – 731 Carrollton St.," cows at 201 Zinnia, a bull at 52 Metairie Heights, and a horse at 102 Oaklawn Drive.

Public education was an early priority, thanks largely to the Bonnabel family. Alfred Bonnabel, who served on the school board for 36 years, dedicated Metairie's first public school in Bucktown in 1908 and donated land for the second on Metairie Road, which opened in 1909. Religious education was introduced by the Theresian Sisters, who set up a mission in 1850. In 1906, Salesian nuns visited one day each week to instruct Italian children on Metairie Ridge (the high land along what is now Metairie Road).

Local lore paints old Bucktown/East End as what could have been known as "The Town that Care Forgot" or "Metairie's Most Interesting 'City.' " It was the most densely populated area of Metairie during the early years, teeming with fishers and trappers, families, drinkers, and gamblers. But mostly, it was rich with families. The Brunings were Bucktown/East End pioneers who settled during the 1850s and acquired much land along the lakeshore. They were followed by the Boutall, Werner, Rapp, Swanson, and Shultz families, to name just a few.

Like New Orleans, Bucktown could have been called "The Birthplace of Jazz," but then so could Metairie Ridge. Both abounded with gambling joints—some plush, some plain—and most providing entertainment with a dance floor and a jazz band. The greats who regularly played here included Peter Bocage, Papa Celestin, Jules Baudic, Albert Brunies, Louis Armstrong, and Armond Piron. Paul Mares, Monk Hazel, Doc Souchon, Johnny Wiggs, Frank, Fred, Papa Jac Assunto, and Betty Owens Assunto performed and lived in Metairie.

Most often turning a blind eye to the gambling were sheriffs John B. Dauenhauer, who served from 1920 to 1928, and Frank Clancy, who was in office for 28 years (1928 to 1956). Clancy testified to a senate crime commission during the 1950s that gambling had flourished here for 100 years and that a candidate could not be elected on an antigambling ticket. And this was the truth, so help him, Gawd.

Metairie became a gambling mecca when Orleans Parish officials cracked down on city gamblers. They merely crossed the parish line to Metairie, where establishments advertised suburban "restaurants" and "clubs." Before there was the exclusive Metairie Country Club in Old Metairie, there was Ballard's "Metairie Country Club" along the Seventeenth Street Canal owned by Fred P. Miller, who was arrested in 1921 by Sheriff Dauenhauer, only after being ordered to do so by Parish district attorney Conrad Buchler because Sen. A.H. Johness had filed a suit alleging that the "Metairie Country Club" was a gambling house. Fred A. Middleton was the defense attorney. Witnesses for the defense included Alexis Dumestre, Eli Watson, Gretna's mayor, alderman, and a candidate running for city marshal, a Jefferson Parish police jurist and grand jury member, and a state board of health inspector. The club's officers were Fred Miller, president; J.M. Bakewell, vice president; C.L. Purcell, secretary-treasurer; E.P Ephram; and T.D. Clark, board member. Jefferson Parish grand jury member J.J. McLachlan was the alleged doorkeeper. Front-page headlines reported the proceedings: "Courthouse Filled With Spectators . . . BALLARD'S FIGHTS FOR LIFE . . . OBJECT OF LEGAL ONSLAUGHT," but in the end Judge Prentice Ellis Edrington Jr. dismissed the case.

Gambling was wide open but was organized by individuals, unlike what evolved later when organized crime stepped into "The Free State of Jefferson." Gov. Huey P. Long, professed foe of gambling, pressured Clancy, and in 1929 the sheriff issued a warning to gaming establishments—but that was temporary at best. In 1951, Sheriff Clancy declared that he still allowed illegal gambling because it provided jobs for about 1,000 aged and otherwise unemployable people. When running for office, he promised voters that, regarding gambling, he would be "as dry as the Sahara Desert." It was not until 1953, after Sen. Estis Kefauver brought Jefferson Parish gambling into the national spotlight, that Clancy declared that he "saw the light." Gambling continued, but it was on a smaller, low-profile scale.

Metairie Road was the first major artery—an ancient naturally occurring ridge through surrounding lowland and swamps. Monsignor Henry C. Bezou, ordained in 1938, pastor of St. Francis Xavier from 1967 to 1983 and the author of *Metairie: A Tongue of Land to Pasture* (the first definitive history of the unincorporated area), when interviewed by the *Times-Picayune* in 1981, said, "I'll tell you my theory for why Metairie Road developed the way it did. Very large tracts of land were held by a few families and very few of them had any desire to sell. It just so happened that many of the older owners were dying out at the time of the boom period that followed World War II. So this led naturally to the development of the land around Metairie Road, as the large old tracts were subdivided."

The 34-block stretch called Metairie has gone by different names through the years. In the early days, it was known as Metairie Ridge Road (which leads to confusion because City Park Avenue was also known as such). During the 1910s, it was often referred to as Jefferson Highway, Shrewsbury, and LA 611-9 (still in use). In the 1920s and 1930s, it was called State Route 1, US 61, and Airline Highway. The last common usage of Metairie Ridge Road occurred around 1947.

Many Metairie street names are family names. The Arnoult streets originate from Pierre Gervais Arnoult's plantation. Beauleau Street recalls the early settler Louis Chauvin de Bealieu. Bore Street is named for the Bore plantation, where sugar cane was first successfully processed. Dwyer Street is named for William Joseph Dwyer, city marshal in 1928 and a leading advocate for incorporation of Metairie as a town. William Mason Smith owned land from the lake to the river next to Lafreniere (also a street) property. William Edenborn was president of the Louisiana Railway & Navigation Company. Frank Fagot, grocer and first modern suburb developer, has a street off Metairie Road named for him. Max Ferran and Joseph A. Neyrey were builders. Before there was a Hessmer Street, there was Hessmer Farm. Harry Papworth, an English horticulturist, bought land at the turn of the 20th century from Metairie Road to the lake with six blocks fronting Metairie Road for $4,000. James and Joseph Turnbull were early-1900s real estate brokers and developers. Builder and real estate developer Fred S. Simonson named a street for his daughter Sena. St. Rene Street comes from the Sainte-Reyne plantations—the earliest in Metairie. Charles Tolmas was also a real estate broker and developer. Other street name origins are included in the following chapters.

Just a few of those who call or called Metairie home included here are entertainers Peter Gennaro, Ellen Degeneres, Becky Allen, John Pela, Phil Anselmo, the Nobles, and the Glory Rhodes. Writers of note include Leon Soniat, Shirley Ann Grau, Helen Prejean, William S. Burroughs, and Bunny Matthews. Sports figures Dave Dixon, Tom Dempsey, Mike Miley, Buddy Dileberto, Craig Steltz, Dick Nolan, Jim

Mora, Otis Smith, and Mel Ott all have lived in Metairie. Entrepreneurs include Al Copeland, Al Scramuzza the Doerr/Mutter family, the Radostas, the Fitzgeralds, the Swansons, the Sclafanis, Merlin Schaefer, John Schwegmann, Alfred Danziger, Phil de Gruy, Jerry Hendrick, and Steven Bel.

Broadcasters Laura Buchtel, Bob Walker, and Scott Walker as well as politicians David Duke and Dave Treen all have lived here. Crime figures David Ferrie, Gordon Novel, Perry Raymond Russo, Dean Andrews, Phil Kastel, and Carlos Marcello made their homes in Metairie.

The route of Veterans Highway was approved in 1953, and in 1956 Jefferson Parish president John J. Holtgreve broke ground for the first span of the Causeway bridge linking Jefferson Parish to Lake Pontchartrain's north shore. Nothing has been the same since. Metairie boomed with new housing, schools, churches, and businesses, many of which still exist today. Had Metairie been incorporated, by 1986 it would have been the second-largest city in Louisiana.

A century earlier, in the spring of 1893, an article appeared in the *Daily Picayune* announcing that George J. Friedrichs, of Baumgarden & Friedrichs, had recently sold 120 acres of land on Metairie Ridge—a mile above Friedrichsruhe (a land development Friedrichs also had a hand in). Friedrichs declared, "It's more than likely that some improvement will be made" there.

Then, on March 13, he auctioned lots on Canal Street on the opposite side of Friedrichsruhe. The land was bounded by Canal, Napoleon (now named South Hennessey), Alexander, and Cleveland Avenues—a full square block, four blocks from the Jewish Cemetery near what was then Metairie Road and is now City Park Avenue. Friedrichs's advertisement for the sale included these words: "Canal Street is the axis upon which the life of the city evolves. Canal Street will continue to be the main artery of the city long after you and I are dead, rotten, and forgotten."

George J. Friedrichs's visionary views came to pass—and made him a very rich man. When streetcars ("electric traction") connected Canal Street to Metairie Road, the once quite country land began to populate with New Orleanians. Large swatches of land in Metairie were subdivided. Old roads were improved and new ones constructed. New businesses, schools, and churches opened to serve the growing population. Swamplands were drained. Unfortunately, verdant, oak-laden, richly fertile country land was converted into streets and sidewalks, residential lots, and parking lots—the price paid for "progress."

Those who built the streets in Metairie as well as those whose names now mark them (including Friedrichs) are included in the following chapters of this book. We must remember, however, that none would exist had not nature formed the first one: the Metairie Ridge. A historical marker proclaims that, had not the Metairie Ridge existed, neither would New Orleans, for it was the high land that linked the city to Bayou St. John and the lake that allowed for early trade and commerce. As important as the geological makeup are the people who formed this community that has endured for centuries. Metairie owes a great debt to New Orleans, which was its cultural lifeblood. The mother-city's offspring now carry new traditions while cherishing the old. This book brings attention to many from Metairie whose talents and efforts have contributed to the richness of New Orleans and the world.

CHAPTER ONE

Visionaries

Claude Joseph Villars Du Breuil was the first European settler in Metairie, arriving in 1710. By 1724, he built a levee (the first in the area) to protect his plantation. This was the predecessor of the Mississippi River's original levee system. Pierre Chartier de Baulne, the French attorney general of the Superior Council of Louisiana, settled in 1719. French Canadian brothers Louis Chauvin de Beaulieu, Nicolas Chauvin de La Frenière, and Joseph Chauvin de Léry came one year later. We can thank Nicolas Chauvin for the word chauvinism, which evolved from the French *chauvinism*, defined as "from a character noted for his excessive patriotism and devotion to Napoleon."

Francois Pascalis de La Barre, a colonial official, was granted a river-to-lake tract in 1750. In 1847, land inherited by his heir, the late J. Volante Labarre, was listed for sale. DuBreuil, Chartier, and Chauvin's land would also be sold and divided, coming into the hands of other families.

Pierre Gervais Arnoult settled in 1827. The Bonnabels came to New Orleans around 1830, but Alfred did not permanently move to Metairie until later. The Trudeaus arrived in the 1840s. Next came the Betz family, who acquired land north of Metairie Road. John N. Betz was born here in 1847. His daughters Louise and Cora married into the Riviere family. Hog Alley was owned by Peter Betz (it became Ingleside Heights). Rosa Avenue is named for John Betz's wife, Rosina. Part of his large tract of land was the Metairie Kennel Club greyhound track. The DeLimons lived on Focis Street in what was one of the oldest homes near Metairie Road and near the Louisiana Kennel Club, whose land they owned. On their property (now DeLimon Place condominiums, formerly Do Drive-In) was an antebellum schoolroom and an early Marconi Wireless Telegraph Company of America wireless radio tower.

Theodore Bruning arrived in Bucktown in the late 1850s and built what would become the third-oldest restaurant in the greater New Orleans area. He married Mabel Hamilton. Sons John and Theodore were well known and loved as rescuers of people in peril on Lake Pontchartrain and the Seventeenth Street Canal. News of John's death in 1963 appeared prominently on the front page of the *Times-Picayune*, memorializing his lifesaving heroics and 20-plus years of service on the Jefferson Parish School Board, his founding of the East End Volunteer Fire Department, and his time served as a deputy sheriff and jailer of his "town."

Next to arrive in Bucktown were the Boutalls. Charles's children, all born in Bucktown, were Jeanette Boutall Woest, whose artwork appears below: Edward D., who married Joseph Bruning's daughter Bertha; and Charles Arthur, who married John Bruning's daughter Lillian. Their son John C. became the judge of the 24th Judicial Court of Jefferson. Lillian's niece Amelia Werner married Sam Urrate. Sam and Amelia ran Bruning's Restaurant until it was destroyed by Hurricane Katrina.

Ralph Shultz, Bucktown commercial fisher and hunter, lived in and opened a general store/bar in what was the town schoolhouse on Lake Avenue. It survived late into the 20th century, as did he. One of his 10 siblings, Grace, married John C. Bruning. Other Bucktown entrepreneurs included William Rapp and members of the Tranchina family who have owned and operated Rapp's Luggage since 1917. Frank William Turan Swanson and wife, Julia Pfeiffer, lakefront residents since the early 1900s, opened Swanson's Seafood in 1926. Half of the building was in Jefferson Parish, the other in Orleans. A line was drawn to indicate which was which, and gambling thrived on the Metairie side. Frank also served as deputy sheriff and operated the Bucktown jail. Swanson's closed in 1979, when grandson Danny Mayer passed away. The Swanson seafood legacy lives on today at Dennis' Seafood, owned and operated by grandson Dennis Lacoste and his wife, June.

Fitzgerald's Seafoods Restaurant was opened in 1932 by Margaret (Bruning) and Maurice J. Fitzgerald, who had married in the old home of her parents on the lake. Their children worked beside them. Maurice Jr. took over after his parents died. He later opened Le Chateau Phylmar in his childhood home on Old Hammond Highway in Bucktown. Maggie Hemard bused tables at Fitzgerald's until 1957, when she opened a little shack, set picnic tables outside, and called the place "Maggie and Smitty's Crabnett."

Back in Old Metairie, horseback-riding constable Charles Root, who used the Camp Parapet powder magazine for a jail, settled in 1888. Frank Fagot came around 1900, acquiring some 200 acres. He opened a general store and in 1911 developed Metairie Heights, the first modern subdivision in Metairie. He was the parish tax collector, and atop the store at Metairie Heights Avenue at Metairie Road he ran a gambling house. In the store, his wife, Florida I. Hanna, was Metairie's first postmistress in 1914.

Eli Watson built his Metairie Road mansion in 1911. He reigned as Rex, "King of Carnival," in 1927 and in 1928 opened the world's longest bridge: the Watson-Williams bridge from New Orleans to Slidell, which he built and owned. It survived Hurricane Katrina and is still used today.

Alfred D. Danziger's name was honored in 1988 when the Danziger Bridge opened over the Industrial Canal as the world's widest lift bridge. The Metairie attorney was also Mayor Robert Maistri's executive council and Gov. Huey P. Long's personal lawyer.

These and other visionaries are included in this chapter highlighting those who settled in the rural area that Metairie was during their lifetimes. These were optimistic people moving to a remote and mostly uncharted place. They whittled homes, farms, and businesses from an ancient forest surrounded by swampland, bayous, Lake Pontchartrain, and the Mississippi River. Some foresaw what was to come. Some actively endeavored to shape Metairie's history. All were pioneers.

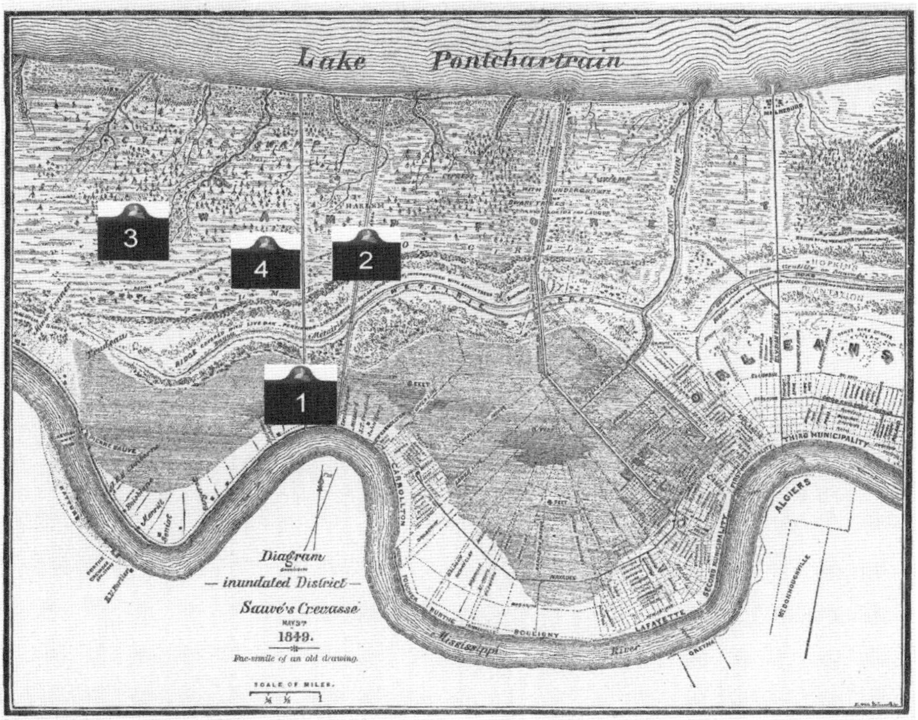

Early Settlers

The land that Friedrichs and many others bought, subdivided, and sold first belonged, of course, to Native Americans. Then came Europeans and French Canadians, who were granted concessions running from the Mississippi River to Lake Pontchartrain. The first of these was Claude Joseph Villars Du Breuil, who settled in 1710 in a home near what is now Ochsner Hospital. He built the first plantation and levee in the area that would become the predecessor of the winding Mississippi River's levee system created in 1724. Du Breuil's land and improvements allowed him to become the wealthiest man in Louisiana. Timber from it was used to construct the Ursuline Convent—the oldest building in the New Orleans area. His home was located near where the number 1 appears on the map.

Pierre Chartier de Baulne, French attorney general of the Superior Council of Louisiana, settled in 1719. He possessed the earliest land grant at the former village of the Colapissa tribe on the Chemin des Chapitoulas (now Metairie Road) in the area near the Jefferson/Orleans Parish line. His land stretched from Bayou Metairie/Metairie Road to Lake Pontchartrain—number 2 on the map.

The following year, Governor Bienville granted a concession to three French Canadian brothers: Louis Chauvin de Beaulieu, Nicolas Chauvin de La Frenière, and Joseph Chauvin de Léry. What is now Lafreniere Park was part of the holding of Nicholas Chauvin LaFreniere, attorney general of Louisiana from 1763 until his death. He led a revolt against the Spanish rulers and was executed by them on October 25, 1769. The Chauvin land is indicated by number 3 on the map.

The Merriam-Webster dictionary notes that the word chauvinism is derived from the French *chauvinisme*, "from Nicolas Chauvin, character noted for his excessive patriotism and devotion to Napoleon in Théodore and Hippolyte Cogniard's play *La Cocarde tricolore,* written in 1831, a full 62 years after his death. La Freniere's sister Barbe Therese and her husband, Ignace Hubert de Bellair, were early settlers; Bellair Drive was named for her.

Colonial official Francois Pascalis de La Barre was granted a river-to-lake tract in 1750. He and his family acquired so much more that, by the 1800s, a large section of Metairie was known as "La Plaine Labarre." The first sheriff in the area was Andres Valsin de la Barre in 1825. Labarre Road is named for the de La Barre family and is designated by number 4 on the map.

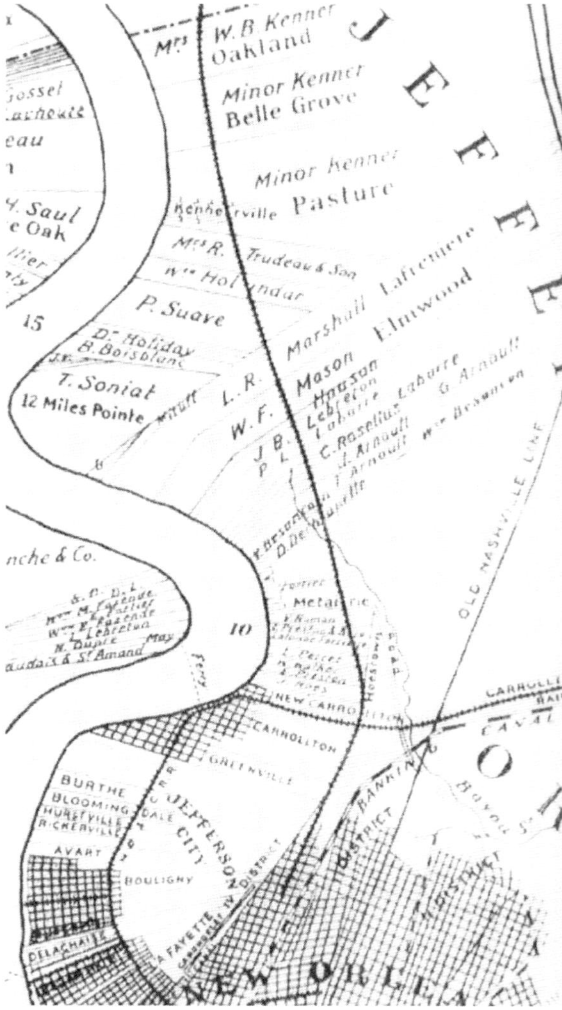

Familiar Names

By the mid-1800s, parcels of the original concessions were sold to those whose names appear on this map. Kenner family lands had been established and familiar Metairie names now seen on street signs include Trudeau, Lafreniere, Elmwood, Labarre, and Arnoult. (Tulane University Special Collections.)

Gen. John Wolcott Phelps

Established in 1861 by the Confederacy, Camp Parapet was captured and used by the Union army for most of the Civil War. General Phelps organized over 300 "contrabands" (escaped slaves from nearby plantations) into three regiments, drilling them daily. He then requested that his superior, Gen. Benjamin Butler, supply them with arms to defend the area. Butler refused and instead sent axes for felling trees and tents to house the men. He proclaimed Phelps "mad as a March hare."

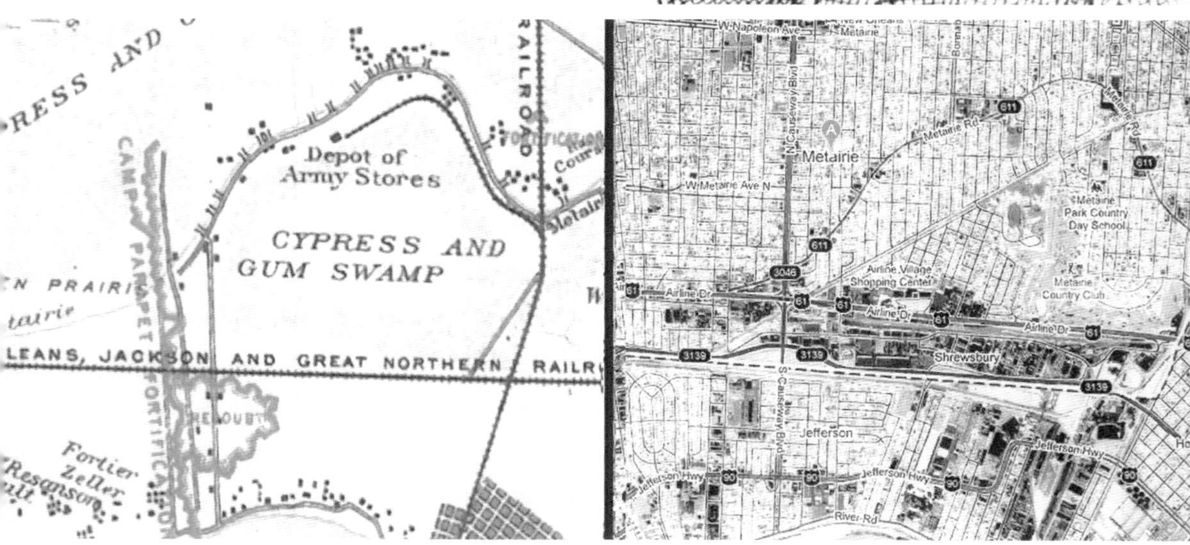

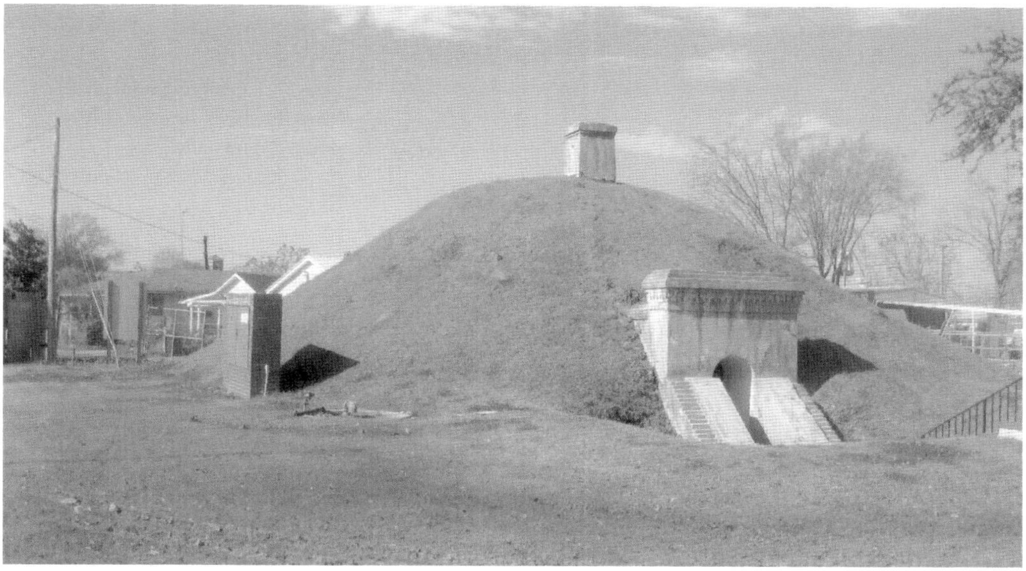

The Root Family

Charles Root moved to Metairie in 1888, built his home on Metairie Road at Dorrington Boulevard, and lived there until his death in 1935. He was a horseback-riding constable who used the Camp Parapet powder magazine (pictured) as a jail. He and his wife, Louise Comment, raised seven children and were blessed with 17 grandchildren. Root was a founding member and deacon of Metairie Ridge Presbyterian Church (established in1920), and an active member and officer in the Democratic Parish Committee for 40 years. (D.C. "Infrogmation" May.)

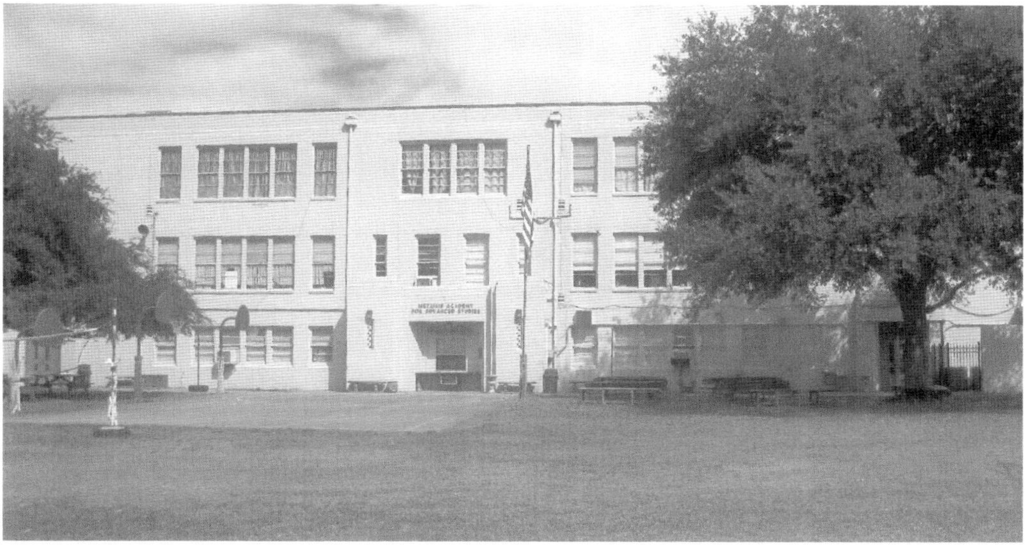

The Riviere Family

Pierre Ernest Riviere married Victoria Rodriguez, acquired this property in1884, and built a one-story farmhouse that was used by his daughter Valentine as a school. Valentine's siblings were Lydia, Joannes, Edwin, Albert, Ernest, and George (page 17). Both Ernest and George married into the Betz family (pages 11, 31, and 34). Since 1972 the Riviere name lives on, as the East End/Bonnabel School was renamed for its longtime principal, Marie B. Riviere.

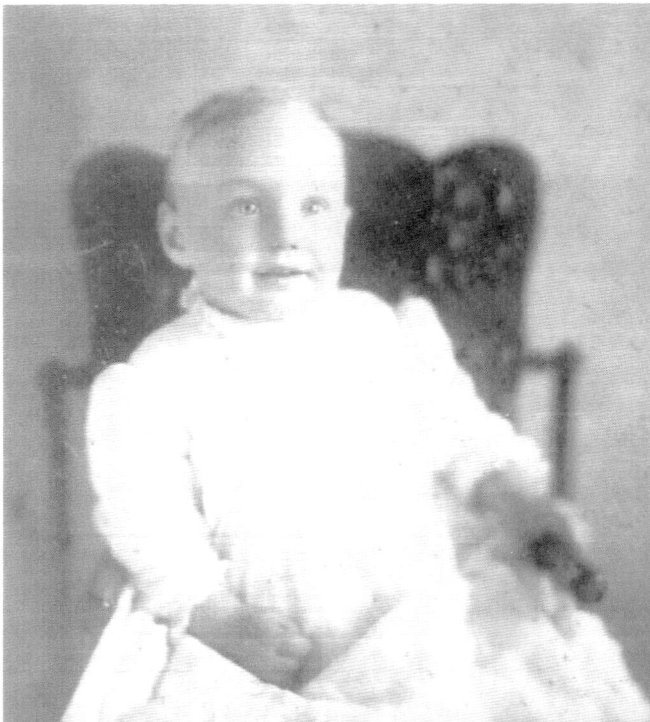

Bonnabel Family
Frenchman Anne Henry Jules Alexandre Bonnabel came to New Orleans around 1830 and married Irish born Julia McCarthy. They had eight children, including Henry Adolph Jules (pictured) and Frederick Eugene Alfred. Frederick's son Alfred (1874–1961) is considered the father of education in Jefferson Parish. (Joan Bonnabel Fasterling Meyers.)

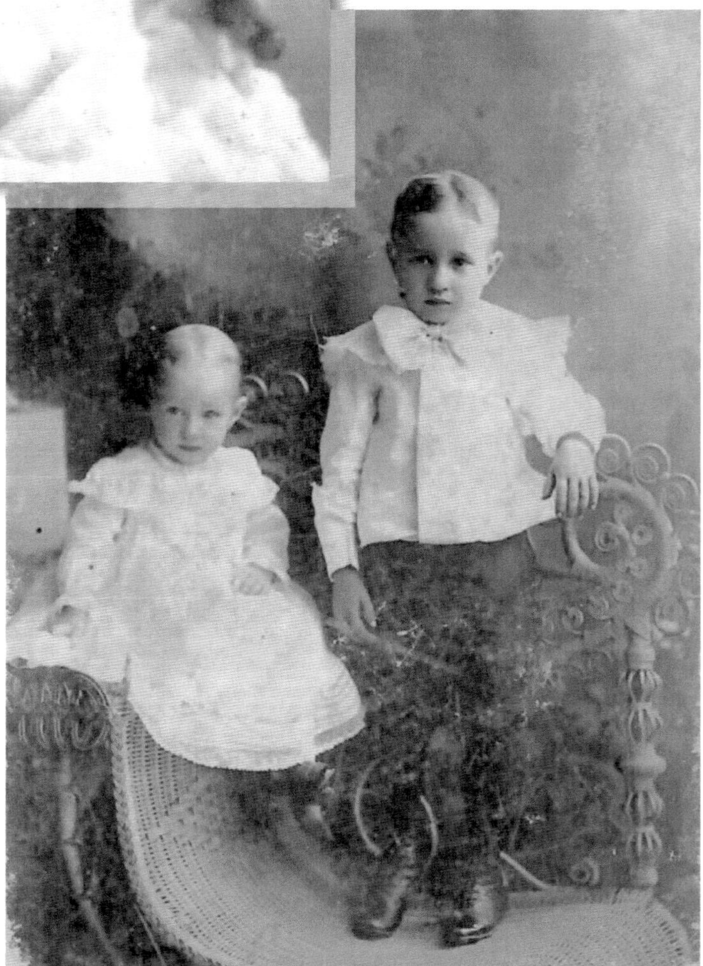

Bruning Family
Bertha Wallace Bruning and her brother Henry Joseph "Sun" Bruning are pictured here in West End in 1910. Bertha married Edward Boutall, brother of Charles, Lillian, and Edward. Members of the large Bruning clan have deep roots in Bucktown and West End. Henry and Bertha are great-grandchildren of Theodore Heinrich Bruning, who came to the area in the late 1850s. (Linda Ohrabka.)

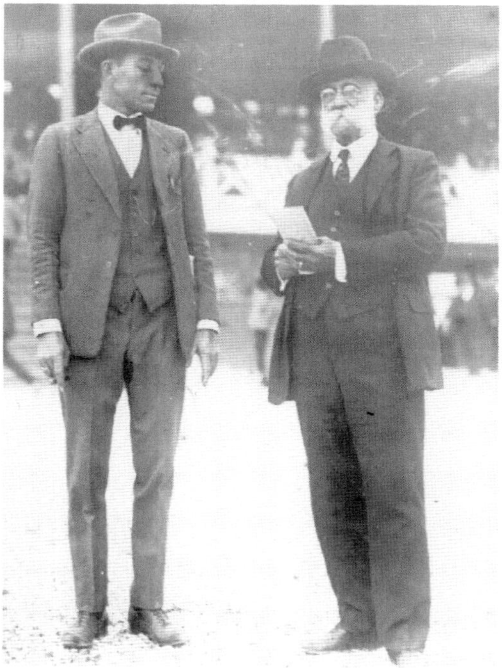

Riviere and Arnoult

Descendants of two of the earliest pioneering families in Metairie, George Riviere, son of Pierre Ernest, is shown here with Louis Edgard Arnoult (right) at the Jefferson Racetrack in 1910. The Arnoults settled in 1827. The Rivieres came a decade later in 1836, when Metairie was still much undeveloped. (John "Jack" Schott.)

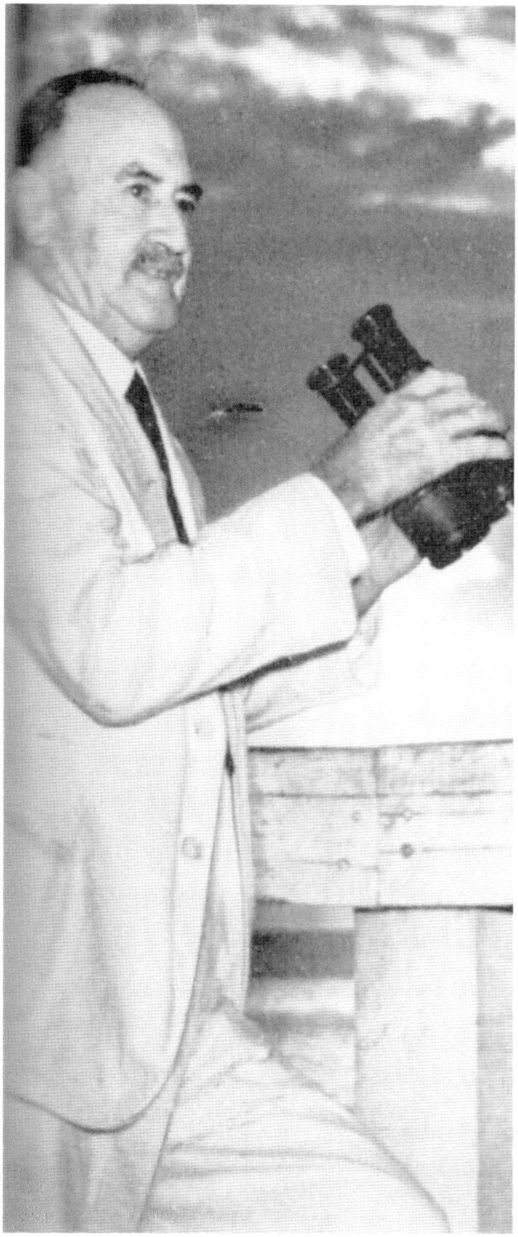

John C. Bruning

Born in Bucktown in 1872, John C. Bruning is pictured here watching out over Lake Pontchartrain, which he called home his entire life. He is the son of Theodore Walter (1847–1917), the son of Theodore Heinrich. He was an honorary captain in the Coast Guard, a commendation he received for rescuing hundreds of people from Lake Pontchartrain. Captain Bruning passed away in 1962. (JPYR.)

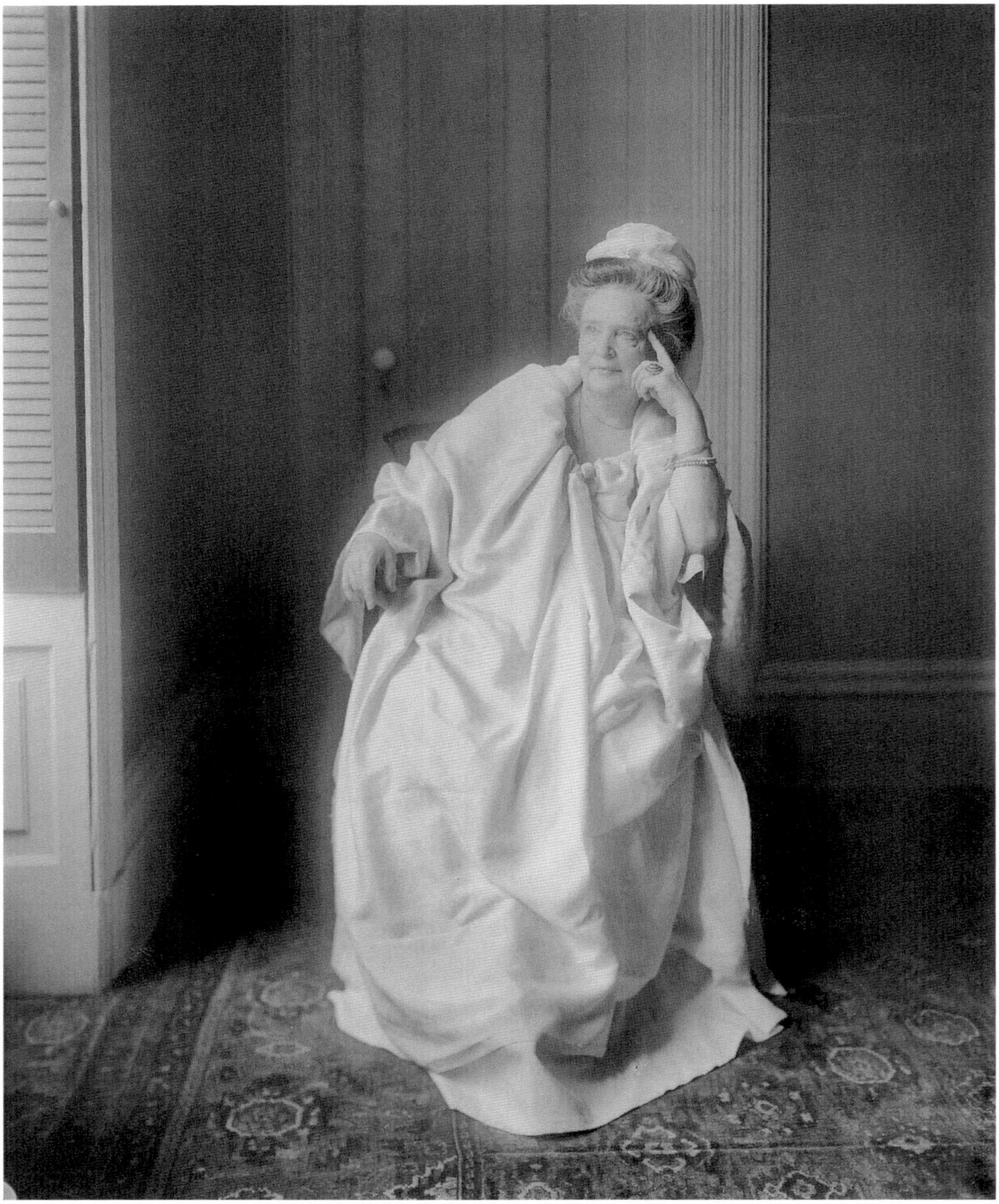

Swami in Bucktown

In New Orleans in the fall of 1898, Frank Dutton Jackson married Widow McGowan, Princess Editha Lolita, Baroness Roschthal, Countess of Lendsfeldt, daughter of Ludwig I King of Bavaria, and Lola Montez Countess of Lendsfeldt. In truth, she was Ann O'Delia Solomon, a swindler with many aliases including Madame Dis De Bar, and Swami Laura Horos. Harry Houdini called her "one of the most extraordinary fake mediums and mystery swindlers the world has ever known."

Mayor Flower ordered the couple to leave town or go to prison. They went to Bucktown, rented a house, and advertised in the local newspapers. Within days, they were told by Jefferson Parish sheriff Marrero to leave or else a committee of citizens would burn them out of their new home. They chose to leave Bucktown, made their way back to New Orleans, and spent 30 days in jail. (*New York Times.*)

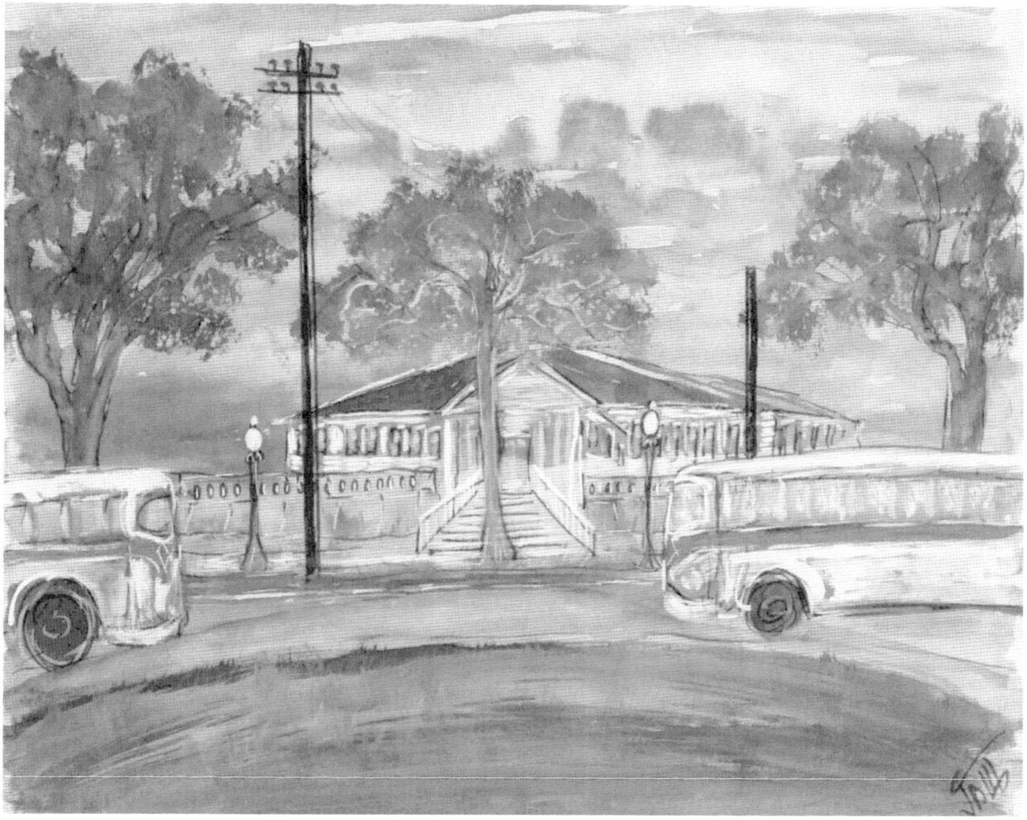

Watercolor Memories
Self-taught artist Jeanette Boutall Woest, born in the fishing village of Bucktown during the early 1900s, documented her community as she remembered it in her youth. Her daughter Dianne Audrey Woest donated her mother's diary as well as 67 of her drawings and paintings to the Historic New Orleans Collection. Four of them are in this chapter, including this one titled "My O My Nite Spot West End Park." (HNOC.)

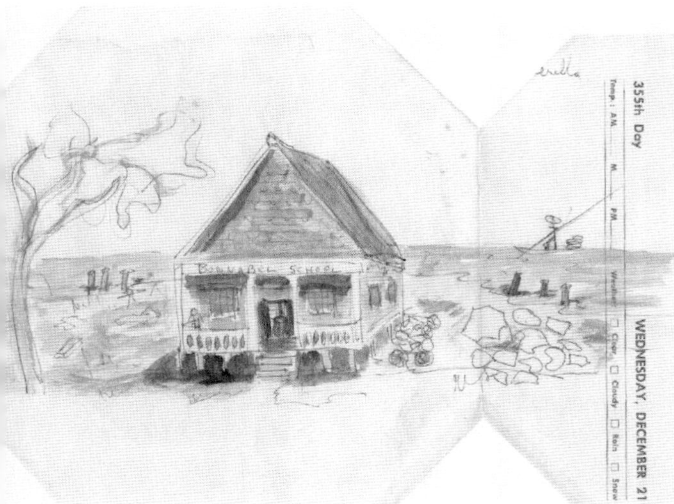

Father of Education
Alfred Bonnabel, parish school director who served on the school board from 1872 through 1918, dedicated this two-room schoolhouse in Bucktown on June 14, 1908. For the occasion, the little building was decorated with palms and flags, a string orchestra played, and food was served by Mrs. John C. (Mabel) Bruning and Mrs. E. (Amelia) Werner. Also in attendance was Adolf W. Shultz, superintendent of schools, whose son Ralph would later call the schoolhouse home. (HNOC.)

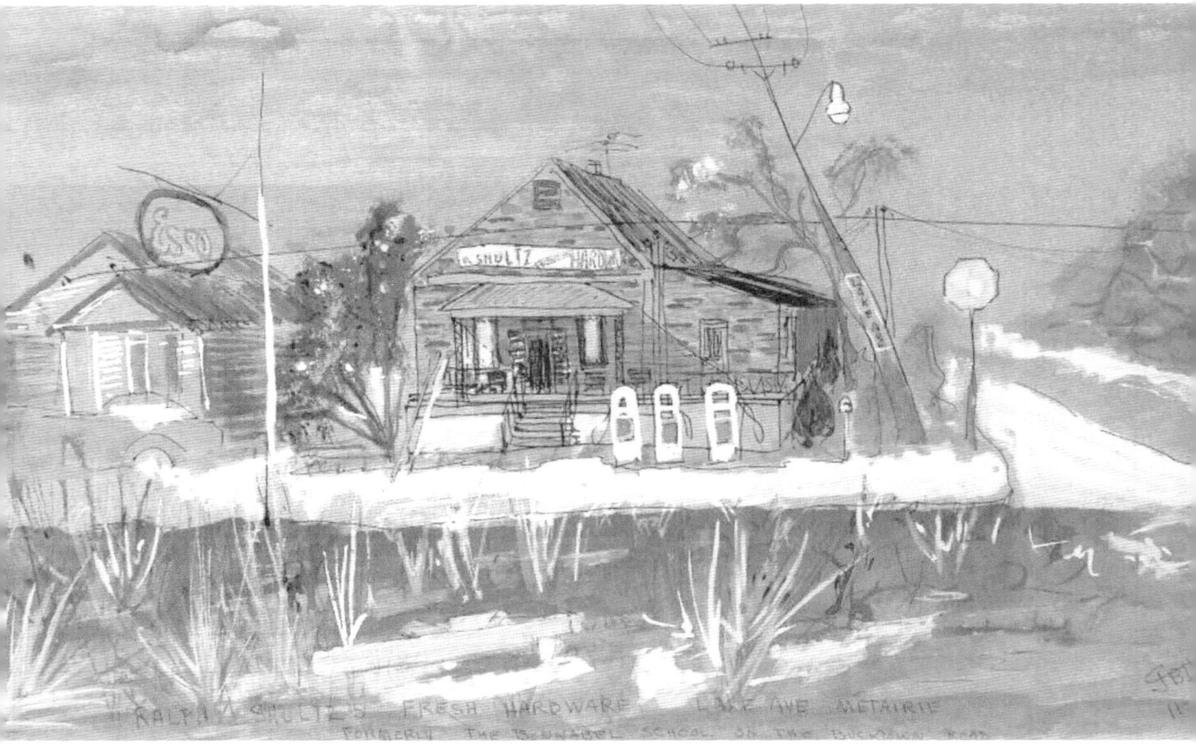

Fresh Hardware

Here is the artist's 1968 painting of R. Shultz's Fresh Hardware and residence at 1720 Lake Avenue. Local legend says that Ralph added "Fresh" to his general store and bar sign during Prohibition to let patrons know he had a fresh keg of home-brewed beer on tap. He also sold trawl, crab, and crawfish nets, bait, tackle, boats, motors . . . just about anything needed to capture the bounty of the lake.

A commercial fisher and hunter, Shultze was also a visionary. During the 1950s, he was an outspoken representative against the banning of commercial fishing in Lake Pontchartrain and for government intervention in improving its ecosystems.

In 1962, while the Mississippi River Gulf Outlet (MRGO) was under construction, he noted, "Surely it can be understood that more water will pour in [into the lake] should a severe hurricane strike" and called for an additional lock at the lake on the Industrial Canal to prevent gulf water from surging into the lake. He also noted that "At present Chef Menteur and the Rigolets channels pour water into the lake."

In 1963, he brought attention to the Louisiana Department of Wild Life and Fisheries (LDWF) that shell dredging allows lime to "sweeten" the lakewater, making it less salty and detrimental to life. He called on the agency to study this issue. In 1965, 1968, 1969, and 1972, he blamed the accidental killing of small shrimp by trawlers on the LDWF's opening the season before the shrimp matured. Always one to buck the system, Shultz sometimes publicly admitted to ignoring LDWF mandates and spent three days in jail in 1960 for killing 11 ducks, one coot, and a rail out of season. In 1961, he opposed a proposed one-mile marina extension into the lake near Bonnabel Boulevard, saying time and money would be saved if it were instead a half-mile long (it was, in fact, built only a few blocks long).

Ralph had 10 siblings, including Mrs. John C. (Grace) Bruning. In 1975, at the age of 76, he was crowned king of the Blessing of the Fleet celebration when he was one of the oldest men in Bucktown still active in fishing and crabbing. He was a founding member of the East End Volunteer Fire Department, a deputy sheriff, and member of the Bucktown Fisherman's Association. He died in 1994 at the age of 95. His home and store are gone. (HNOC.)

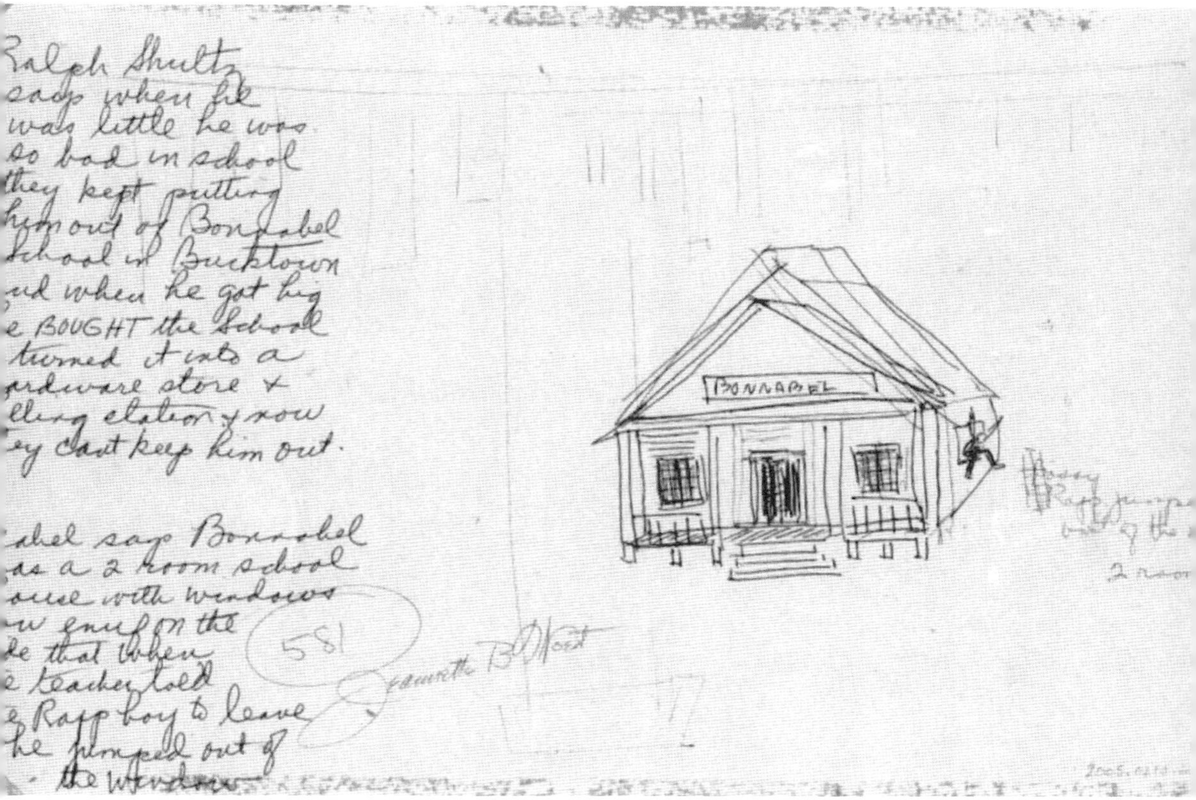

First Families in Bucktown

The artist wrote on the back of this painting, "Ralph Shultz says when he was little he was so bad in school they kept putting him out of Bonnabel School in Bucktown and when he got big he BOUGHT the School & turned it into a hardware store & filling station & now they can't keep him out . . . Mabel [Hamilton Bruning] says Bonnabel was a 2 room school house with windows low enuf on the side that when the teacher told the Rapp boy to leave he jumped out of the window."

William Rapp and Shultz grew up to serve together as officers of the East End Democratic Club in 1927 along with fellow Bucktownians Charles Root Jr., Frank Swanson, Jules Swanson, Charles Boutall (the artist's father), and Theodore and John C. Bruning (who married Ralph's sister Grace).

Around the turn of the century, William Rapp's father, John, and uncle George took over John's father-in-law's Duffy Trunk Store on Baronne Street, which had been established in 1865, and renamed it Rapp's Trunk Store. George's daughter Estelle married Anton C. Tranchina (also of Bucktown), who became a partner in the business. The Tranchina/Rapp family has operated Rapp's Luggage since 1917 with as many as six locations including one not far from Bucktown at 3250 Severn Avenue.

The Boutall family had long lived in Bucktown in a large home on the water. Jeanette's brother Edward D. married Bertha Bruning (daughter of Joseph Bruning). Brother Charles Arthur married Lillian Bruning (daughter of John C. Bruning and Mabel Hamilton) and became executive assistant and vice-president of the East Bank Water Works. His son John C. was the judge of the 24th Judicial Court of Jefferson. Lillian's niece Amelia Werner married Sam Urrate, who kept Bruning's Restaurant alive until Hurricane Katrina destroyed it and the Bruning home completely in 2005. (HNOC.)

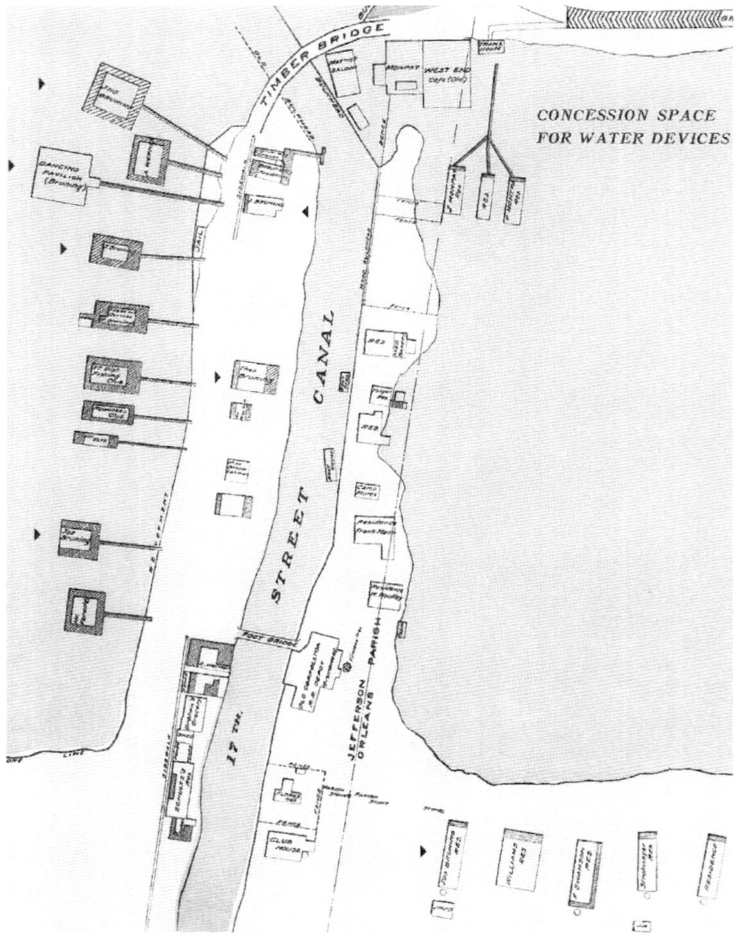

Guardians of the Lake

For several generations in Bucktown and West End history, the Brunings were known and loved for their volunteer efforts to save lives along the shores they called home. When Theodore Bruning III died in 1914 of typhoid malaria, the headline included, "He saved others, himself he could not save." The article included the fact that "father, son, and grandson, all with the same name 'Theodore' and John C. have been heroic life savors in Lake Pontchartrain for years." When Capt. John Charles Bruning died at age 91 in 1963, the news appeared on the front page of the *Times-Picayune*, noting his 20-plus years of service on the Jefferson Parish School Board, the one-day closing of the schools in his memory, and the many lives he and his family had saved through the years.

These quiet heroics (they did not accept monetary thanks and seldom acknowledged awards) began in 1859 when several restaurants were opened along the shoreline near the Seventeenth Street Canal. In that year, Theodore Bruning moved his Carrollton restaurant to Bucktown/East End. In 1882, he leased No.16, Revetment Levee, West End from the City of New Orleans for $150 per year. His son continued the restaurant business, and his grandsons opened a boathouse and fishing supply business. A storm destroyed the restaurant, which was rebuilt on the Jefferson Parish side of the peninsula that jutted out past the canal. The Original Bruning's Restaurant, which, for a time, featured dancing waitresses and rows of slot machines, operated over the lake until Hurricane Georges badly damaged it in 1998. The restaurant moved to Federico's on-land building next door, where Bruning's served seafood until Hurricane Katrina decimated the area. Bruning's was the third-oldest restaurant in New Orleans; only Antoine's and Tujaques predated it.

In 1893, Capt. John C. Bruning built the landmark family home, which was later washed away in Hurricane Katrina. This property can be viewed on the map, along with six other structures (all marked with an arrow) built by members of the Bruning family as of 1914. The jail, which the family operated as sheriffs, is also included. From his lookout on the roof of his home, Captain Johnny continued to watch over swimmers and boaters. During the early 1900s, he owned and operated the White Squadron: 42 white fishing boats (16 and 18 feet long) that he rented for 50¢ per day. After a 1910 fire devastated his community, he organized Bucktown's volunteer department.

Note on this 1914 map that the Ralph Shultz home/schoolhouse is included in the lower left. (LDL.)

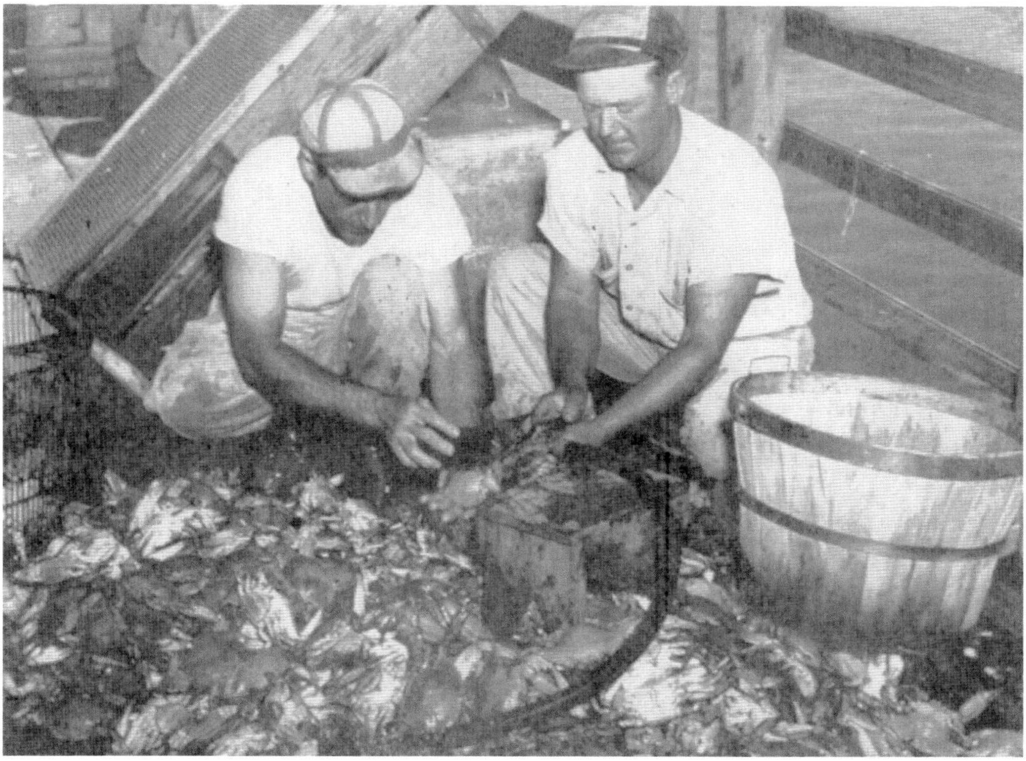

Swanson's Sea Food

In 1922, Frank William Turan Swanson (whose residence appears on the 1914 map in the lower right) opened the Yellow Dog Saloon, serving all the boiled seafood customers could eat as long as they imbibed his 10¢ schooners of beer. In 1926 he opened Swanson's Sea Food Restaurant, whose floor was clearly marked with a line designating which half of the building was located in Jefferson Parish where gambling was illegal, which was mostly ignored by local authorities. He fished and hunted to supply the restaurant in which his wife, Julia Pfeiffer, worked. Frank is seen here preparing crabs for cooking.

A May 1948 fire destroyed the restaurant and the neighboring My-O-My Club (Bruning's had minor damage). Frank and Julia rebuilt the business, which became so popular that celebrities such as Guy Lombardo dined there. By 1953, Swanson's boasted of "Delicious seafood in air-conditioned bliss." Frank passed away in 1956 at the age of 64. As a youth he had been an outstanding swimmer with the East End Athletic Club and had hunted ducks and snipe for market, bringing large bags of birds to buyers at East End who shipped the goods far and wide. He was known as one of the best marksmen in the area and was widely acknowledged as an outstanding fisherman—one of the first to catch a tarpon within city limits on Lake Pontchartrain. He also served the community as deputy sheriff and operated the Bucktown jail. The Swansons had lived at 1849 Orpheum Street.

In 1968, Vincent Aiavolasiti took over the restaurant and added "aged K.C. Steaks and authentic Italian food." In 1975, Bill Summers stepped in and renamed it "Swanson's Flagship." The restaurant returned to Swanson ownership in 1978 when Danny Mayer, grandson of Frank and Julia, bought the business. When Danny passed away in 1979, the doors were closed for good. In October 1984, the building burned to the ground.

The Swanson family legacy lives on. In 1975, Frank and Julia's grandson Dennis Lacoste and his wife, June, opened Dennis' Seafood on Lorino Street, some 4.5 miles from the original Swanson's Restaurant. (LDL.)

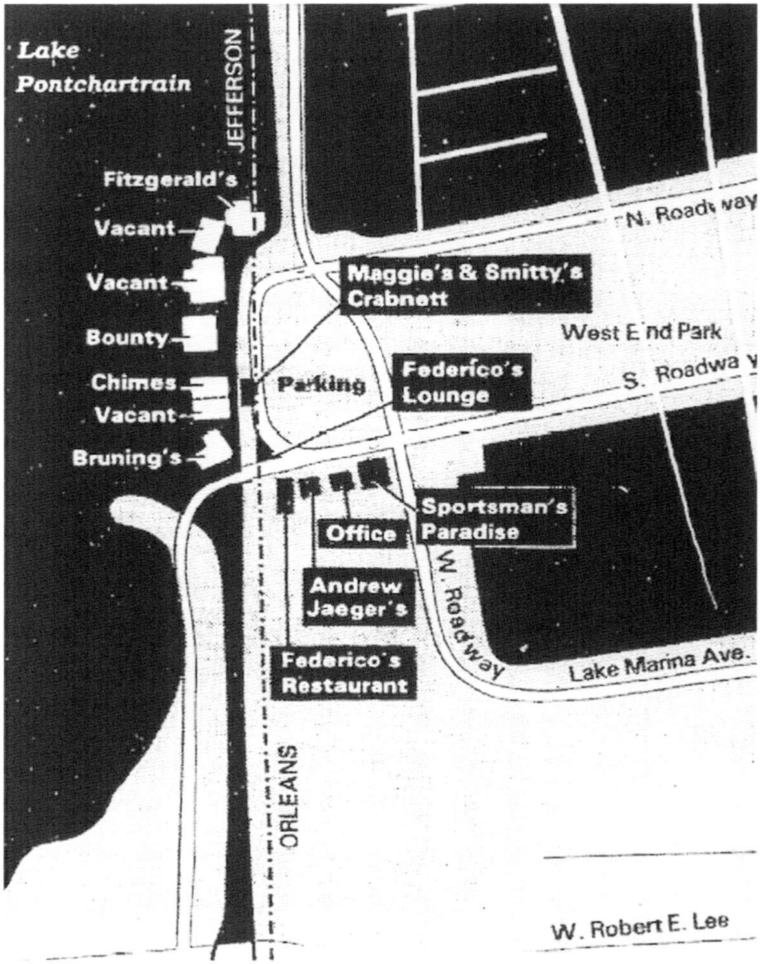

Fitzgerald's

In 1915, Margaret Bruning and Maurice J. Fitzgerald celebrated their wedding at the Bucktown home of her parents. They opened Fitzgerald's Seafoods Restaurant in 1932 and later moved to a larger, 7,000-square-foot building at 1928 West End Park (shown on the map of restaurants existing in 1987). Their son, daughter, and their spouses joined the ranks. For a time, there were gambling and slot machines as readily available as the fried softshell crabs and boiled seafood. In 1960, the wide porches were enclosed, and a 30-ton air-conditioner was added—gone were the lake breezes. Hurricane Hilda damaged the restaurant in 1964, but the family repaired it and kept it going strong. Margaret and Maurice celebrated their 50th wedding anniversary there in 1965 at the ages of 67 and 78 years. Margaret passed away in 1966. Maurice died in 1976.

Maurice Jr. took over the kitchen and management and ran the business very well, but by the 1980s, the glory days of West End had come to an end. Maurice sold the restaurant in 1989, but it continued in operation until Hurricane Georges damaged it beyond repair in 1998.

In 1981, Maurice Jr. converted his parents' home at 324 Hammond Highway into "an exquisite, small French Chateau" he named Le Chateau Phylmar. In 1985, he and his wife, Patricia, enlarged and renovated it, printed the menu in French, and continued to serve fine food. He was the first certified executive chef in Louisiana and taught in the Delgago College Culinary Arts Program. He passed away in 2008 at the age of 85.

Also in the illustration, labeled in the center, is Maggie and Smitty's Crabnett—a very casual on-land location for hot boiled seafood and cold beer. Maggie Hemard opened the little place in 1957 after learning the trade busing tables at Fitzgerald's. Co-owner Lloyd "Mr. Red" Hemard said in 1987 while lamenting the demise of business at West End, "It's very depressing out here. It was a great thing we had. We had good business, a family trade, we made a good living. But that's pretty much over. I'm burned out. The good days are gone. I'd sell it tomorrow if it weren't for Maggie but she wants to stay." (TP.)

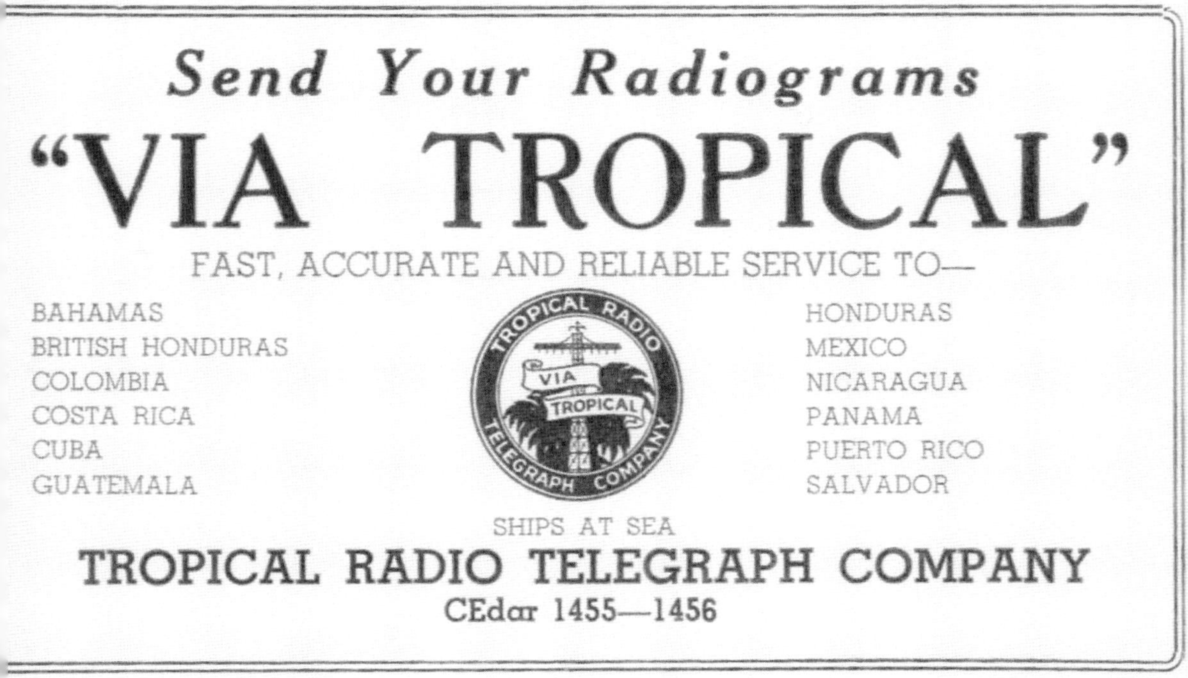

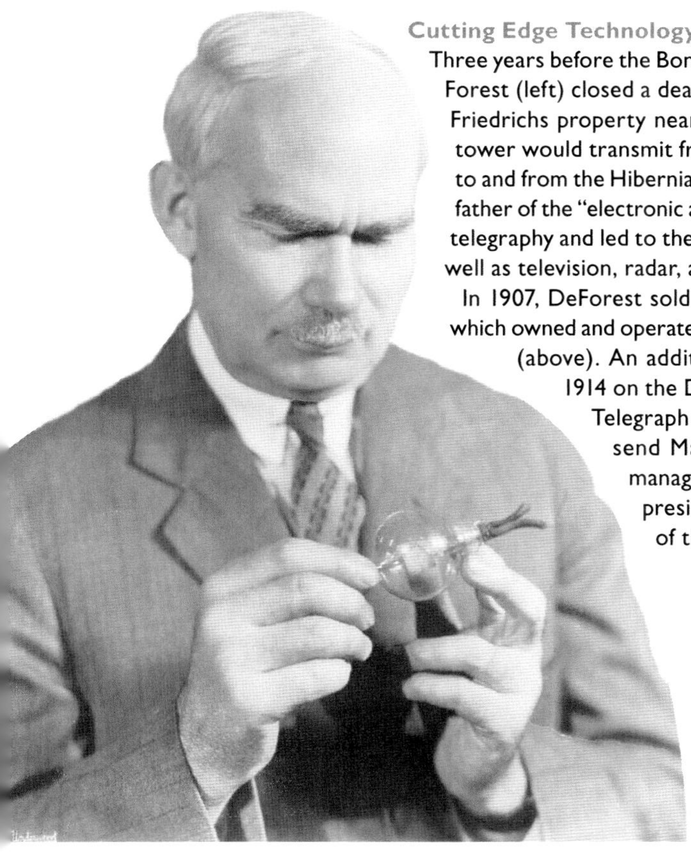

Cutting Edge Technology

Three years before the Bonnabel schoolhouse was built, Dr. Lee De Forest (left) closed a deal for a wireless telegraph station on the Friedrichs property near the Orleans Parish line. The 216-foot tower would transmit from the highest point on Metairie Ridge to and from the Hibernia Bank Building. De Forest is considered a father of the "electronic age"—his Audion tube improved wireless telegraphy and led to the development of radio as we know it, as well as television, radar, and long-distance telephony.

In 1907, DeForest sold his holdings to United Fruit Company, which owned and operated the Tropical Radio Telegraph Company (above). An additional tower was added to Metairie in 1914 on the DeLimon property by Marconi Wireless Telegraph Company of America. Metairians could send Marconigrams! David Sarnoff, contract manager of the Gulf South Division and future president of RCA, oversaw the construction of this station. (Left, LOC; above, JPYR.)

First Modern Subdivision

Frank Fagot settled in Metairie around 1900 on some 200 acres. In 1911, he sold 87 acres to Fidelity Land Company, which, with him, developed the first modern subdivision in Jefferson Parish. Named Metairie Heights, it consisted of 100 lots that were 25 feet wide and 120 feet deep. Frank, a major stockholder, proclaimed that he would move his general merchandise store to a different location on the property and would add another story to the building. (TP.)

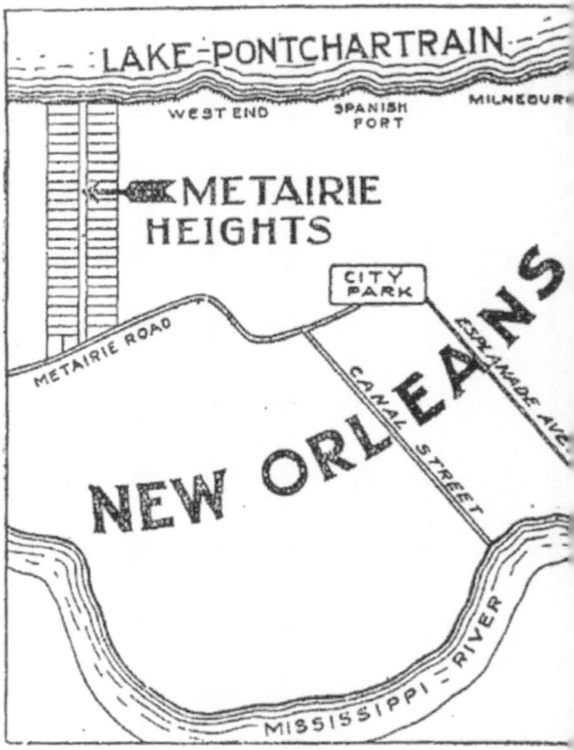

Streetcar Named Royal Blue

As early as 1912, allegations were passed that Fagot had been running a "blind tiger" (illegal bar) out of his store. That same year, he ran for the position of school director but was beaten by Alfred Bonnabel by eight votes. In 1913, he was appointed parish commissioner of tax collection and advocated for a street railway to Kenner and New Orleans (the Orleans-Kenner Traction Company's O-K line), which came to be in 1916. In Metairie, it was called the Royal Blue Line. (LDL.)

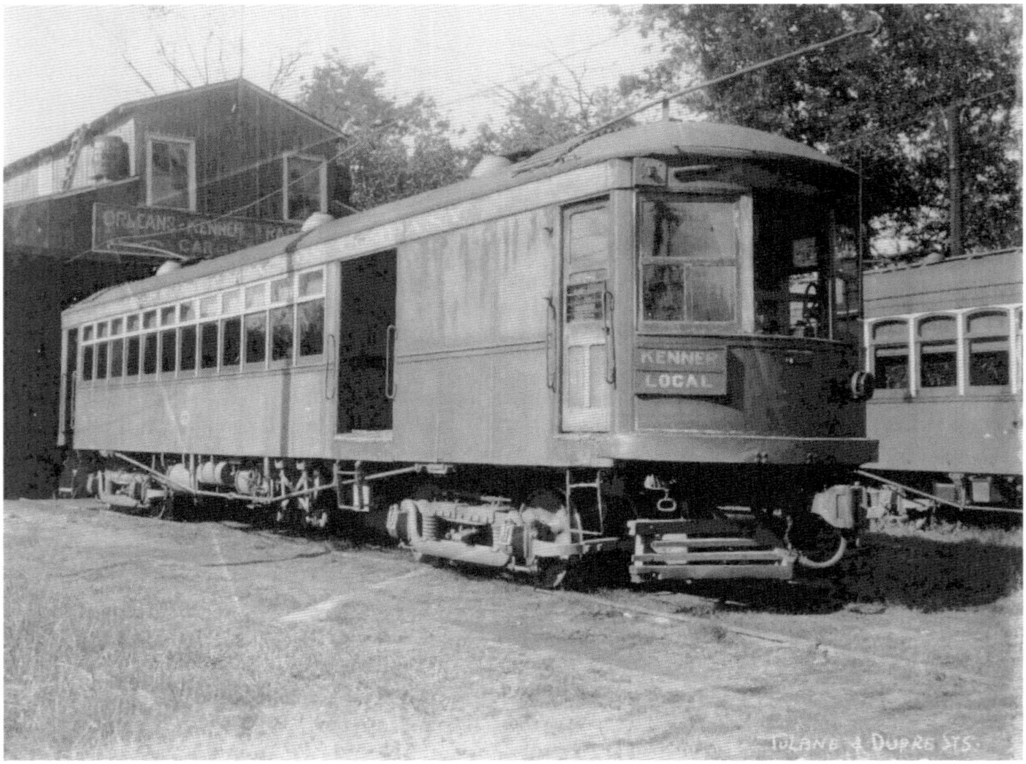

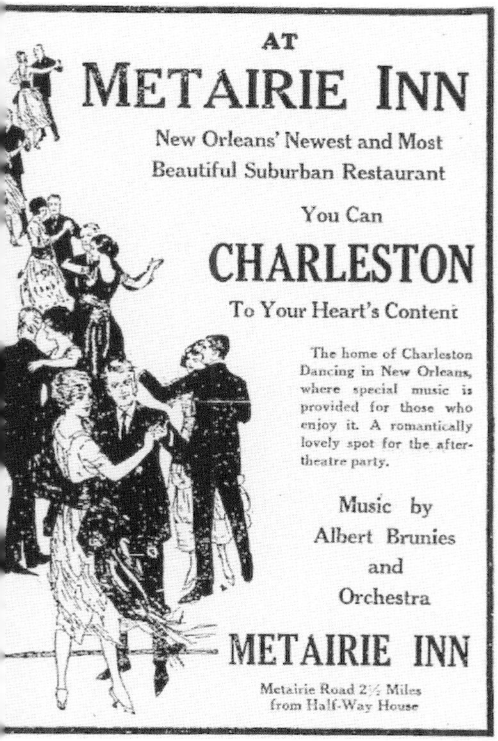

First Postmistress with Gambling Upstairs

In 1914, the fourth-class Metairie Post Office was established in Fagot's store with his wife, Florida I. Hanna, serving as Metairie's first postmistress. In 1928, Gov. Huey P. Long sent the National Guard to raid his Metairie Inn: a gambling hall on the second floor of his business on his property bounded by Metairie Heights, Fagot Street, and Metairie Road. Fagot leased the store to A&P in 1934. (TP.)

Brothers

Frank Fagot Jr. was an agent for the Parish Department of Conservation (a game warden). On November 29, 1927, he was shot and killed at the age of 37 while chasing a man in Crestmont Park who was allegedly shining rabbits. Younger brother Allen was a deputy sheriff at that time. This 1931 photograph of Louis Armstrong and his orchestra was autographed for Allen and his family by banjoist Ruben (Mike) McKendricks when the band played at Suburban Gardens. (LDL.)

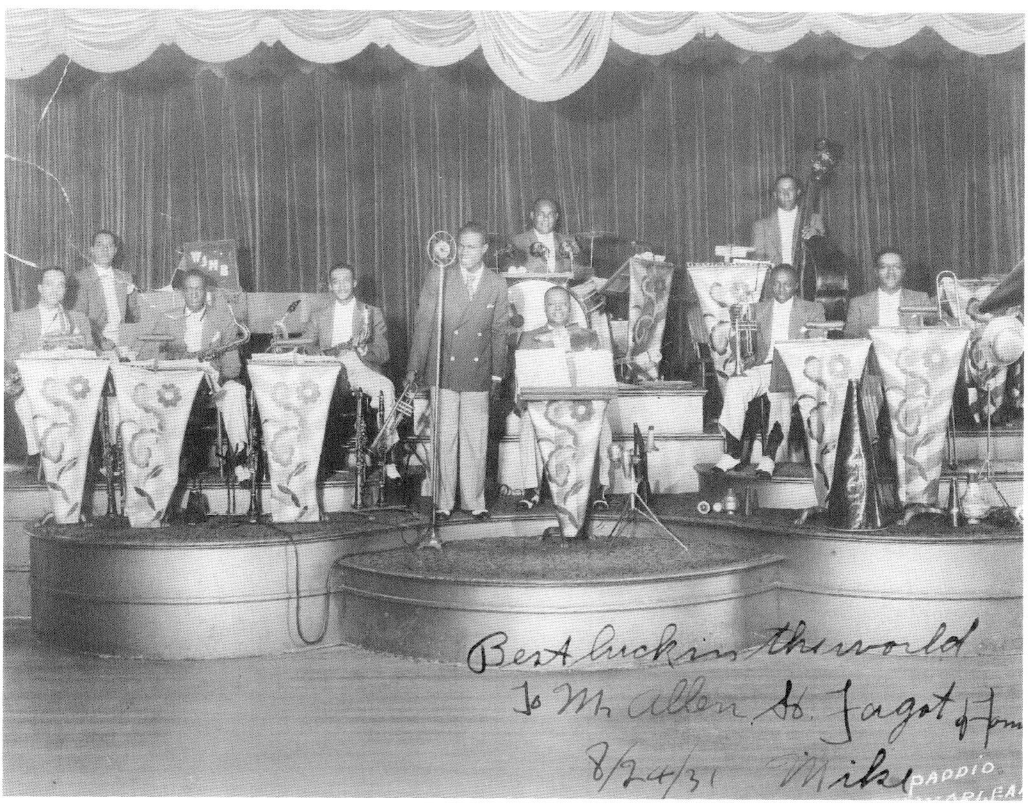

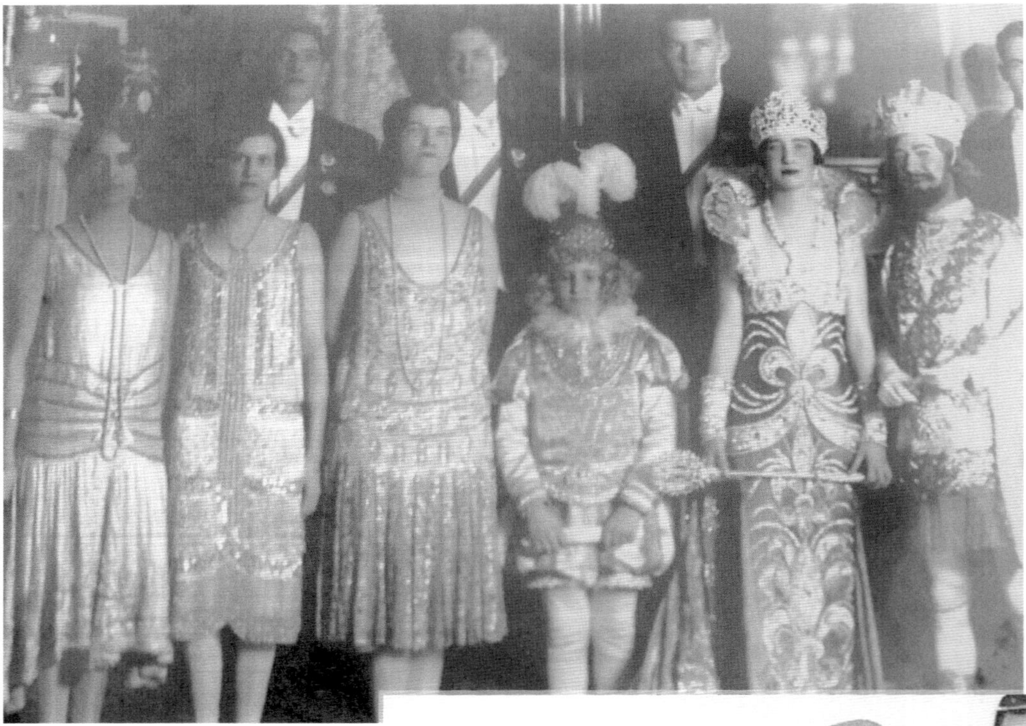

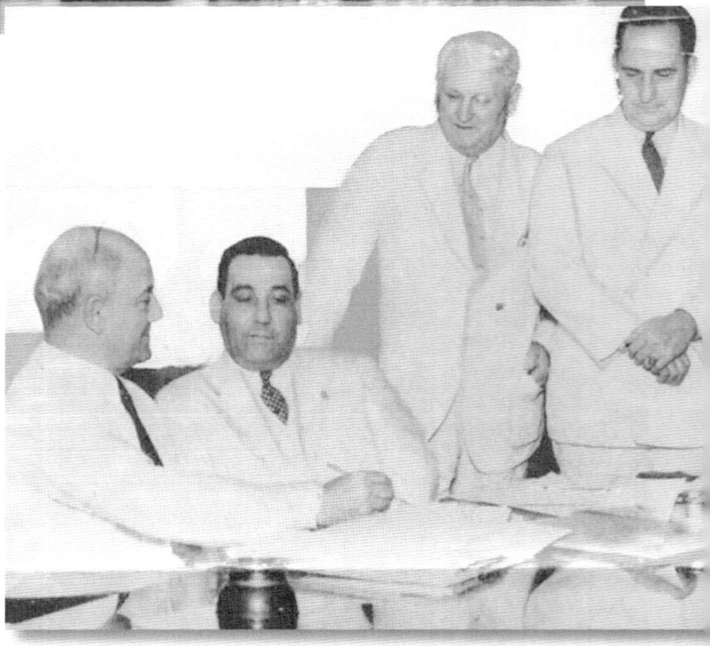

Longest and Widest Bridges

In 1911, Eli Watson built his mansion in the 400 block of Metairie Road on land measuring 150 by 318 by 270 feet bounded by a brick garden wall at a cost of $15,000. By 1928 (the year after he reigned as Rex, pictured above), he had built and owned the first bridge across Lake Pontchartrain, which was the longest bridge in the world. At a cost of $5 million, it was named the Watson-Williams Bridge for his company of investment bankers headed by him and his partner George Williams.

The Danziger Bridge, when completed in 1988, was the widest lift bridge in the world. It was named for Metairie attorney Alfred D. Danziger (pictured to the right, on the right, in 1936) who was Huey P. Long's personal lawyer and executive counsel to Mayor Robert Maistri. Danziger also acquired massive land holdings including the area near the bridge. (Both, LDL.)

CHAPTER TWO

Movers and Shakers

By 1920, the vast majority of Metairie was still uninhabited. A 1923 advertisement by United Realty noted that "New Orleans is one of the few cities in the U.S. having no suburbs. This condition can not go on forever." During the 1920s, Crestmont Park, Beverly Knoll, Livingston Place, and Metairie Club Gardens opened on the riverside of Metairie Road, encompassing land roughly from the parish line to Labarre Road. Enormous profits came to many. For example, Peter Stifft, who was custodian of notarial records for Orleans Parish, purchased land known as Crestmont Park in 1908 for $20,000, sold some in 1915, and the remainder in 1923 to Guaranty Investment Company for $100,000.

In 1923, Crestmont Park developer Alfred F. Theard boasted "city convenience, or better, at suburban prices" with "the beauty & attractiveness of the country" on "homesites of 50 foot frontage from $600 to $1650 . . . at the Crest of the Ridge." Real estate salesman James C. Everhardt noted "Metairie is the St. Charles Avenue of the future" and that a Catholic church (St. Catherine) would be erected in Crestmont Park (he was wrong). The streets in the subdivision were named Glenwood, Hollywood, Rosewood, Ridgewood, Ellis, Fairmont, and Crestmont.

Wealthy wholesale grocer Henry Thomas Cottam Jr. donated 50 acres of his Metairie Road fronting property plus $100,000 in 1923 for construction of a Charity Hospital convalescent facility. The parish school board petitioned to secure 9.14 acres of it to expand Metairie High School, add a gymnasium, and build athletic fields. The police jury voted against a hospital of any kind near a residential neighborhood, but the school did expand. Not until 1946 were Cottam Park lots offered for sale (by Dale & Northrup). Favored advertising lingo noted it was "Adjoining Farnham Place" and added the typical "Enjoy Country Life in the City." A new home sold there in 1947 for $14,000. The streets were named Holly, Cedar, Mulberry, Sycamore, Magnolia, Fairmont, and Cottam Drive.

Beverly Knoll, subdivided in 1923 by the Elvis Realty Co. and marketed by United Realty, is bounded by Metairie Road, Loumor Avenue, Jefferson Avenue, and Labarre Drive. Beverly Knoll streets also include Beverly, Glendale, Arlington, Dorrington, Atherton, Mildred, Dolores, Avalon, Elshor, and Brentwood.

Undeveloped land between Beverly Knoll and Crestmont Park was owned by Dominican College of Louisiana. The archdiocese planned to build its seminary there but instead sold the land for $65,000 to a residential developer who would market Livingston Place subdivision. Its first property (two 25-foot lots) was sold in 1926 by J.L. Ornarato for $3,750. Streets include Livingston, Mildred, Dolores, and Loumar.

Metairie Club Gardens, bounded by Airline Highway, Duplessis Street, and Friedrichs Avenue, was developed in 1926. Early transactions included a home-site purchased by Dr. Leo Burthe from Pipes and Johnson and Friedrichs and Dupas for $10,000. A Mr. Ludwigs completed a home at a cost of $35,000. The 13.5-acre Metairie Park Country Day school was founded in 1929. Before it opened, headmaster Ralph E. Boothby moved from Hudson, Ohio, to 319 Metairie Ridge Road.

Bridgedale was named for a structure that had yet to exist: The Huey P. Long bridge. Streets were being constructed in 1925, but only south of Airline Highway between Transcontinental, Central, and Jefferson Highway.

Movement to the north of Metairie Road was heralded by United Realty, which gushed in 1924, "The Riviera of New Orleans lies right at your door—The Hammond Highway (planned from New Orleans to Hammond) will put New Orleans on the coast" and informed in 1925 that the proposed 180-foot-wide Harlem Drive (now Causeway Boulevard) would connect Metairie Road to the highway. Although Causeway now needs no introduction, United Realty played it safe: "Drive two blocks past the new Cumberland Telephone building [on the still unpaved Metairie Road] and you will notice two large signs on the right. That is Harlem Avenue." Lots in the new development were a bargain at $135. Metairie Nursery sites were also on the market in 1924 for $75 to $300, as were Brockenbraugh Court subdivision sites from $350 to $600, and Old Homestead lots for $425 to $900.

By 1927, Brockenbraugh Court, north of Cottam Park, had been fully developed. An extension with 400 lots at 25 by 120 feet was planned by Albert J. Vallon & Co. Inc. Meanwhile, 38 lots in Sierra Place were marketed by Sierra Realty Co., owned by F.V. Sierra, H.G. Hollander, and J.B. Garvey. They sold property on Metairie Road at $90 per foot and on Causeway for $80 per foot. Sierra Place boundaries are Metairie Road, Causeway Boulevard, and Roman Street.

By 1927, the Bonnabel Place suburb, east of Bonnabel Boulevard running from Metairie Road to the lake, was marketed by Joseph F. Turnbull with lots selling from $200 to $400. Bonnabel Boulevard was under construction, but Metairie Road had been paved and the streetcar still ran along it. Turnbull touted his community as amenable for young families by advertising the nearby Metairie Ridge School, St. Catherine's church and school, and Metairie Presbyterian Church.

The Jefferson Parish Police Jury opened the first section of Airline Highway in 1927. It ran from Williams Boulevard to Shrewsbury Road and continued along Metairie Road to the city. Airline Highway south of Metairie Road was not completed until 1928. With other new major roads built or proposed during the 1920s (Harlem/Causeway, Transcontinental, Clearview Parkway) a commute to the city was much more palatable. Metairie's first building boom occurred in this decade.

While new folks moved into Metairie, gambling was thriving. A 1925 *Times-Picayune* article noted, "Out in the suburbs, but patronized by Orleanians, are the de luxe places." It described one of many—Dominick Tranchina's Beverly Gardens on Metairie Road where "the gambling equipment is the finest" and an "excellent orchestra" fronts a "brilliantly polished dance floor," while "a few hundred yards down Metairie Road" was the Victory Inn.

Some newly arrived residents lobbied to remove the gambling establishments, formed a committee, and petitioned to incorporate as a municipality that could enforce laws ignored by Jefferson Parish officials. In 1926, a charter was issued for the town of Metairie Ridge. C.P. Aicklen was chosen as their mayor and promptly announced that he would shut down the gambling houses. Gaming figures then lobbied to overturn the charter. In November 1928, the Supreme Court of Louisiana decided that the city had been illegally incorporated because too few residents had signed the petition.

Aside from gambling in the 1920s, Metairie was relatively crime free, but some ladies were upset by the actions of some visitors as described in an August 19, 1927, article that read, "Plans were discussed, to rid the streets and roads of the city of Metairie of the numerous petting parties of young men and women of New Orleans who are using these dimly lighted places as parking grounds, at a meeting of the Women's Civic Auxiliary of Metairie Thursday night at the home of Mrs. G.L. Sheen, Friedrichs Avenue." This chapter rings in the Roaring Twenties and meanders into the late 1950s, when even newer subdivisions, businesses, schools, churches, and gambling houses were born.

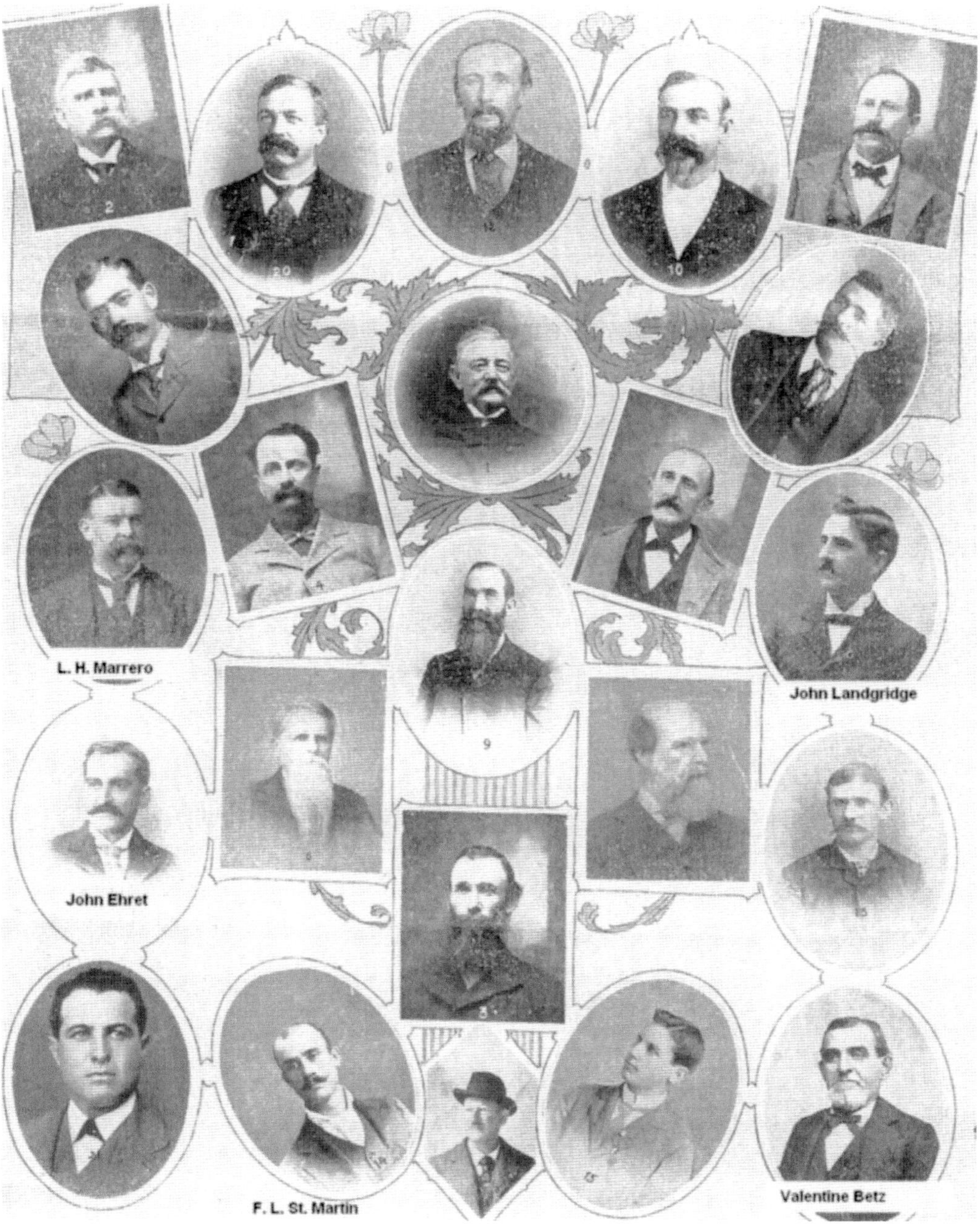

Early Leaders

Jefferson Parish leaders, who would serve in different offices for years to come, appear in this montage. They are Louis H. Marrero, sheriff; John Reuben Langridge Sr., clerk of court; police jurists F.L. St. Martin, Valentine Betz, and John Ehret, future mayor of Gretna. The original photographs appeared in Frank Tomkins's 1901 *Riparian lands of the Mississippi River.*

Gambling Houses

In a 1959 interview, jazz musician Peter Edwin Bocage (pictured here in 1961) recalled playing at Dominick J. Tranchina's Metairie Road clubs. "There was plenty of money in those days," Bocage said. "We used to make high as 20, 30 dollars a-piece, just collections [tips] from gamblers. Money was like water with them." Tranchina died in 1937 at the age of 63 after having owned and operated many restaurants and clubs where illegal drinking and gambling were featured. He had maintained a residence on six lots at Dorrington Boulevard at Elshor Avenue. His *Times-Picayune* obituary noted that he retired briefly "during the period of prohibition" but went on to open another "store." (LDC.)

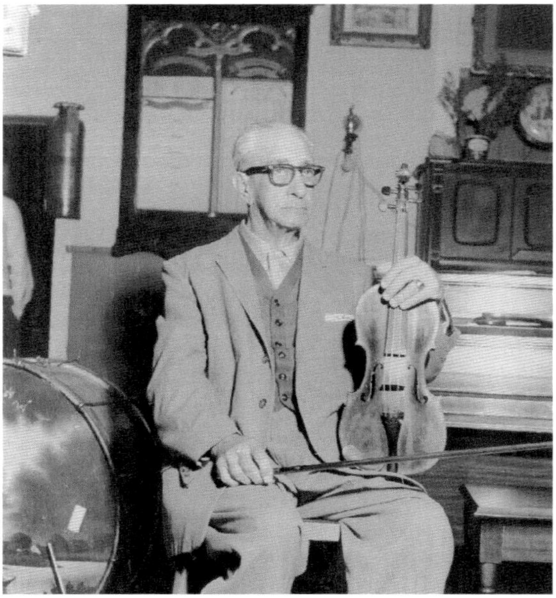

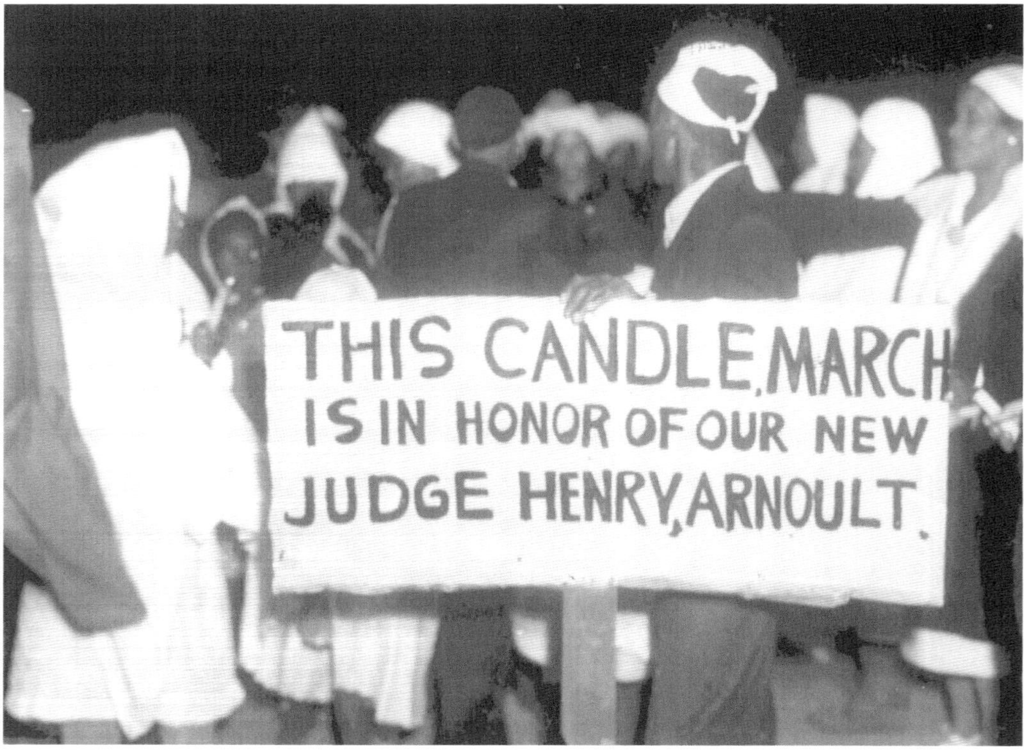

Henry Arnoult

During the 1930s, the congregation of the First Mission Baptist Church honored Judge Henry Arnoult with a candle march from their church to his home at 402 Arnoult Road in gratitude for his service to the parish and his donations to the church. Henry was the son of Judge Louis Edgard Arnoult (see page 17) and Louise Jeanne Durel, who was the first president of the Shrewsbury/Jefferson Elementary School Mothers Club in 1909.

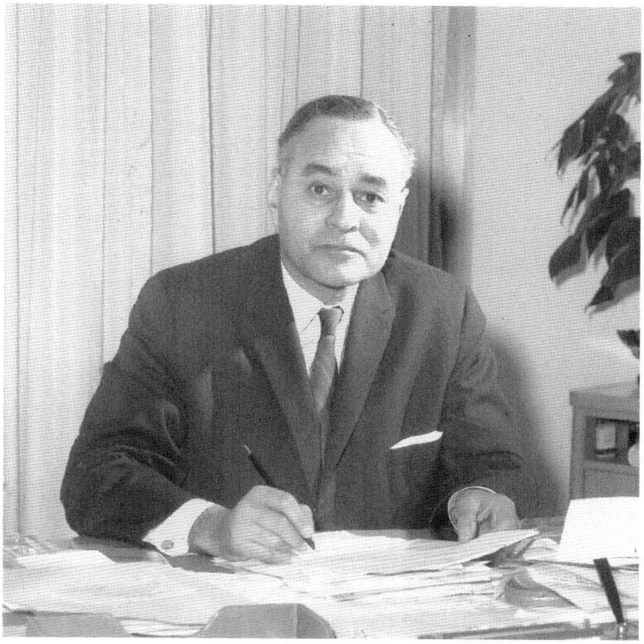

Ralph Johnson Bunche

Raised by a paternal grandmother who had been a slave, Ralph Bunche was the first African American to win a Nobel Peace Prize. Born in Detroit in 1904 to Fred Bunche (a barber) and Olive Johnson Bunche, who both died when he was a young teenager, Ralph was also the first African American to earn a PhD in political science from an American university.

He graduated as the valedictorian of Jefferson High School in Los Angeles and then attended the University of California at Los Angeles on an athletic scholarship, graduating in 1927 as a summa cum laude valedictorian with a major in international relations. With funds raised by neighbors and a scholarship to Harvard University, he earned a master's degree in 1928. While teaching at Howard University, he worked toward a doctorate at Harvard, where he also received a Rosenwald Fellowship for 1932 through 1933 to do research in Africa. His 1934 dissertation was awarded the Toppan Prize for outstanding research in social studies. Postdoctoral work from 1936 to 1938 included a Social Science Research Council fellowship in anthropology at Northwestern University, the London School of Economics, and South Africa's Capetown University. His interest in education lasted throughout his life. He chaired the Department of Political Science at Howard University (1928–1950), was codirector of the Institute of Race Relations at Swarthmore College (1936), and taught at Harvard from 1950 to 1952. He was a member of the New York City Board of Education (1958–1964), the Board of Overseers of Harvard University (1960–1965), and the Board of the Institute of International Education. He was also a trustee of Oberlin College, Lincoln University, and New Lincoln School.

His views on civil rights were based on academics and pragmatism—that there are no scientific or anthropological differences between races. He wrote *A World View of Races* in 1936 and, with Eleanor Roosevelt, helped create the Universal Decree of Human Rights, which was adopted by the United Nations General Assembly in 1948.

After serving various positions with the Department of State and the United Nations, he was appointed principal secretary of the UN Palestine Commission, which negotiated the armistice agreements between Israel and the Arab states, ending the 1947–1949 Jewish/Arab conflicts. In 1950, he received the Nobel Peace Prize for these efforts.

In New York City he was given a ticker-tape parade. In Los Angeles, he was honored with the naming of a "Ralph Bunche Day." And in Metairie, in 1954, Bunche Village ("New Orleans' best planned colored subdivision") opened. Reverend A.L. Davis officiated the grand dedication of the 256 homes in 1955.

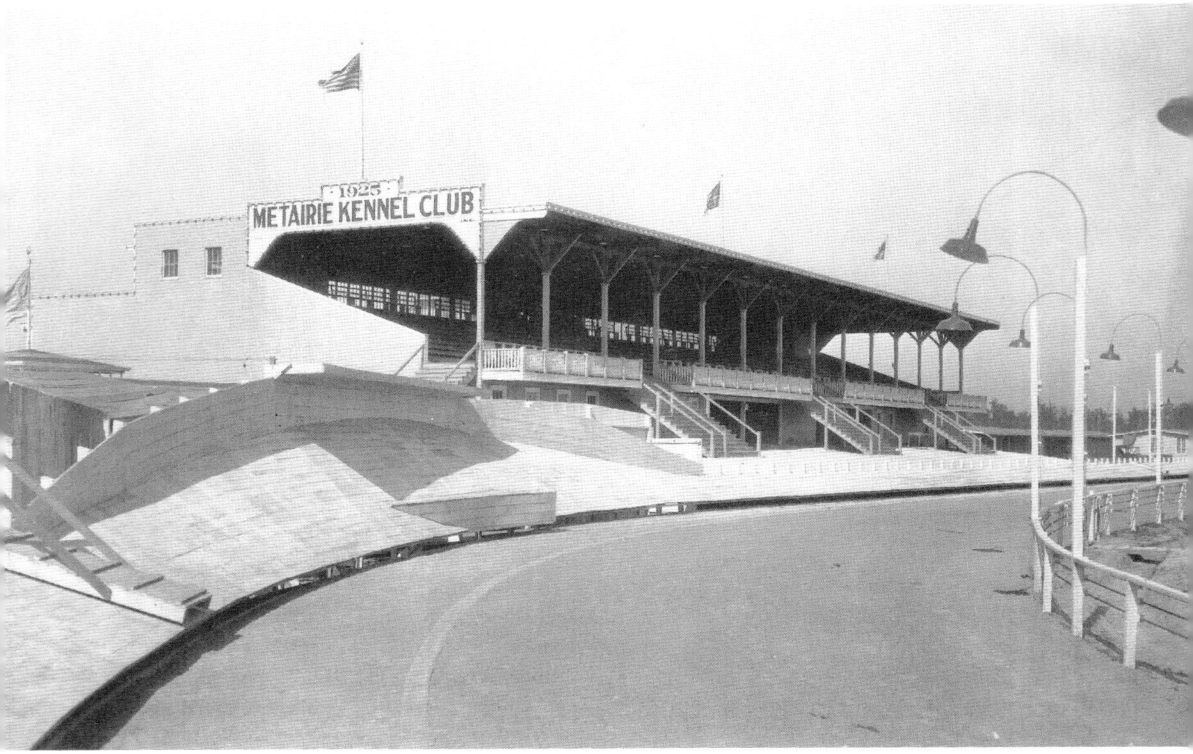

8,000 Visitors Per Day

The Metairie Kennel Club opened on September 29, 1925, on the lakeside of Metairie Ridge between Rosa and Oaklawn Avenues on the property of John Betz near the railroad tracks approximately 1.5 miles from the Halfway House/New Basin Canal (now City Park Avenue at the Pontchartrain Expressway). The huge facility could accommodate 400 dogs. The *Times-Picayune* reported that, during the days leading to its formal opening, more than 8,000 men, women, and children visited each day to take a look at the new track and facilities, which included electrical lighting installed by local electrician Charles Argo and the mechanical pace-setting rabbit "of the newest pattern." Argo predicted that "when the lights first go on local people in the vicinity would imagine there was some conflagration."

Anthony "Pop" Rouprich served as the club's first president. Theodore Walgrem was the secretary/treasurer. The first season called for seven events nightly, with nine dogs per race and a Saturday matinee. Local businesses contributing trophy cups included the Monteleone Hotel and Loubat's Glassware Company (Walter Loubat was a founding member of the club). Groundskeeper C.G. Fitzgerald boasted that the Metairie Kennel Club was "the finest in the country."

The following year, a neighboring greyhound track, DeLimon Park, opened on Metairie Road between Rosa Avenue and Focis Street on Louis DeLimon's farm property. The year 1928 brought tougher legislation against dog racing and the closing of both tracks. In 1932, Smith's Golf Driving Range opened and advertised "golf practice at its best" at the former Metairie Kennel Club, where nighttime lighting allowed for long hours for owners Harry Turple and William Roux, who were contemplating also building a nine-hole golf course on the property (which they did). DeLimon Park was also used for car racing and occasional illegal greyhound competitions. In 1941, part of the DeLimon property was subdivided for housing. After World War II, DeLimon Park was converted into the Do Drive-In, which closed in 1981. It would become the Old Metairie Village and the DeLimon Place condominium complex. (LDL.)

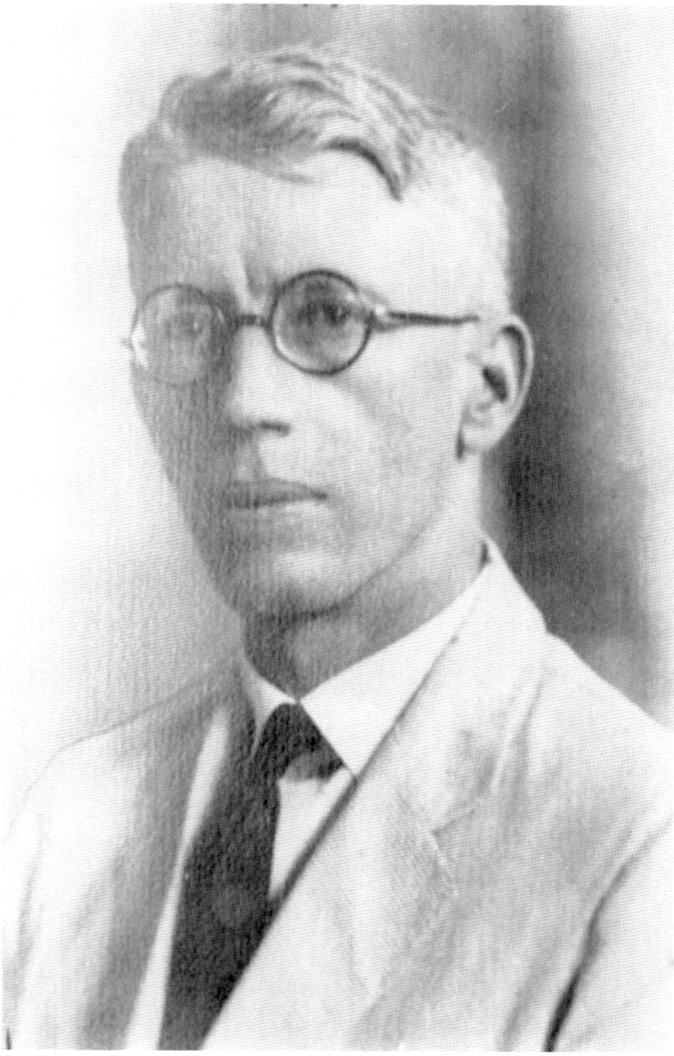

C.P. Aicklen

Some Metairie residents lobbied to remove the gambling houses, which came before them from their new upscale neighborhoods. C.P. Aicklen, co-owner of Borden-Aicklen Auto Supply Company, was selected as chairman of the Metropolitan Municipal League, which circulated a petition for incorporation as a town disassociated from Jefferson Parish government officials who flagrantly turned a blind eye to gambling and liquor laws.

The boundaries of the new town would be Shrewsbury Road, the Illinois-Central Rail Road tracks, the Bonnabel Canal, and the Orleans Parish line. This would include the Metairie Road gambling houses and dog tracks that contributed the vast majority of taxes collected in the area. Incorporation as a town would allow more tax revenue for municipal improvements, which made the prospect a double-edged sword to both sides of the gambling issue.

Aicklen, as chosen president/mayor of the town/corporation, announced his hopes for a city hall with stone steps and marble pillars, general street lighting, regular garbage collections, police protection, and street repairs. "We have instructed the city attorneys to draft laws against the operation of gambling houses . . . These ordinances will bar gambling . . . and will mean that alleged dice and poker resorts now operating along Metairie Road must go," he said.

Gov. Henry L. Fuqua received the petition and approved it in 1926. The new City of Metairie Ridge, Louisiana, would be headed by Mayor Aicklen; W.J. Dwyer, marshal; F.W. Bogel, clerk; and E. Howard McCaleb, city attorney. The first ordinance adopted by Mayor Aicklen and endorsed by new governor O.H. Simpson created the City of Metairie Ridge on July 9, 1927.

In November 1928, the Supreme Court of Louisiana decided that the City of Metairie Ridge had been illegally incorporated because not enough signatures were included on the petition. Jefferson Parish district attorney Archie T. Higgens and Judge L. Robert Rivarde, along with pro-gambling factions, had prevailed. The city was dissolved in December 1928, and gambling remained active, although the largest operations moved to Jefferson Highway and River Road. In January 1929, taxes collected by the defunct city, amounting to $22,000, were turned over to Jefferson Parish. The only notable official action by Mayor Charles Philip Aicklen Sr. had been the turning of a valve in 1928 at the Seventeenth Street Canal near Metairie Road, which brought natural gas to all constituents via a nine-mile pipe.

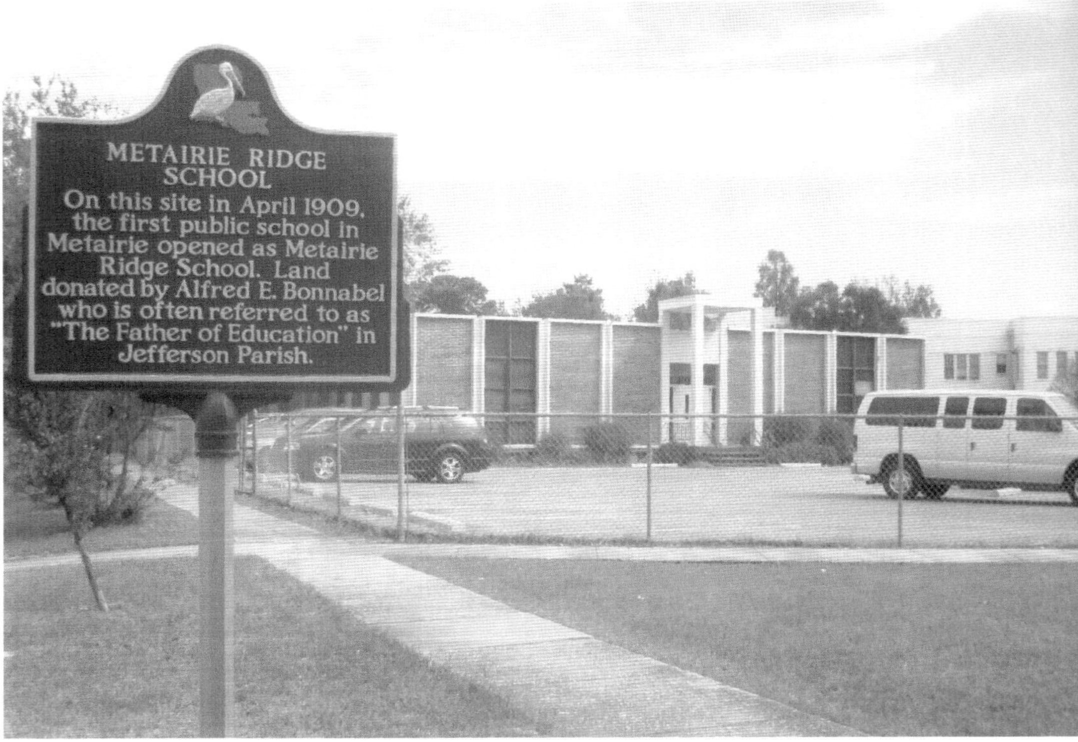

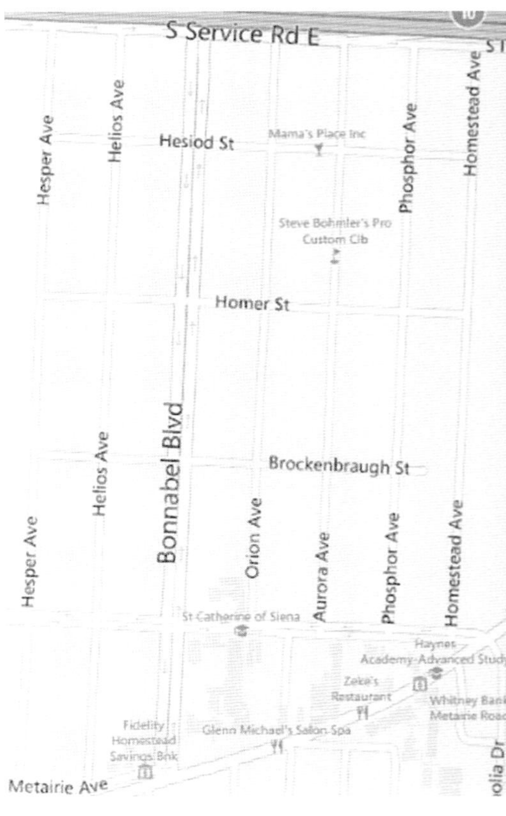

Alfred Bonnabel and the First Public School

Alfred Bonnabel donated land for the first public school in Metairie at what is now 1416 Metairie Road. The two-room structure built there in 1909 was named Metairie Ridge School. In 1911, its principal Miss Luella Van Vrancken married Bonnabel's son Alfred Jr. Today, Haynes Academy for Advanced Studies occupies the property. Pictured above are the historical marker commemorating the original school, with the school as it stands today in the background.

Alfred and Luella had seven children: Laura Elby, Louella, Dorothy, Guion, Miriam, Lea May, and Alfred Jr. Alfred Bonnabel High School was named for him in 1971. Luella named the north–south streets of Alfred's Bonnabel Place development after figures in Greek mythology: Hesper, Helios, Orion, Aurora, and Phosphor. Homestead is the location of the Bonnabel mansion, and Brockenbraugh was named for Alfred's mother, Laura Brockenbraugh Rappleye. Luella named the east–west streets for poets Homer and Hesiod, statesman and orator Demosthenes, the Roman goddesses of fertility and abundance Pomona and Feronia, and emperors Nero and Claudius. Haynes Academy is included on the map in the lower right.

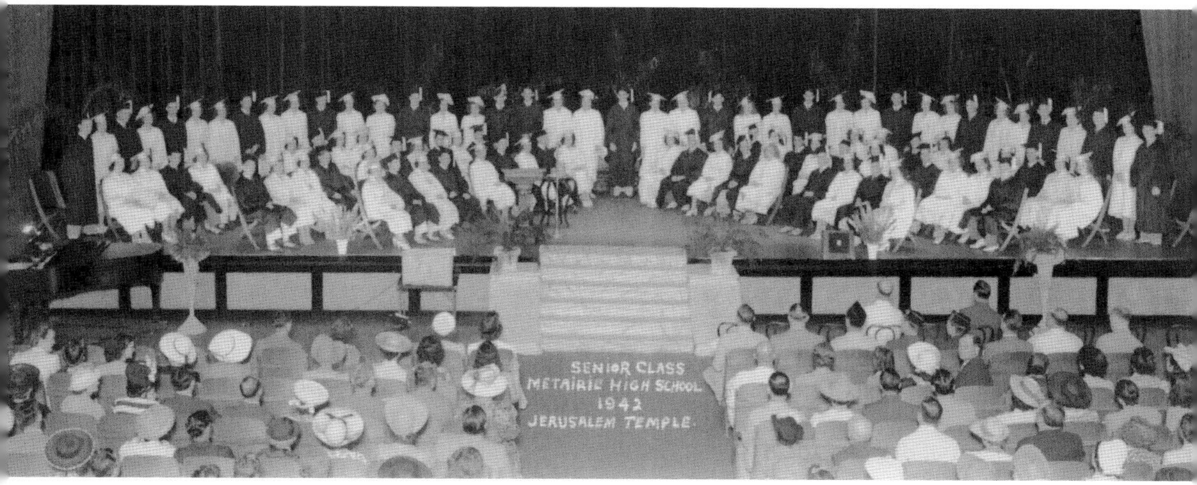

The Haynes and the Bonnabels and Metairie High School

The 95-member Metairie High School class of 1942 is pictured at commencement in Jerusalem Temple. Their school replaced the schoolhouse in 1924. In 1955, after 1,716 students had graduated, the school became Metairie Junior High under the leadership of Vernon C. Haynes. Newly opened East Jefferson High would then serve as Metairie's secondary school.

The building was demolished in 1968, and many of the current structures were built. Through the years, it has been named Metairie Middle School (1969), Vernon C. Haynes Middle School (1974), Vernon C. and Gilda P. Haynes Middle School (1995), Metairie Academy for Advanced Students, and Haynes Academy for Advanced Studies.

When the school celebrated its 100th anniversary in 2009, in attendance were retired teacher Miriam Bonnabel Lacy Buchler (a granddaughter of Alfred Bonnabel; see pages 19 and 36), and school principal Jerome Helmstetter, whose father appears in the 1942 graduation photographs. (LDL.)

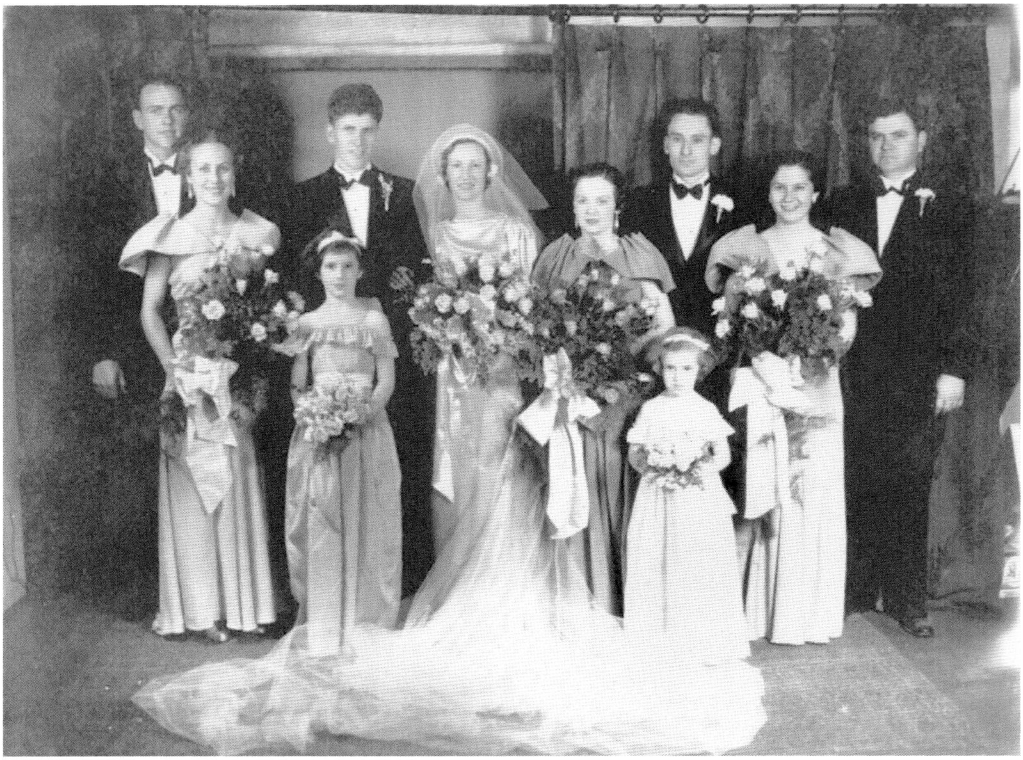

A Match Made in Metairie

The couple whose memory is honored by the school on Metairie Road was a most interesting pair. Arkansas native Vernon "Lefty" Carlton Haynes was a man of few words. Metairie born Gilda Dorothia Pohlig was an outspoken ball of fire. They met when he was officiating a basketball game in which she was a player. He called a foul on her, and she became foul with him.

He had a BA from Tulane and an M.Ed in administration from LSU. She dropped out of Tulane to take a job modeling swimwear. He made a living coaching sports, while she dreamed of becoming a professional basketball player—a prospect her father would not allow.

These opposites attracted and were married on November 2, 1935, at Metairie Presbyterian Church. Lefty said he picked the date because his father and grandfather had also had their weddings on the second day of November. Vernon and Gilda were married for 38 years.

He was a principal at Metairie High who oversaw hundreds of students. She was an alumna (class of 1928, which included nine graduates) who said, while slamming her fist on a table, "We didn't have all these electives. That was the ruination of the schools. They need to get back to basics." Despite the different ideologies, they both were tireless in working with and for young people.

Vernon was an All-American football star at Tulane who played in the 1932 Rose Bowl. Gilda, who was a student in the Metairie Ridge Schoolhouse, was a standout basketball player and one of the best bowlers in the South. He was inducted into the Tulane Athletic Hall of Fame posthumously in 1982. She was named to the Louisiana State US Congress of Bowlers Women's Bowling Association Hall of Fame in 1987.

Together, they owned Bowl-A-Rama at 1008 Jefferson Highway, which she managed from 1956 until his death in 1973 at age 62. She then served on the Jefferson Parish School Board from 1974 through 1980. Gilda passed away in 1995.

Their home at 126 Brockenbraugh Court is gone, the property long taken over by Munholland Methodist Church. But their memory lives on a few blocks away in the school named for them. (Carlyle Dana Vann.)

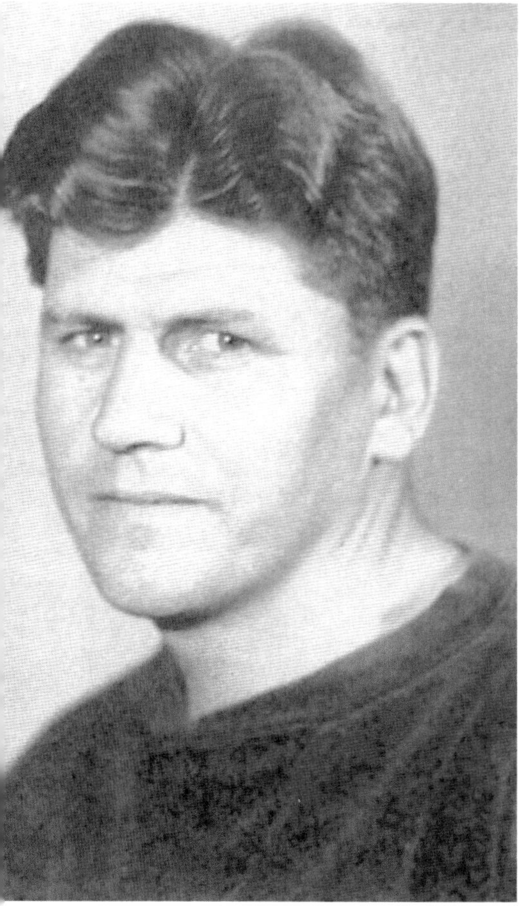

Vernon and Gilda Haynes

His first coaching jobs were at Fortier (1932), then at Warren Easton (1933–1935), where he also taught. After a stint in Ouachita Parish schools (1935–1940) he coached at Tulane (1941–1949), where he was head basketball coach. From 1949 to 1951, he coached in Newport News, Virginia, then moved back home in 1951 to teach and coach in public schools. He served on the parish council from 1958 to 1960 and was a superintendent of schools from 1961 to 1973. Lefty was also an avid bowler.

The first manager of Airline Bowl at 7401 Airline (1962), Gilda was a charter member of the Louisiana Women's Bowling Association (1966), the first woman chairman of a local Professional Bowling Association tournament (at Pelican Lanes in 1974), and recipient of an LWBA outstanding service to female bowling award in recognition of two decades of work with children. Vernon and Gilda's Bowl-A-Rama is pictured below in 1963. (JPYR.)

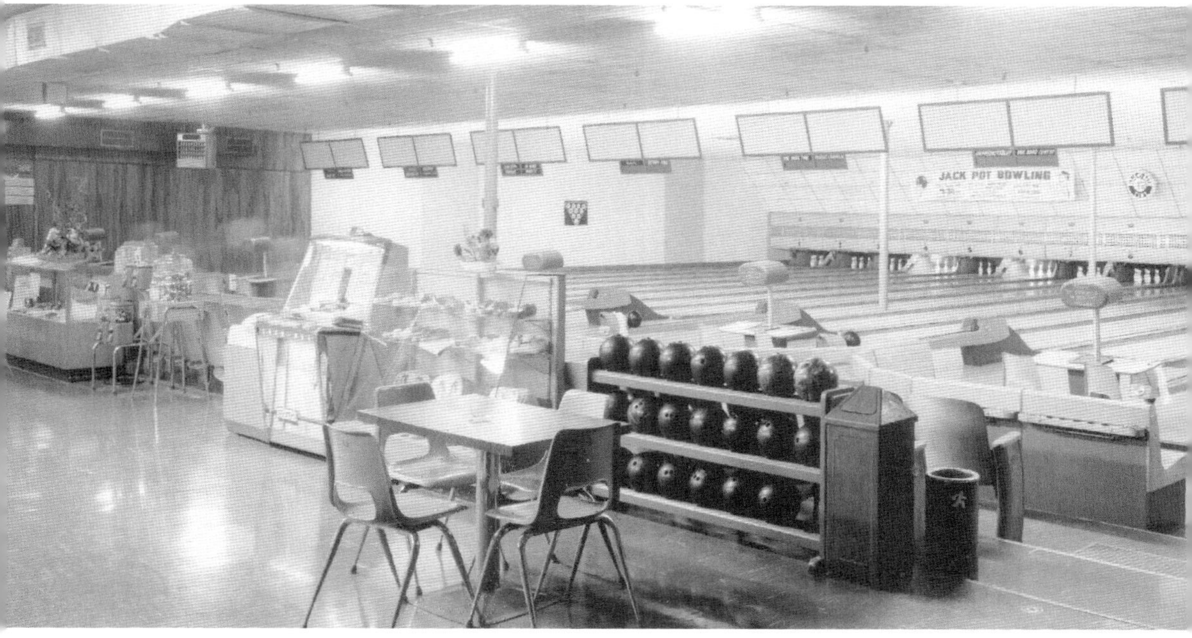

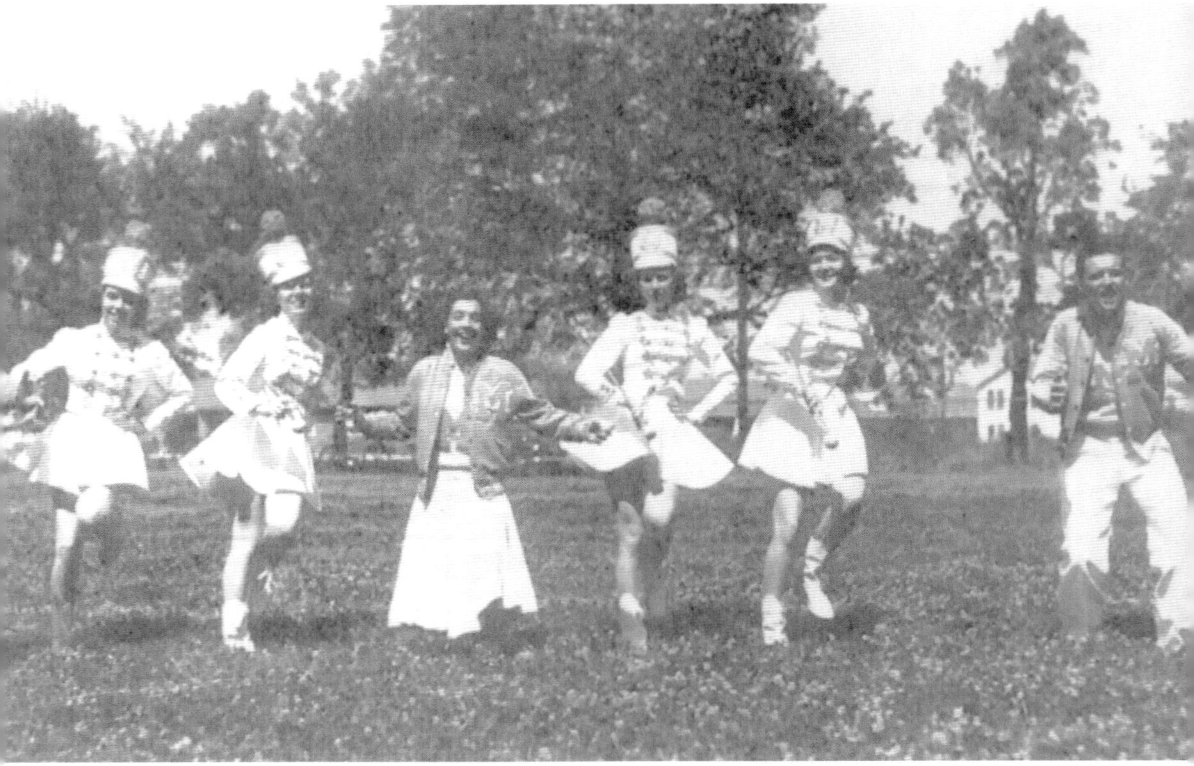

Ashley Schexnaildre

The 1950 Metairie High cheerleaders and majorettes displayed their enthusiasm for teams coached by H. Ashley Schexnaildre. He taught and coached all sports at Metairie High from 1942 through 1956. With him as head coach, the Yellow Jacket football squad won five championships from 1948 to 1953. In 1954, students dedicated the yearbook to their beloved teacher and coach. In 1953, he wrote *The History of Metairie High School, 1924–1952*. A World War II vet and Loyola graduate with an MA from Tulane, Hobart Ashley Schexnaildre died in 1985 at the age of 62. He is pictured below (standing second from right) on the school board with Paul Hubbel (see page 76), John C. Bruning (page 17), Emile Gennaro (page 78), and Leon Soniat (page 71).

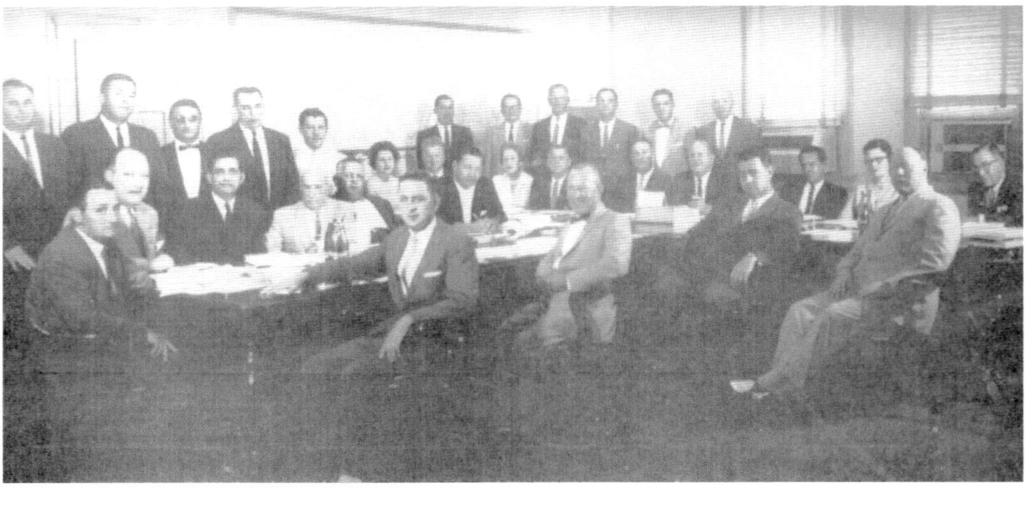

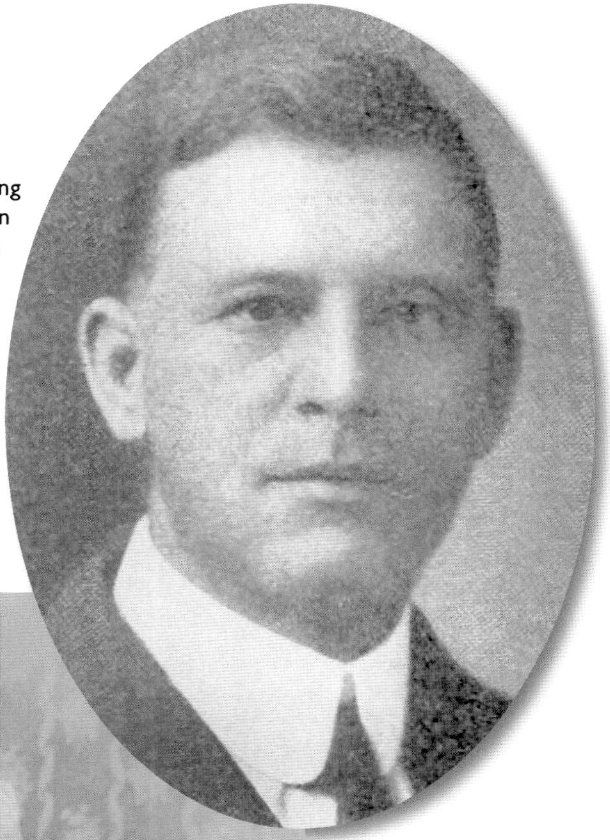

Sheriff Dauenhauer
John Baptise Dauenhauer Jr. was traveling auditor for the Louisiana Conservation Commission (1906–1911), Jefferson Parish assessor (1911), and sheriff (1920–1928). Never a personal enemy of gambling, the sheriff was ordered to enforce the laws in Metairie during the administration of Gov. Oramel Simpson. (JPYR.)

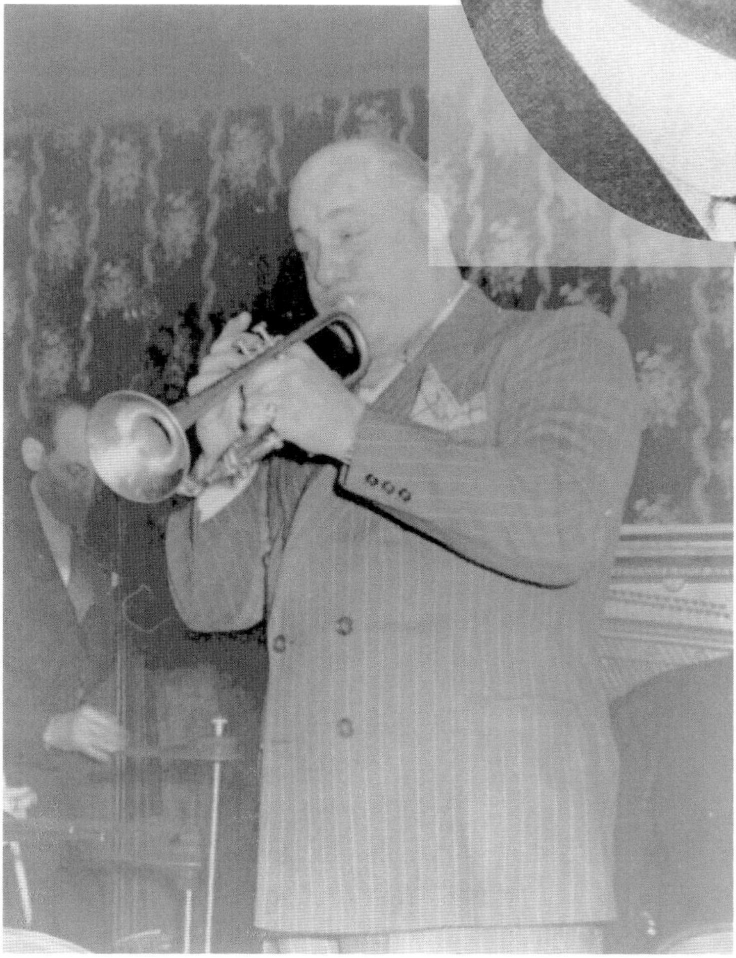

Historic Jazz Moment
Paul Mares is pictured here when he was the leader of the New Orleans Rhythm Kings in 1945. At his home at 118 Glenwood Drive, he hosted a historic 1929 party during which members of Paul Whiteman's band jammed with local jazz musicians. The photograph is signed on the back, "To Dr. Souchon" (see page 57). (LDL.)

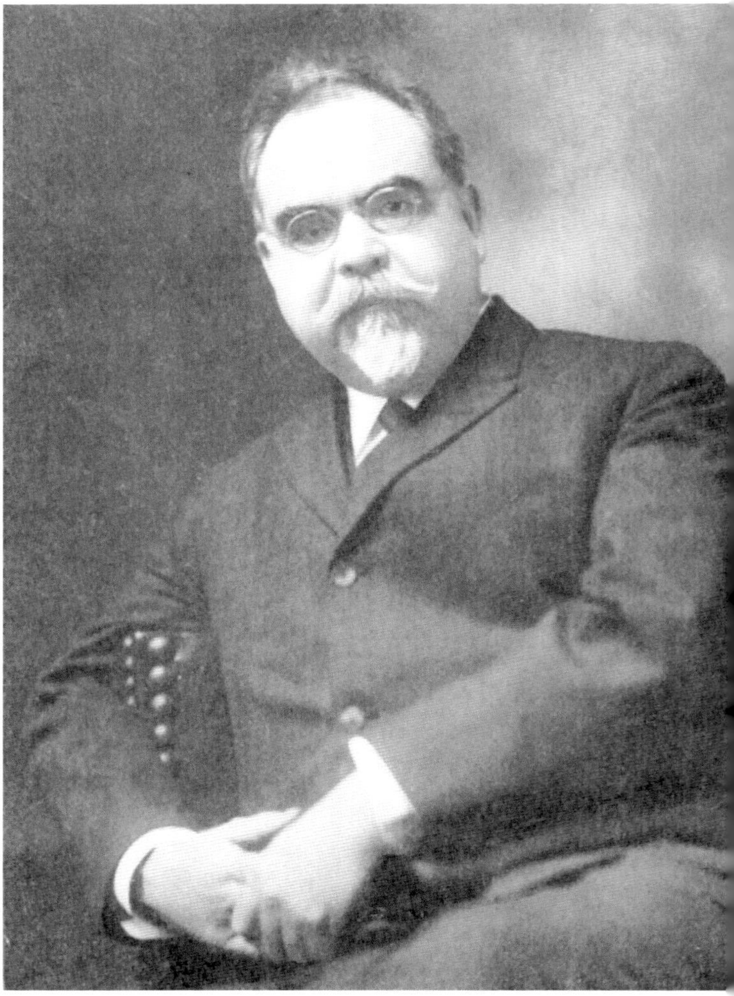

Surgeon and Butcher
Nineteen-year-old Rudolph Matas (right) earned his degree from the Medical School of the University of Louisiana in 1880. In 1889, he was the first surgeon in the United States to use spinal anesthesia. During his career, he developed the IV drip technique and was the first to surgically repair aneurysms. Dr. Matas died on September 23, 1957, at the age of 97. Rudolph Matas Elementary School is named in his honor.

The Garsaud family has long roots in the community. Octave Garsaud had a fine food store at 521 Metairie Road. Pictured here is a 1949 advertisement for it. His father Jean Octave Garsaud was an avid supporter of French culture, a 50-year butcher in the French Market (beginning in the 1890s), and a leader in the market's preservation. (Right, Tulane University; below, JPYR.)

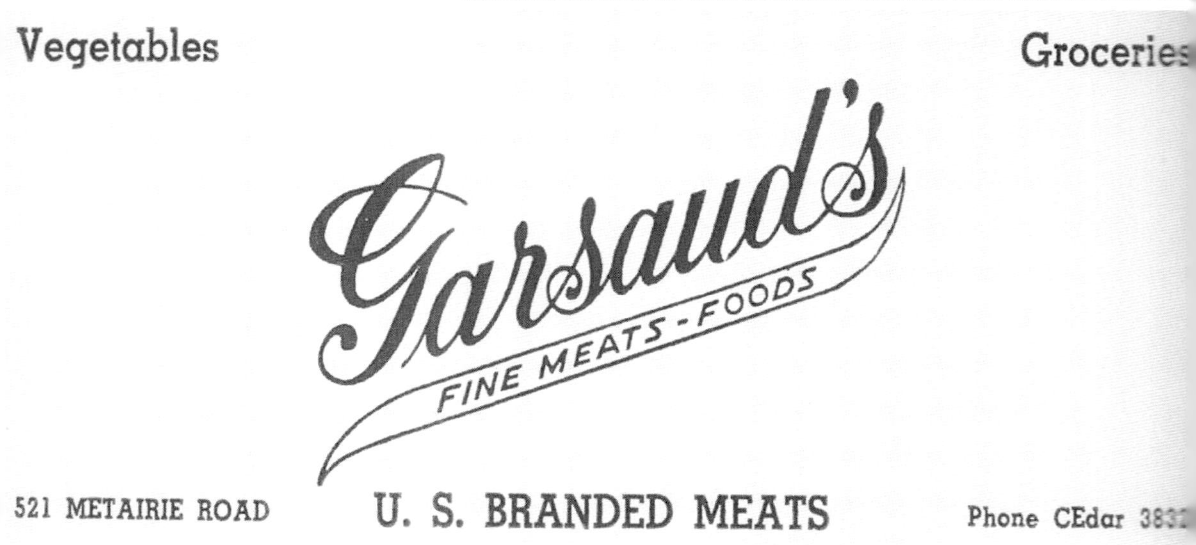

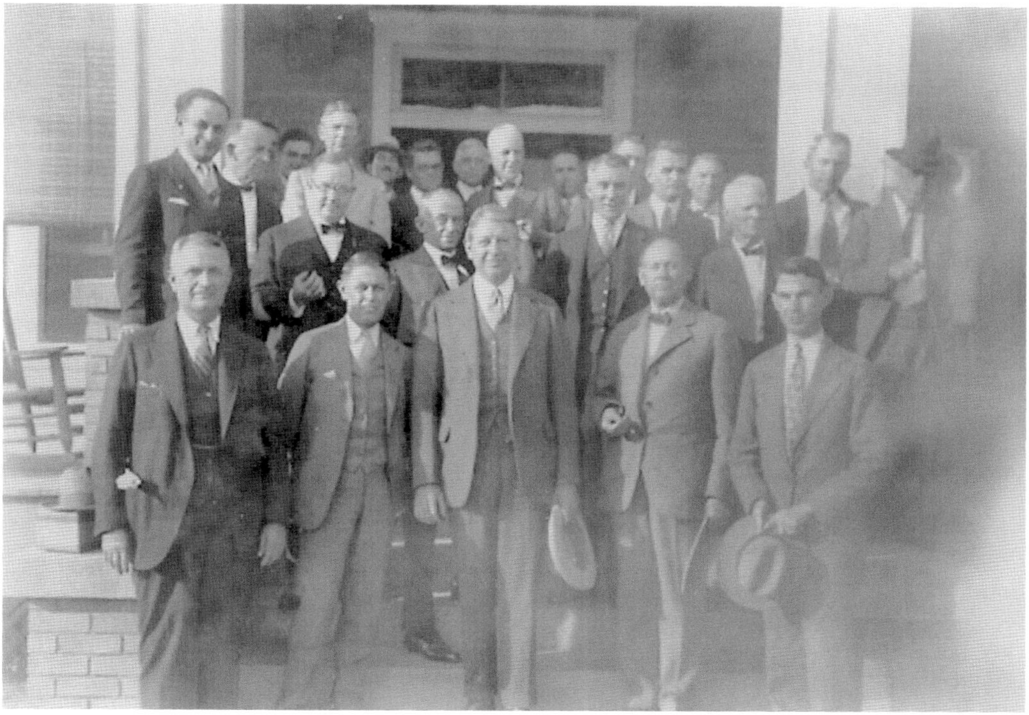

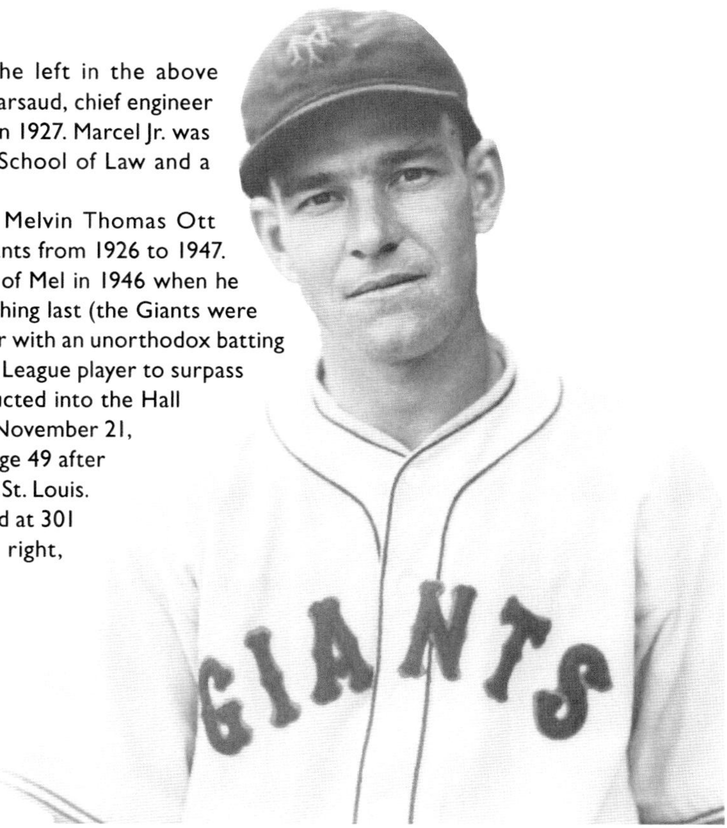

Nice Guys

Front row, second from the left in the above photograph is Col. Marcel Garsaud, chief engineer of the Orleans Levee Board in 1927. Marcel Jr. was Dean of Loyola University School of Law and a Louisiana appellate judge.

Born in Gretna in 1909, Melvin Thomas Ott played for the New York Giants from 1926 to 1947. Leo Durocher was speaking of Mel in 1946 when he quipped about nice guys finishing last (the Giants were in last place). The right fielder with an unorthodox batting stance was the first National League player to surpass 500 home runs and was inducted into the Hall of Fame in 1951. He died on November 21, 1958, at Touro Infirmary at age 49 after an automobile accident in Bay St. Louis. He and his wife, Mildred, lived at 301 Cedar Drive. (Above, LDL; right, Martin Conlin.)

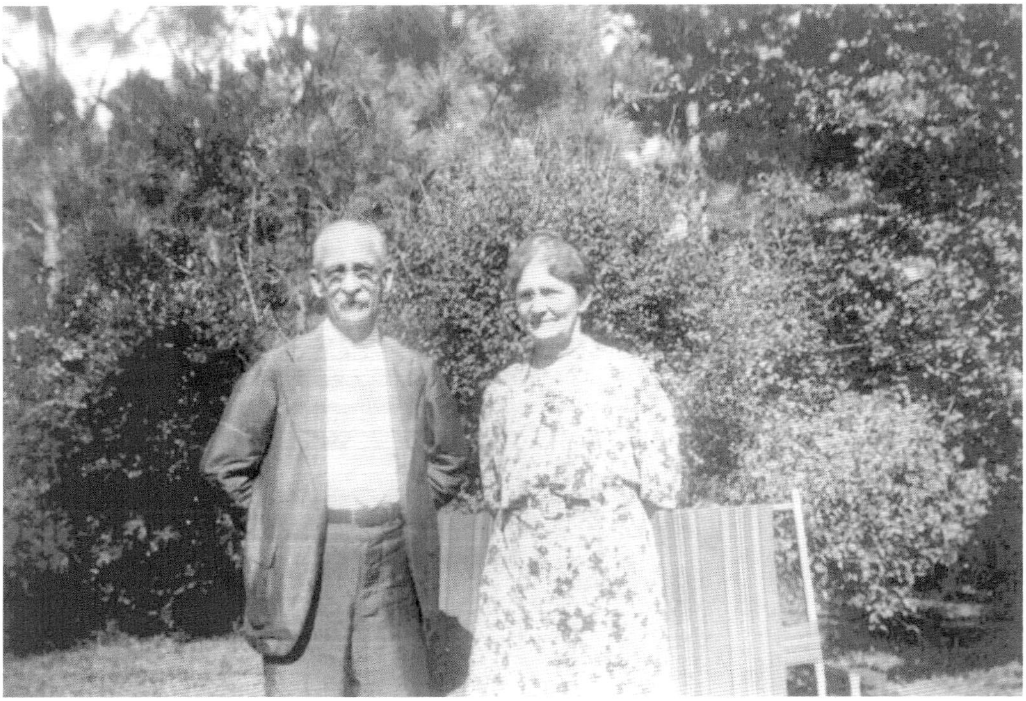

The Metairie Theater

When Metairie Theater opened at Metairie Road between Frisco and Aris Avenues on January 5, 1926, Eli T. Watson was the proprietor. In addition to stage shows and motion pictures, the theater was used for political meetings and rallies, including meetings of the 8th Ward Dumestre Club in support of Alexis Casimir Dumestre's run for police jurist. A 1928 *Times-Picayune* article described Dumestre as the "owner and manager of the show" holding a benefit with proceeds supporting the neighborhood Boy Scout troop. During 1929, meetings were held to discuss a proposed water plant, exorbitant gas rates, better streetcar service, lower telephone rates, and improved roads. Dumestre is pictured here in 1937 with his wife, Winona, at their home on Iona Street.

C.E. Strause and H.A. Johnson took over management of the theater, added heating, and reopened it on April 29, 1930, touting an RCA Photophone to show *The Cock-Eyed World* starring Victor McLaglen, Lily Damata, and Edmund Lowe.

In 1932, C.F. Bullard leased the building and Joseph Gruner became the manager. A highlight of that year was a rally on February 21 at DeLimon Park for the 8th Ward Democratic Club, with motion pictures run before and after the speakers' presentations. It culminated with Dumestre's speech from the theater that was broadcast on WTBO radio at 6:30 p.m. Meetings and benefit shows continued, and in 1935, the theater was used to distribute tax forms.

The building was sold in 1937 to the United Theatres chain. It reopened the evening of June 11, 1937, with interior and exterior renovations along with updated equipment, a new screen, and sloped floors. "Various special features for the comfort of the patrons have been introduced, and an effort has been made to have the theater one of the most artistic in the United Chain," boasted the owners' advertisement. Another advertisement announced "Rogers & Astaire to open new Metry Theater with Shall We Dance with 8 fresh songs – one of the most attractive playhouses in the City – 6:30 Admission 10 cents & 20 cents."

On June 30, 1940, Miss New Orleans candidates were chosen at all local United theaters, including the Metry. By 1952, the theater was unused but made front-page headlines: "Jefferson Boys Nazi Club Bared – Nazi Storm Trooper Club." Nine teenage boys were arrested for allegedly planning to bomb it. It has been alleged that Gordon Novel (see page 82) was one of these boys. (LDL.)

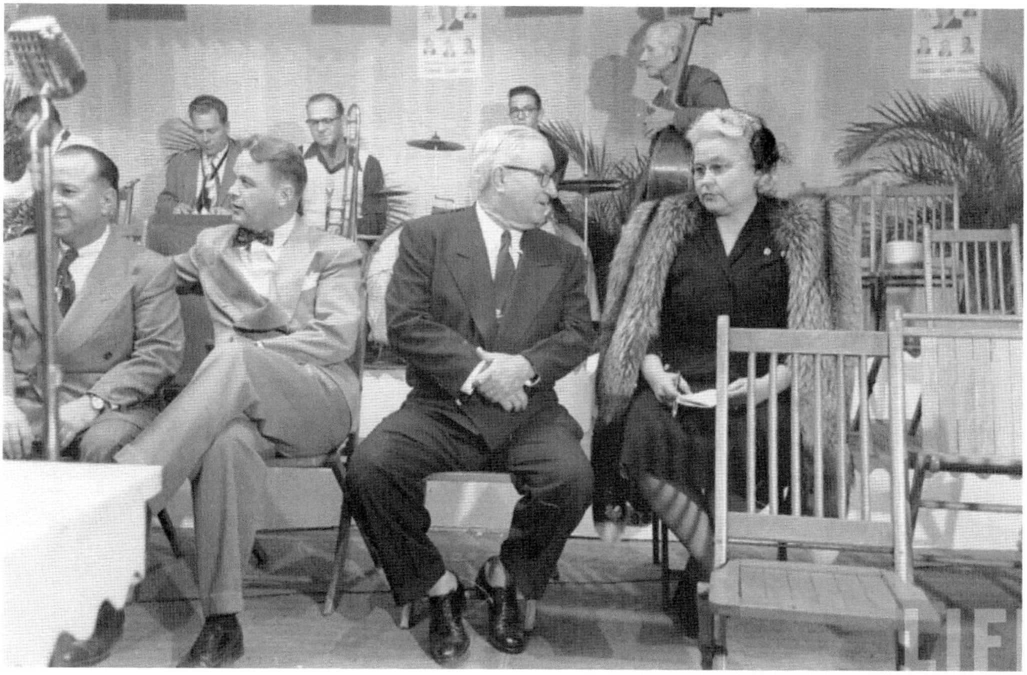

King Clancy

Frank James "King Clancy" was a young lawyer in 1915, the Jefferson Parish clerk of court from 1920 to 1928, and sheriff from 1928 to 1956. When speaking in 1953 about his lack of initiative in enforcing gambling laws, he said, "We just wait till a fellow loses his wad. Then he's bound to tell his wife, and she calls us." He is pictured here with his wife in 1952. (Time-Warner.)

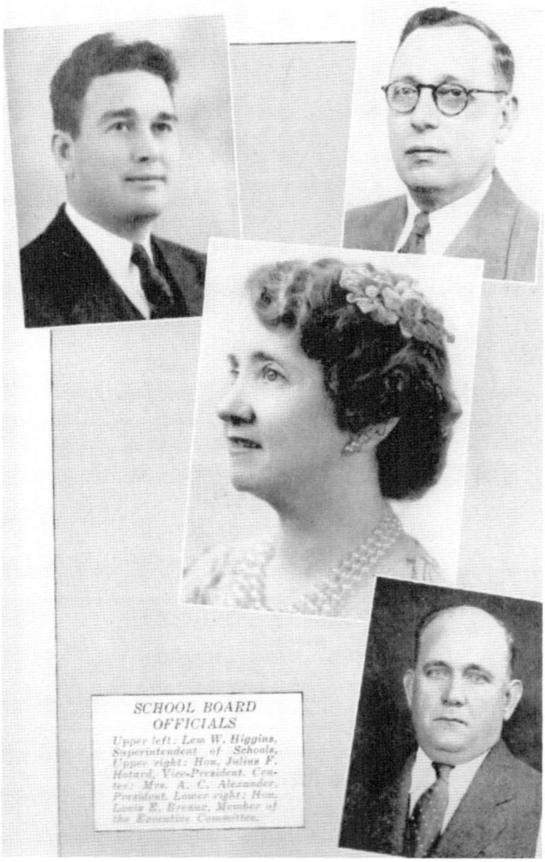

Clancy Family

The sister of Sheriff Frank Clancy, Anastasia Clancy Alexander (center) served on the Jefferson Parish School Board for 29 years, with 20 years as president. Wife of Richard J. Alexander, she was the daughter of John Clancy, first president of the board. She is pictured here in 1950. Jefferson parish schools have been named for her and her father. (JPYR.)

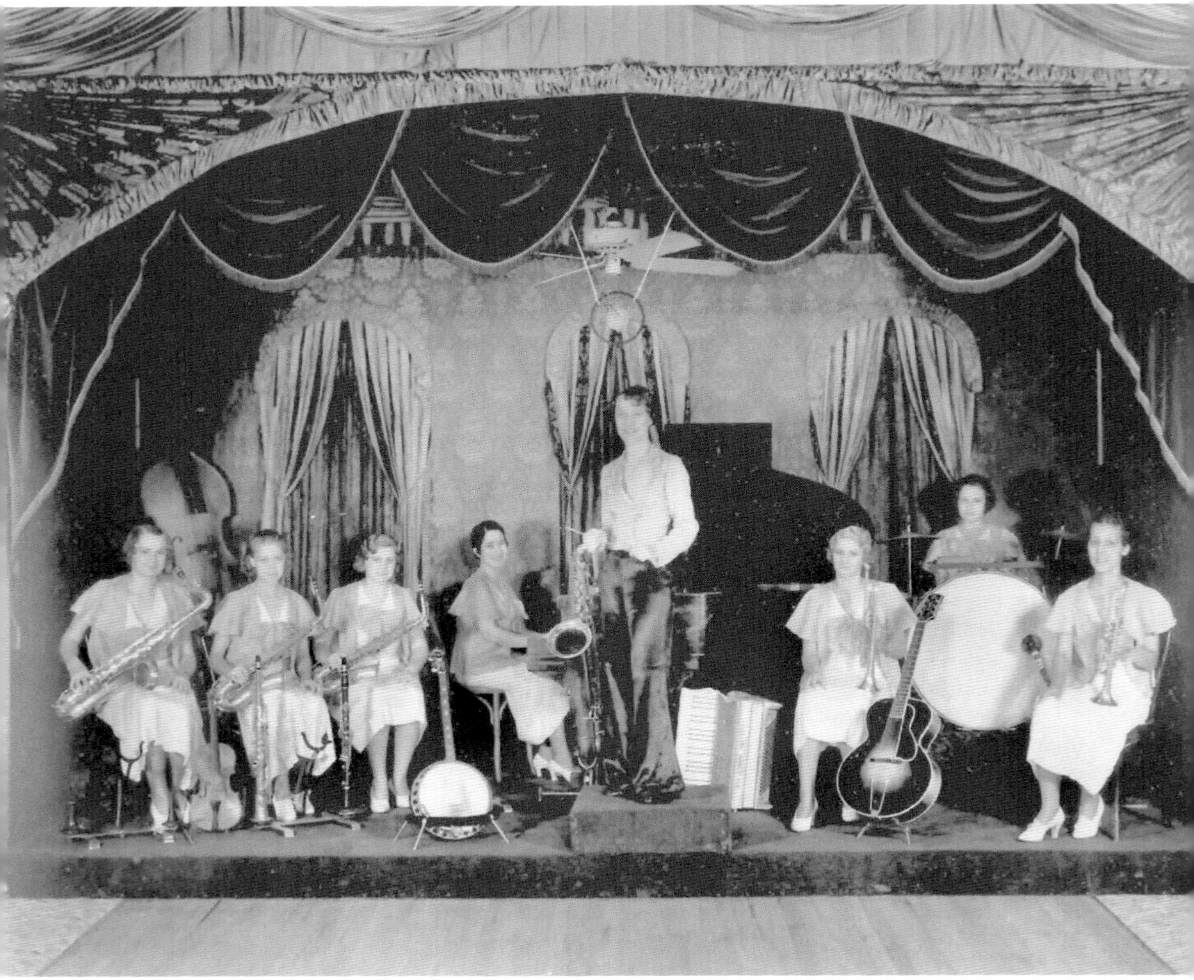

All-Girl Band (Almost)

Likely the earliest "all-girl band" in the greater New Orleans area, the Original Shades of Blue orchestra was formed in 1929 by seven local women, all in their early twenties . . . and Ernie the drummer, who wore a dress matching theirs and a wig. They played big-band music, which was just becoming popular at the time, performing at the Roosevelt Hotel Blue Room and the Parisian Room on Royal Street as well as Jefferson Parish venues like the Beverly, the Avalon, and the Cotton Club. The orchestra also performed on WWL radio's *Dawnbusters* show and on WDSU radio until the mid-1930s, when they moved to Chicago in an attempt to broaden their audience. Pictured here from left to right are Lorraine Ziblich, Maeceil Petersen, and Myrtle Bentin, saxophones; Thelma MacDonald, piano; Julie Huth, director; Jeanie Spato, trumpet; Ernie ?, drums; and Norma Latino (a longtime Metairie resident who is also pictured on the cover), trumpet. (Henry and Anne Harmison.)

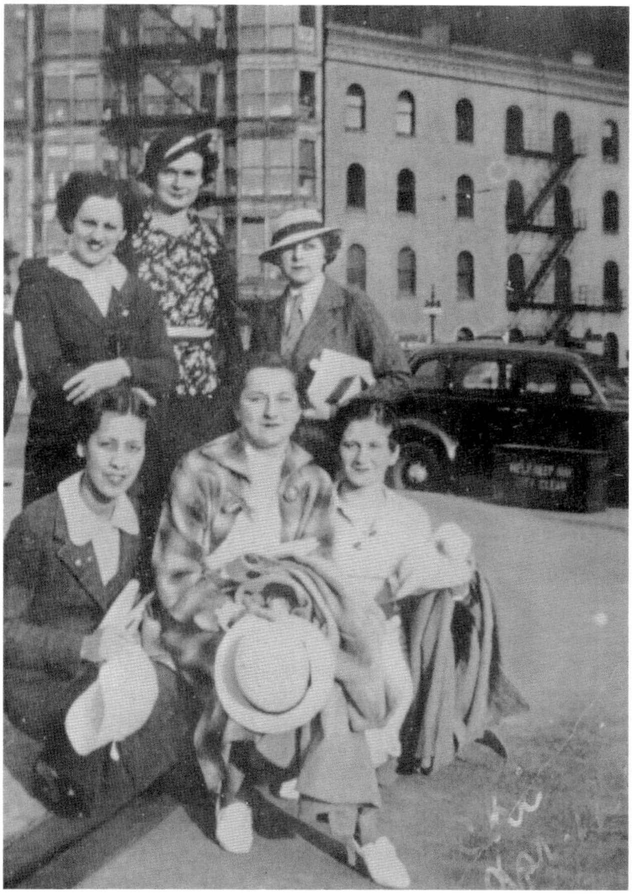

End of an Era
Times were tough during the Great Depression, and speakeasies featuring live performers were no longer in vogue. Shades of Blue disbanded in Chicago, where this photograph was taken. Pictured from left to right are (first row) Norma Latino, Josie Berger, and Jennie Spato; (second row) Skippy Kieran, Lorraine Zibilich, and Myrtle Bentin. (Henry and Anne Harmison.)

Monk Hazel
Arthur "Monk" Hazel, born in 1903, played with Johnny Wiggs, Albert Brunies, and many other local jazz greats. His New Orleans Jazz Kings helped launch the careers of Al Hurt and Pete Fountain. He is pictured here (left) in a c. 1932 photograph with Jules Bauduc's Orchestra at Metairie Inn. Monk passed away in 1968. (LDL.)

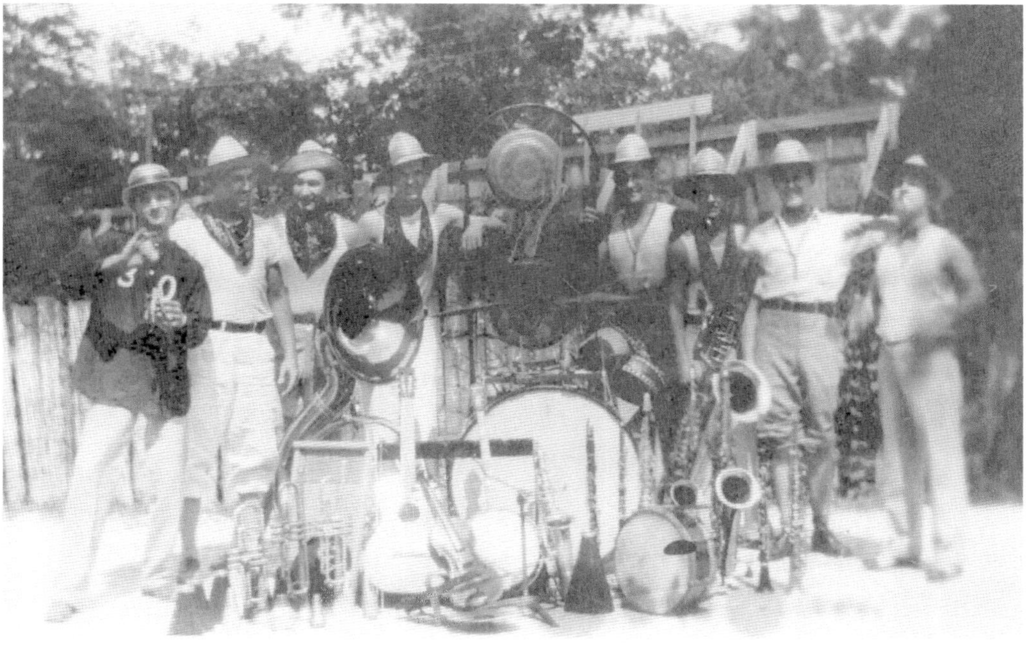

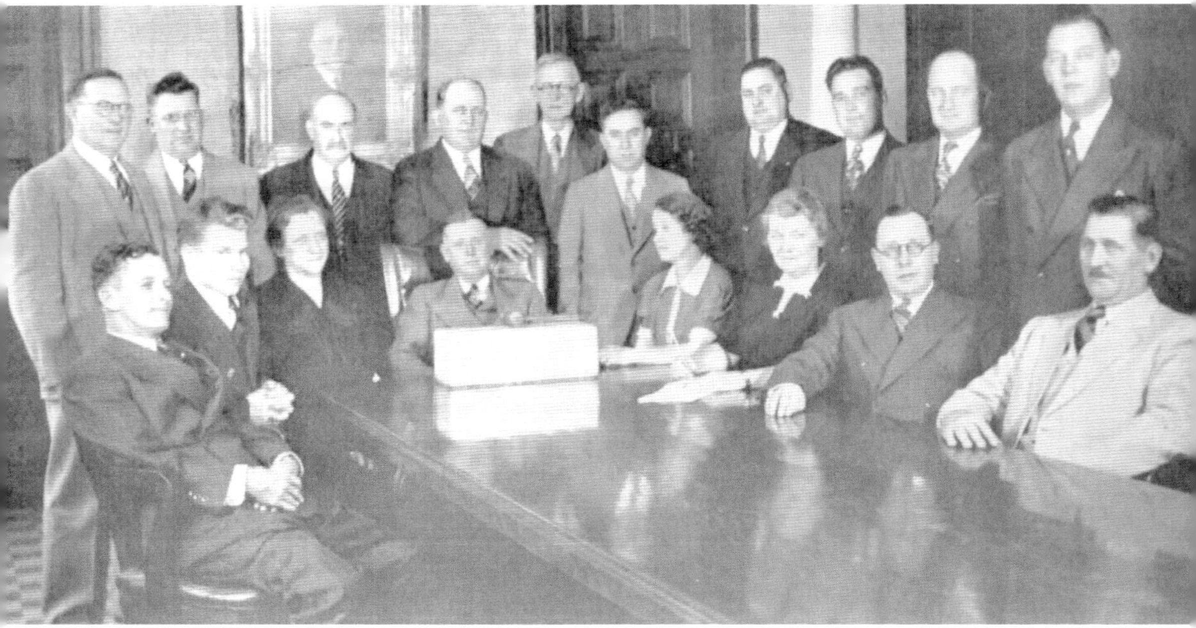

First School Superintendent
From 1908 until his death in 1940, J.C. Ellis (standing center, in 1939) oversaw tremendous growth in the public schools. During his 32 years in office, the student population grew to 8,511. Physical education classes and school buses were introduced. In 1940 alone, 11 new schools were built. Ellis lived in the 400 block of Metairie Road. J.C. Ellis Elementary school is named for him. (JPYR.)

CHAS. EBLE, FLORIST
Established Over 50 Years
152 Baronne St. Pere Marquette Bldg.
Phone MAin 1175—MAin 1223
Night UPtown 7446—CEdar 1261
Nurseries—Arnault Road—Jefferson Parish

"Say It With Flowers"
Metairie Ridge Nursery Co., Ltd.
FLORISTS
135 CARONDELET STREET NEW ORLEANS, LA.
NURSERY—METAIRIE RIDGE

Nurserymen
His storefront was on Baronne Street, but Charles Eble's nursery was and had been on Arnoult Road since before the turn of the 20th century. This advertisement was printed in 1939. Harry Papworth was a competing Metairie nurseryman, as the lower advertisement from 1941 indicates. Papworth Street now indicates where his home and lands were located. (JPYR.)

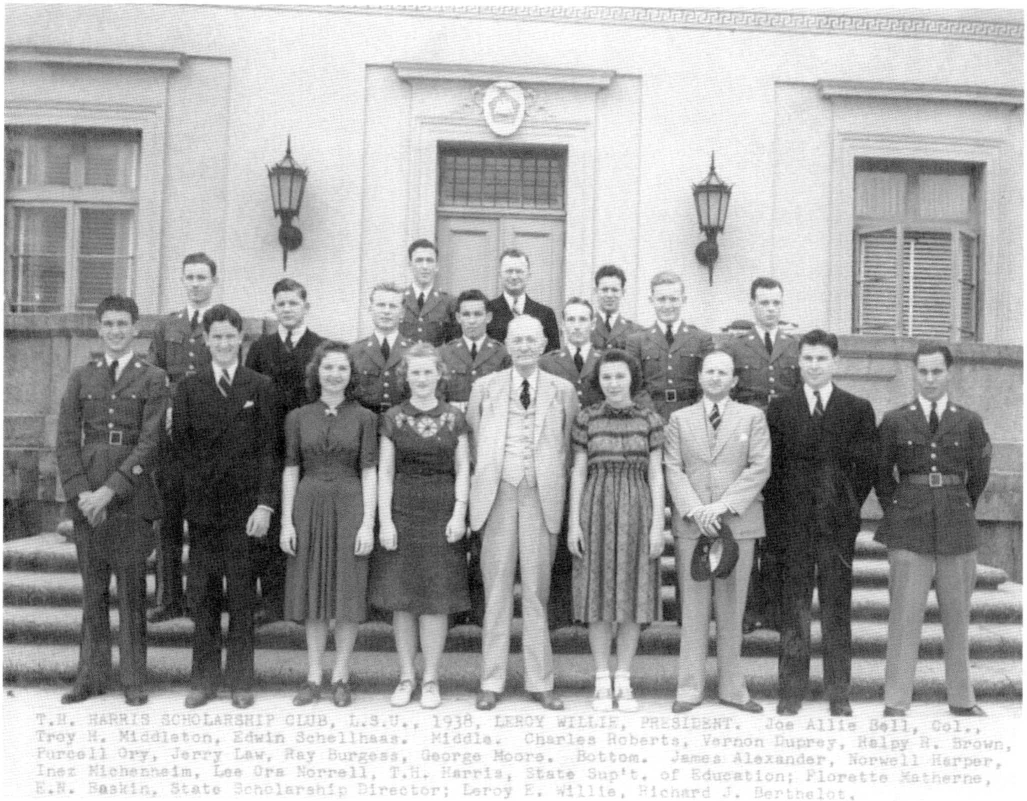

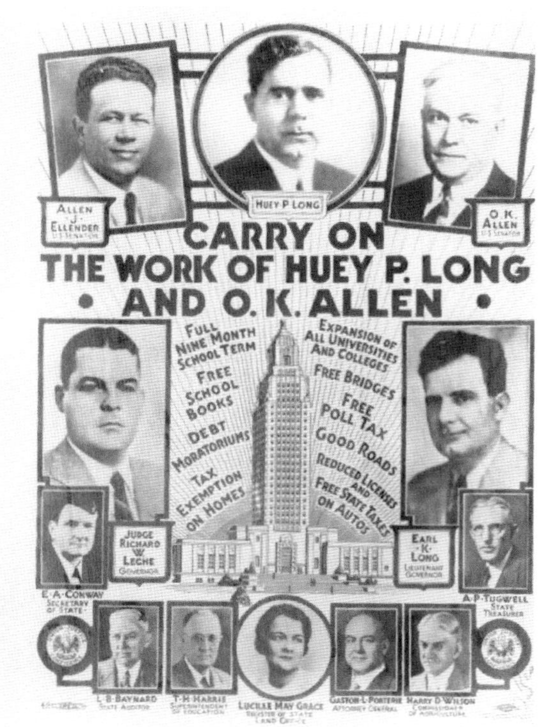

32-Year School Superintendent

Members of the T.H. Harris LSU Scholarship Club of Louisiana State University flank its namesake in Baton Rouge in this 1938 photograph. Harris was the state superintendent of education for 32 years, from 1908 to 1940. The middle school on Elise Avenue is named for him. (LDL.)

Under 12 Governors

Harris served under 12 governors while in office as superintendent of state schools. He is included in this 1936 political poster with Huey P. Long, O.K. Allen, Earl K. Long, and Richard Leche. Allen and Leche continued Long's nine-month school years, free textbooks for students, and improved colleges and universities. (LDL.)

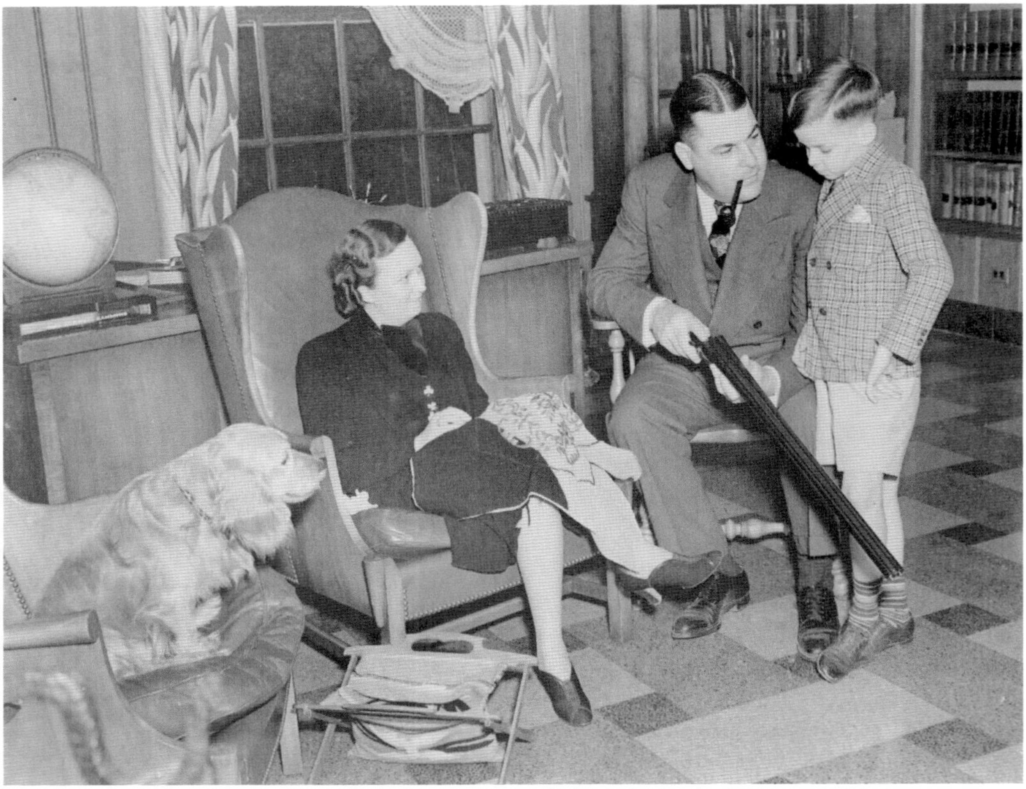

The Louisiana Scandals

On June 9, 1939, the *New Orleans States-Item* reported on the front page that a truck owned by LSU delivered building materials to a home under construction at 170 West Oak Ridge Park Avenue in Old Metairie. The property belonged to Catherine McLachlan (wife of James J. McLachlan), a close friend of Gov. Richard Leche. Associate editor Meigs Oliver Frost and photographer Willie d'Aquin had hid in a field to document this incident of state-owned materials being used for a private residence. This revelation led to what was and is still known as the Louisiana Scandals.

The governor resigned on June 26 for "health reasons." In 1940, he was convicted of mail fraud for taking kickbacks on state purchases and given a 10-year sentence, of which he served fewer than four years in a federal prison. LSU president James Monroe Smith fled to Canada to no avail; he spent 10 months in prison for misuse of university funds. This was only the beginning. Further investigation into the Leche administration and his political allies resulted in 200 indictments, several suicides, and the discovery that millions of dollars in state funds had been stolen. Leche was pardoned by Pres. Harry Truman in 1953. He is pictured here in Old Metairie (not far from the McLachlan property) with his wife and son in 1930.

Soon after he was elected governor in 1936, Leche began acquiring land on the Tchefuncte River. He commissioned Leon Charles Weiss (who had designed Huey Long's new state capitol, governor's mansion, LSU buildings, and LSU Medical School) to design a baronial home with a 40-foot great room 22 feet high, a 30-foot dining room, pegged heart-of-pine floors, and pecky cypress walls 13 inches thick on a governor's salary of $7,500 per year. A caretaker recalled seeing prisoners in striped uniforms working during the construction of the home. The Leche family spent much time there, and the governor often ran the state long-distance from the lodge, which employed a cook, housekeeper, gardener, stableman, and two chauffeurs who drove a Cadillac and a Packard (a gift of the Louisiana State Democratic Committee).

Leche's son Richard Jr. remembered a Scotsman named James McLachlan who "was like a member of the family and lived in the house with us. 'Mr. Mac' had a heart attack and died the night before my father returned from the Atlanta Federal Penitentiary in June 1945," he said. (LDC.)

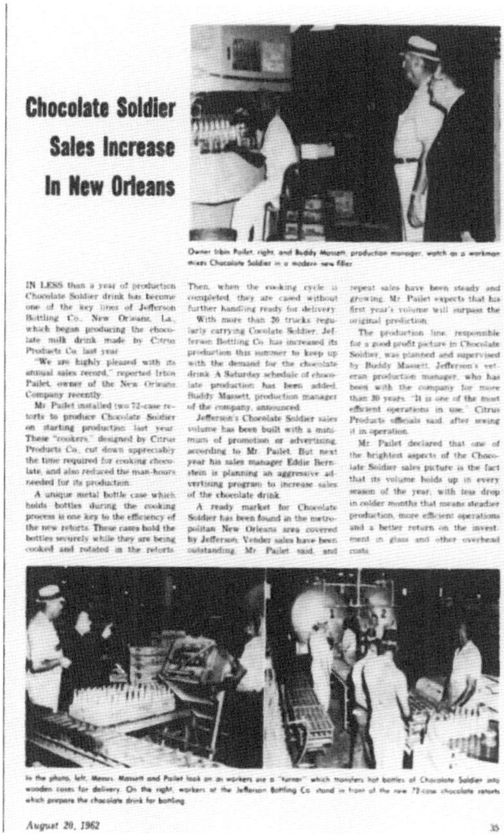
Chocolate Soldier Sales Increase In New Orleans

Owner Irbin Pailet, right, and Buddy Massett, production manager, watch as a workman mixes Chocolate Soldier in a modern new filler

IN LESS than a year of production Chocolate Soldier drink has become one of the key lines of Jefferson Bottling Co., New Orleans, La., which began producing the chocolate milk drink made by Citrus Products Co. last year.

"We are highly pleased with its annual sales record," reported Irbin Pailet, owner of the New Orleans Company recently.

Mr. Pailet installed two 72-case retorts to produce Chocolate Soldier on starting production last year. These "cookers," designed by Citrus Products Co., cut down appreciably the time required for cooking chocolate, and also reduced the man-hours needed for its production.

A unique metal bottle case which holds bottles during the cooking process is one key to the efficiency of the new retorts. These cases hold the bottles securely while they are being cooked and rotated in the retorts. Then, when the cooking cycle is completed, they are cased without further handling ready for delivery.

With more than 20 trucks regularly carrying Cocolate Soldier, Jefferson Bottling Co. has increased its production this summer to keep up with the demand for the chocolate drink. A Saturday schedule of chocolate production has been added, Buddy Massett, production manager of the company, announced.

Jefferson's Chocolate Soldier sales volume has been built with a minimum of promotion or advertising, according to Mr. Pailet. But next year his sales manager Eddie Bernstein is planning an aggressive advertising program to increase sales of the chocolate drink.

A ready market for Chocolate Soldier has been found in the metropolitan New Orleans area covered by Jefferson. Vender sales have been outstanding, Mr. Pailet said, and repeat sales have been steady and growing. Mr. Pailet expects that his first year's volume will surpass the original prediction.

The production line, responsible for a good profit picture in Chocolate Soldier, was planned and supervised by Buddy Massett, Jefferson's veteran production manager, who has been with the company for more than 30 years. "It is one of the most efficient operations in use," Citrus Products officials said, after seeing it in operation.

Mr. Pailet declared that one of the brightest aspects of the Chocolate Soldier sales picture is the fact that its volume holds up in every season of the year, with less drop in colder months that means steadier production, more efficient operations and a better return on the investment in glass and other overhead costs.

In the photo, left, Messrs. Massett and Pailet look on as workers use a "turner" which transfers hot bottles of Chocolate Soldier into wooden cases for delivery. On the right, workers at the Jefferson Bottling Co. stand in front of the new 72-case chocolate retorts which prepare the chocolate drink for bottling.

August 20, 1962 35

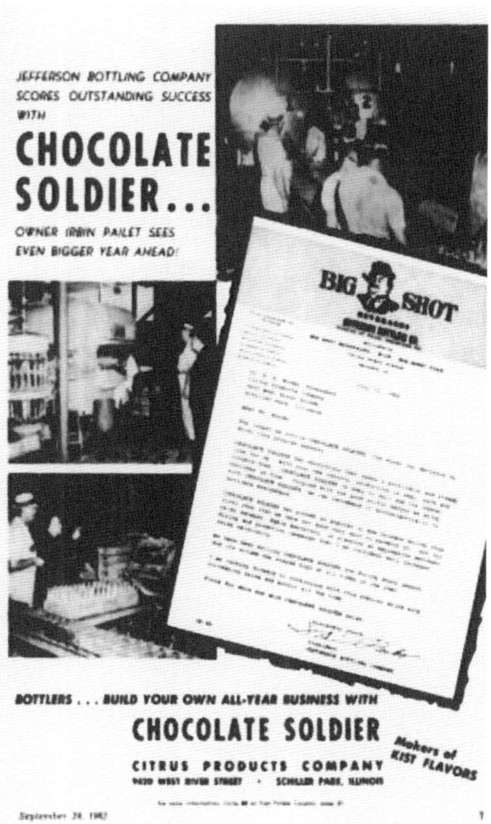

The Ice Man Cometh

In 1946, Leche (see page 49) sold his Tchefuncte estate to Irbin Pailet. He swapped it for Irbin Pailet's home on 112 acres on Bayou Lacombe plus $175,000. In 1920, with one horse and a wagon, Pailet had built an ice and soft-drink empire—Jefferson Bottling Company—pictured here in 1962 at 716–724 Frisco Avenue off Metairie Road.

Big Shot

During the early days, the family business also included Metairie Ridge Ice Company on Labarre at Metairie Road and employed sister Fannie and brothers Morris and Samuel Pailet Jr. Irbin's brother Maurice served as president. Brother-in-law H.J. Wallick was director of sales. In 1928, Irbin bought the Orange Crush bottling company at 3500 Tulane Avenue. By 1935, the Pailets introduced the iconic Big Shot cola.

METAIRIE RIDGE ICE CO., INC.
JEFFERSON BOTTLING CO., INC.
THE CITY ICE CO.
ARCTIC PURE ICE CO.

CEdar 1126

DRINK—

BIG SHOT ROOT BEER

DOUBLE COLA • TOM COLLINS, JR.

Round the Clock Ice

Pailet's business expanded from 1941 (above) to 1955 (below) to include Claiborne Ice, Arctic Ice on Bienville, Riverside Ice on Chartres Street, American Ice on St. Philip, and City Ice House at 3535 Tulane Avenue (later to become the laboratory of Dr. Morgus). The company pioneered 24-hour service via coin-operated machines. Pailet also owned Marada Stock Farms and Countryside Nursery in Covington.

In 1960, on the company's 40th anniversary, the local paper reported that Pailet Industries was "one of the states' and city's largest tax-payers . . . using raw materials principally from Louisiana resources." Irbin's death on November 4, 1962, was reported as front-page news. He had owned interests in livestock, nurseries, and oil production, was president of Metairie Bank, a member of the Metairie Business Men's Association, president of Congregation Chevra Thilim, and a philanthropic supporter of the Jewish Community.

THE JEFFERSON BOTTLING CO.

—BOTTLERS OF—

BIG SHOT BEVERAGES AND HIRES ROOT BEER

Metairie Road and Frisco Crossing New Orleans, La.

PAILET INDUSTRIES DIVISIONS

The Jefferson Bottling Company—Metairie Ridge Ice Company—Arctic Pure Ice Company, 3701 Bienville Ave.—Riverside Ice Company, 2731 Chartres St.—Claiborne Ice Company, 2816 S. Claiborne Ave. American Ice Company, 2801 St. Philip St.—Marada Stock Farms, Covington, La.—Countryside Nursery, Covington, La.

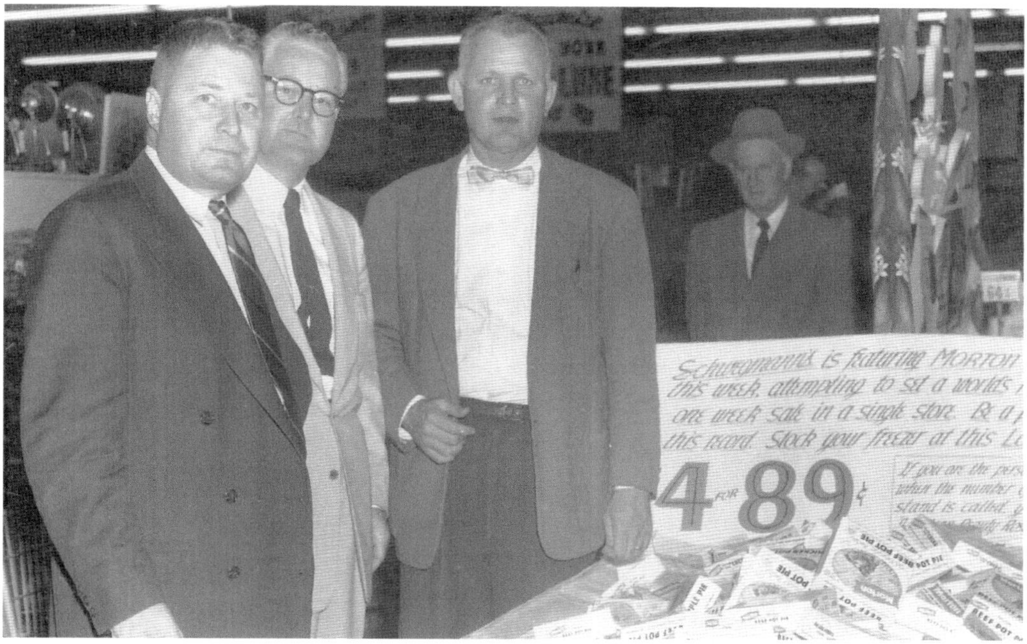

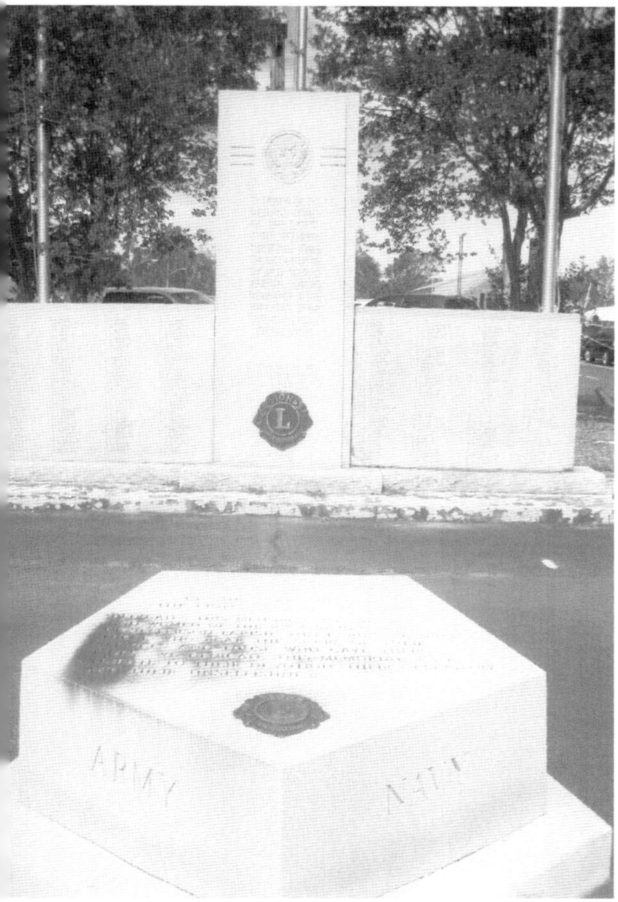

John Schwegmann Jr.
Having learned the grocery business in their father's store at Piety and Burgundy, Anthony, Paul, and John Gerald Schwegmann Jr. (pictured at the Airline Highway Schwegmann's location, which opened in 1941) built an empire of 18 stores, based in Metairie, with 5,000 employees. John was also a state representative (1960 to 1968), state senator (1968 to 1972), and Louisiana public service commissioner (1975 to 1980). He could have lived anywhere but chose a home in Metairie. (LDL.)

In Memory
On May 25, 1947, the Metairie Lions Club dedicated this memorial to the 728 men from Metairie who served in the armed forces. Of them, 27 names are starred to signify that they died in service to our country. The Reverends Paul Melancon, J.W. Bracy, and David Colomy participated in the opening ceremonies. The monument still stands on the Bonnabel neutral ground at Metairie Road where each Memorial Day they and others are honored.

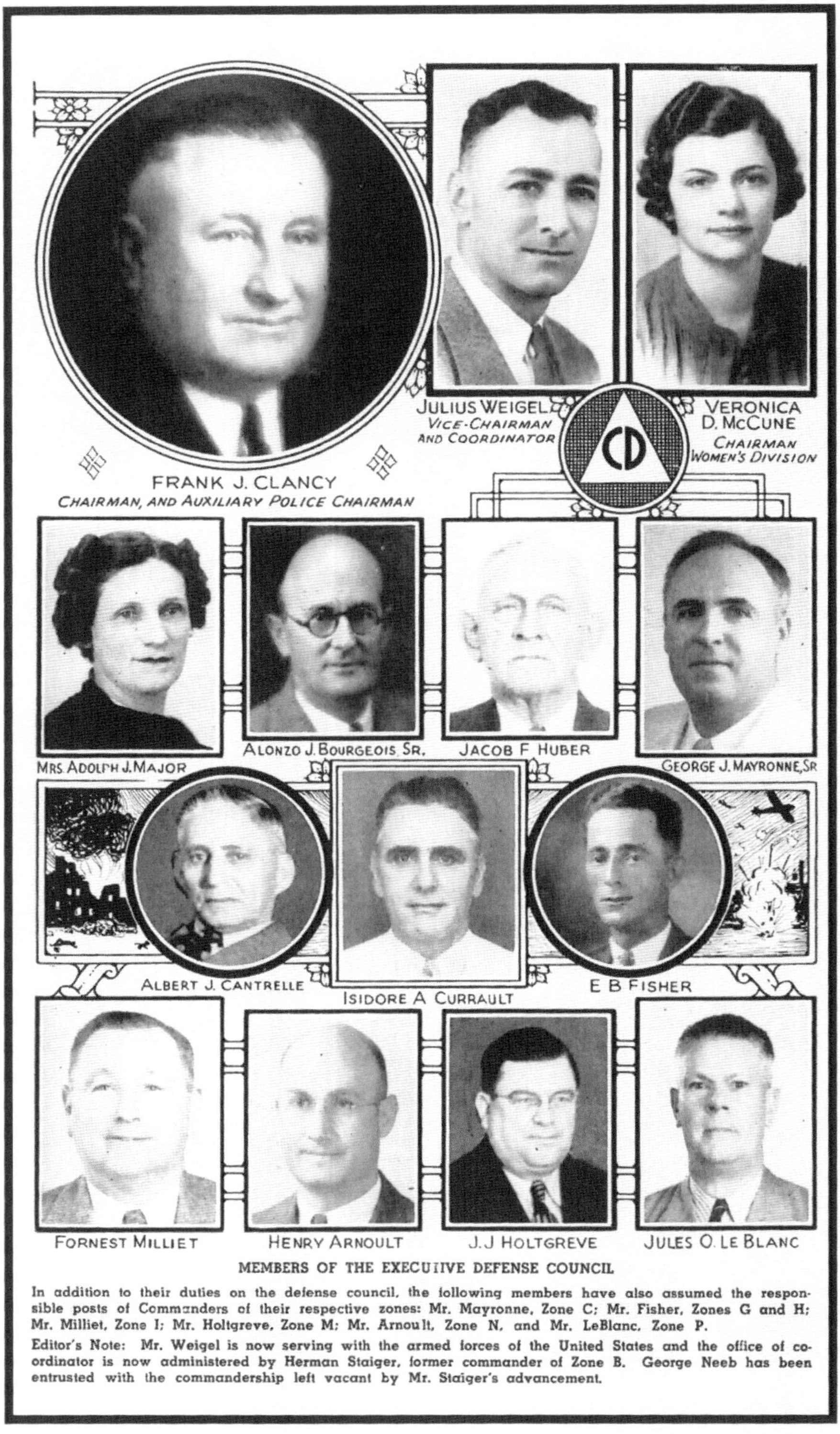

FRANK J. CLANCY
CHAIRMAN, AND AUXILIARY POLICE CHAIRMAN

JULIUS WEIGEL
VICE-CHAIRMAN AND COORDINATOR

VERONICA D. McCUNE
CHAIRMAN WOMEN'S DIVISION

CD

MRS. ADOLPH J. MAJOR

ALONZO J. BOURGEOIS, SR.

JACOB F. HUBER

GEORGE J. MAYRONNE, SR.

ALBERT J. CANTRELLE

ISIDORE A CURRAULT

E B FISHER

FORNEST MILLIET

HENRY ARNOULT

J. J HOLTGREVE

JULES O. LE BLANC

MEMBERS OF THE EXECUTIVE DEFENSE COUNCIL

In addition to their duties on the defense council, the following members have also assumed the responsible posts of Commanders of their respective zones: Mr. Mayronne, Zone C; Mr. Fisher, Zones G and H; Mr. Milliet, Zone I; Mr. Holtgreve, Zone M; Mr. Arnoult, Zone N, and Mr. LeBlanc, Zone P.

Editor's Note: Mr. Weigel is now serving with the armed forces of the United States and the office of coordinator is now administered by Herman Staiger, former commander of Zone B. George Neeb has been entrusted with the commandership left vacant by Mr. Staiger's advancement.

Parish Officials

Jefferson Parish officials during the 1940s included Sheriff Frank Clancy (top left; see page 52); Weaver R. Toledano, police jury president (bottom left); Edward M. Thomassie, president pro tem (bottom middle). In the right column, beginning at the top, are Vic A. Pitre, clerk of court; Vernon J. Wilty, assessor (see page 72); James E. Beeson, state representative; and Dr. Charles F. Gelbke, coroner.

PARISH OFFICIALS

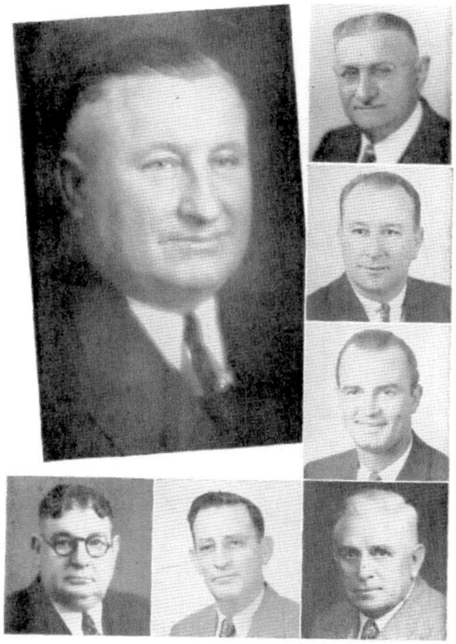

Hon. Frank J. Clancy, Sheriff

Reading from top to bottom: Hon. Vic A. Pitre, Clerk of Court; Hon. Vernon J. Wilty, Assessor; Hon. James E. Beeson, State Representative; Dr. Charles F. Gelbke, Coroner; Hon. Edward M. Thomassie, President Pro-Temp., Police Jury; and Hon. Weaver R. Toledano, President, Police Jury.

Weaver Romanus Toledano served on the police jury for 32 years (1920–1952) and was president from 1925 until his retirement in 1952. A 45-year resident, he was also a longtime publisher of the *Jefferson Parish Yearly Review*, an annual synopsis of the growth that had occurred during the previous year. Toledano died in 1962 at the age of 82.

Born in 1888, Edward M. Thomassie served on the police jury from 1944 through 1946. Husband of Jeanne Cassou, he owned and operated the Hollywood Theater in Gretna and the Royal Theater in Marerro. When Thomassie died at the age of 43 in 1956, Weaver Toledano was a pallbearer.

Grocer Augustin "Victorin" Pitre was born in 1878. He sat on the school board (1912–1928), where he served as president and vice president; was the parish clerk of court (1928–1952); and served as mayor of Westwego (1921–1941). He and his wife, Jewell Assenheimer, had two daughters: Ruth was a supervisor of elementary schools, and Thelma Gray was a parish home demonstration agent. His business interests were in real estate, trucking, poultry farming, and manufacturing. Pitre died in 1957 in an automobile accident.

State representative James E. Beeson held that position continuously from 1944 until 1972, working alongside John Schwegmann (see page 53). William Dwyer (see page 77), Leon Soniat (see page 71), and Hank Lauricella (see page 58). One of his most important pieces of legislation was the $9 million allocation in 1960 to LSUNO for the construction of the library, classrooms, and the administration building, which allowed for expanded enrollment. Husband of Carolyn Case, he was a partner in Beeson Warner Inc. and a director of Enterprise Federal Savings and Loan. He passed away in 1966.

Dr. Charles F. Gelbke, born in 1878, graduated from Tulane Medical School in 1900 and became Jefferson Parish coroner in 1904. He served in that position until 1908. From 1916 to 1920, he was both the mayor of Gretna and the parish coroner. Elected mayor again in 1922, he held the office for 10 years. He was elected again by Gretna voters from 1940 to 1949 and also took on the job of coroner from 1944 to 1946. The husband of Mary E. Koebel, he was also appointed as a colonel by Gov. Luther F. Hall in 1913 and as an administrator in the Works Progress Administration by Pres. Franklin Roosevelt. Retired from politics in 1949, Dr. Gelbke died in 1951.

John Joseph Holtgreve (OPPOSITE PAGE)

Positioned second from right in the bottom row of this 1942 composite of the members of the Executive Civil Defense Council, John Holtgreve also served for 20 years on the police jury, as president from 1952 to 1956, when he resigned to manage the Causeway Bridge's first span. He had worked on the project since 1944, when the Greater New Orleans Expressway Commission was incorporated to oversee the planning and construction of the structure. Married to Marie Lafargue, he lived at 155 Metairie Court. Holtgreve was in the Army Signal Corps during World War I and had managed the Helois Street sewerage plant before he died in 1960.

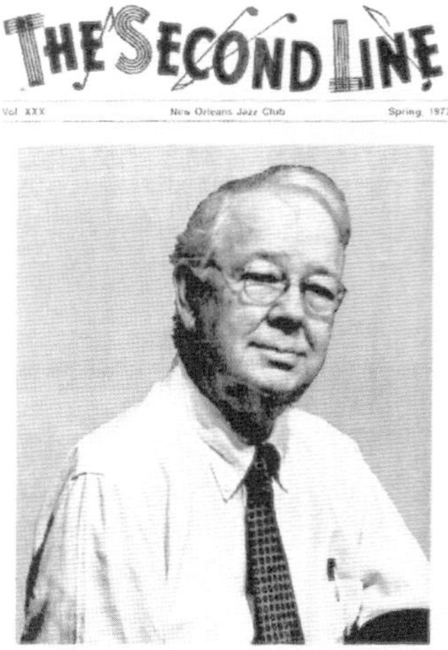

JOHNNY WIGGS

Johnny Wiggs

Pete Fountain was John Wiggington Hyman's most famous student, but he also taught Vince Campanella to play the clarinet at his State Band School of Music. He performed as Johnny Wiggs and in 1948 founded the New Orleans Jazz Club, a civic nonprofit organization that revived national interest in Dixieland jazz and reinvigorated the careers of many originators of the genre. His family owned land running from Lake Pontchartrain to the Mississippi River that would become Causeway Boulevard. At right, he graces the spring 1977 cover of *The Second Line*, the publication of his New Orleans Jazz Club. Below, he performs at a club meeting in 1950 with Sherman Mangiapane. (Both, LDL.)

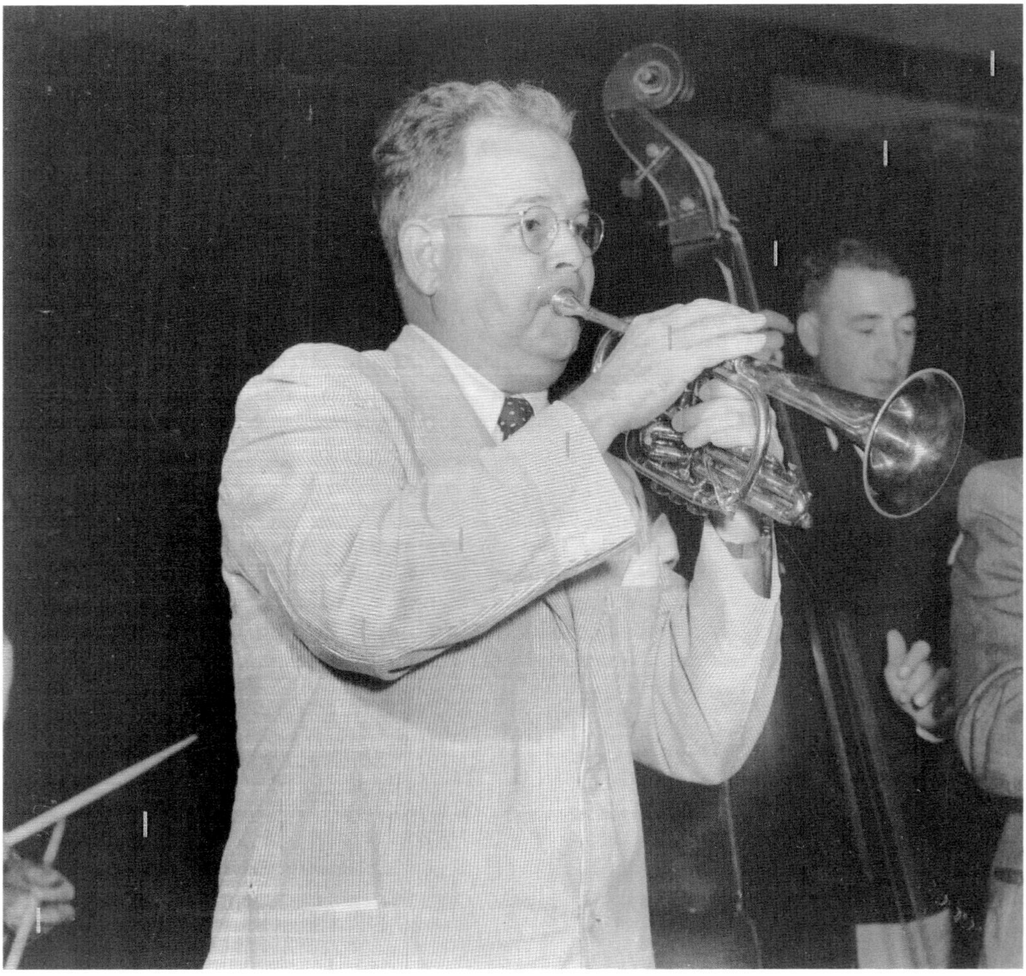

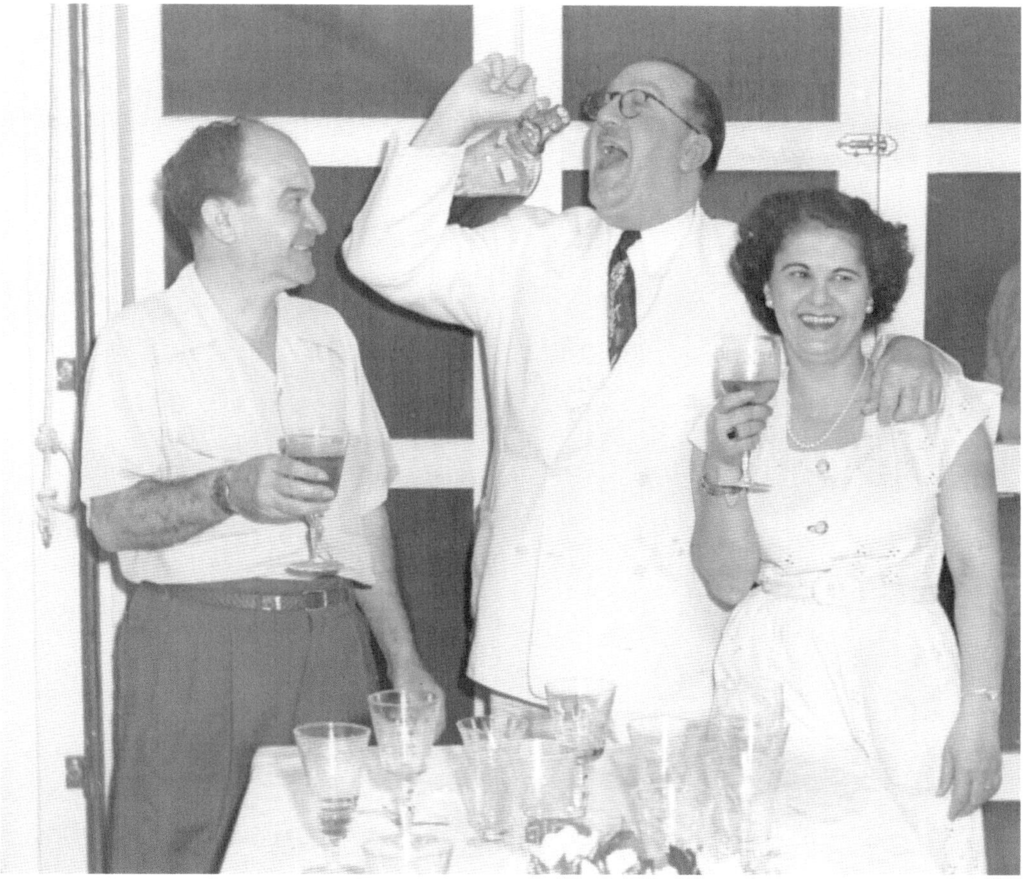

Doc Souchon

Born on October 25, 1897, to a prominent New Orleans family, Edmond Souchon II was a passionate lover of jazz and a dedicated physician. He practiced medicine at Hotel Dieu (as chief of staff), Charity, De Paul, Mercy, and Crippled Children's Hospitals. He was a founding member of the Louisiana Surgical Association, a pioneer user of sodium thiopental as a general anesthetic, and a life fellow of the American and the International College of Surgeons. He was a director of Pan American Life Insurance Company and the Krewe of Rex.

"Doc" formed his first band, The Six and 7/8 String Band (which played music akin to jazz before the term had been coined) while attending Tulane University. He played guitar and banjo with many of jazz's best musicians, including Johnny Wiggs, Sherwood Mangiapane, Papa Jack Laine, and Paul Barbarin.

He is credited with the historical preservation of jazz during his lifetime. To accomplish that, he featured great local musicians and their music on a WWL radio show, contributed to *Life*, *Newsweek*, and *Time* magazines, lectured, and appeared on national radio and television programs. He had become so well known for his avocation as a local jazz enthusiast that, on May 5, 1961, he appeared on the popular *This is Your Life!* television show, hosted by Ralph Edwards.

Souchon played benefits for Crippled Children's Hospital, established the National Jazz Foundation and the New Orleans Jazz Museum, recorded some 500 songs, was a president of the New Orleans Jazz Club, and edited *Second Line* from 1951 until his death. He could not read a note of music.

In 1967, with Al Rose, he wrote *New Orleans Jazz: A Family Album*. "Doc" Souchon died, playing his guitar for friends and family, on August 24, 1968, in his home at 523 Betz Place. He bequeathed 5,000 records and a library of literature to the New Orleans Public Library and the William Ransom Hogan Jazz Archives at Tulane. He is pictured here (center) with Sharkey and Mildred Bonano at a party in their home.

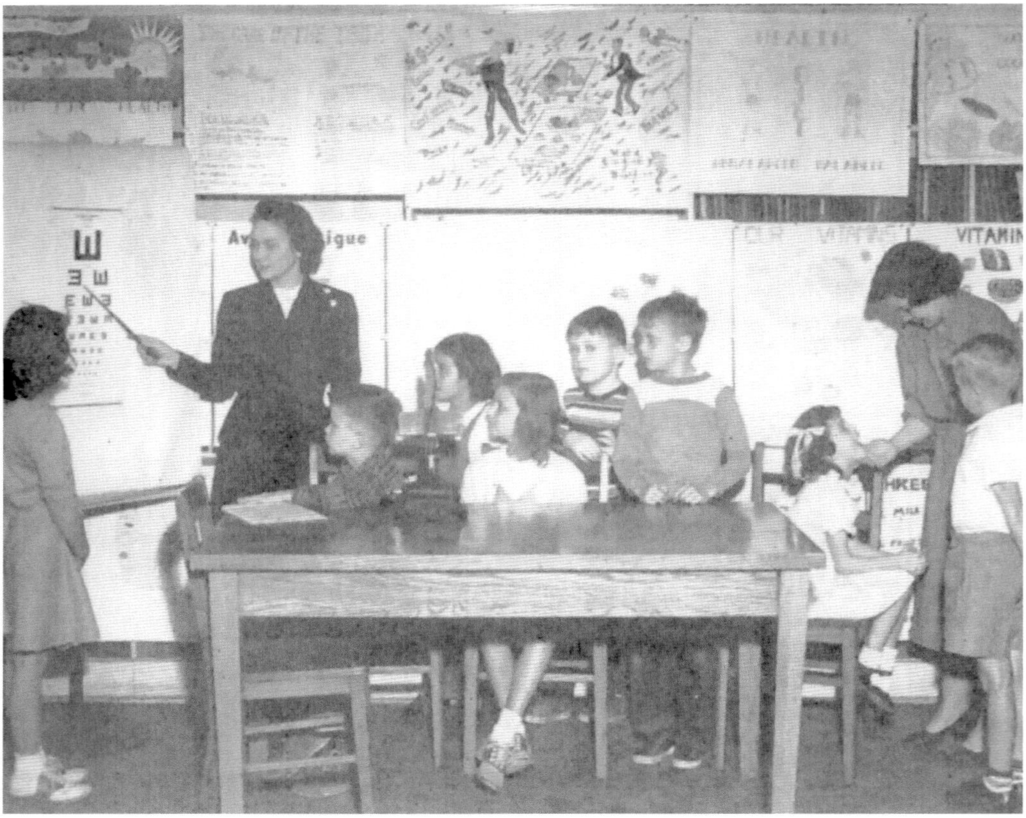

Codifer Family

Armantine Codifer is shown here in 1950 demonstrating use of an eye chart at Metairie Grammar School. The daughter of Louis Pascal Codifer Sr. and Esther Stutzman, she later married James Leroy Smith Jr. and had two daughters, Armantine M. and Celeste M. Smith. Codifer Boulevard is named for her family, who donated the property upon which St. Catherine of Sienna school and church located in 1924. (LDL.)

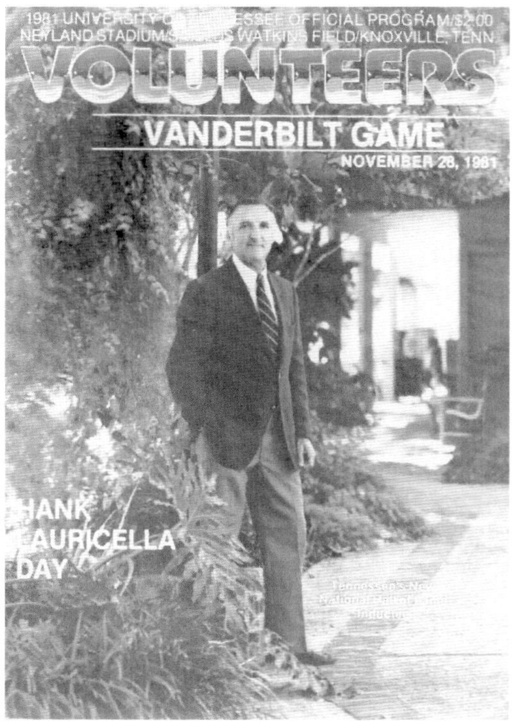

Football Star and Senator

"They're ready to move in," proclaimed Lauricella & Sizeler Company in 1951, builders of Airline Park Subdivision, offering 18 models at $500 down for $58 per month. Meanwhile, Lauricella's son Francis E. ("Hank") was named an All American halfback. Hank joined his father's business, which became Lauricella Land Company. He was a state representative (1964 to 1972) and senator (1972 to 1996). In 1981, Hank was inducted into the College Football Hall of Fame. (The University of Tennessee.)

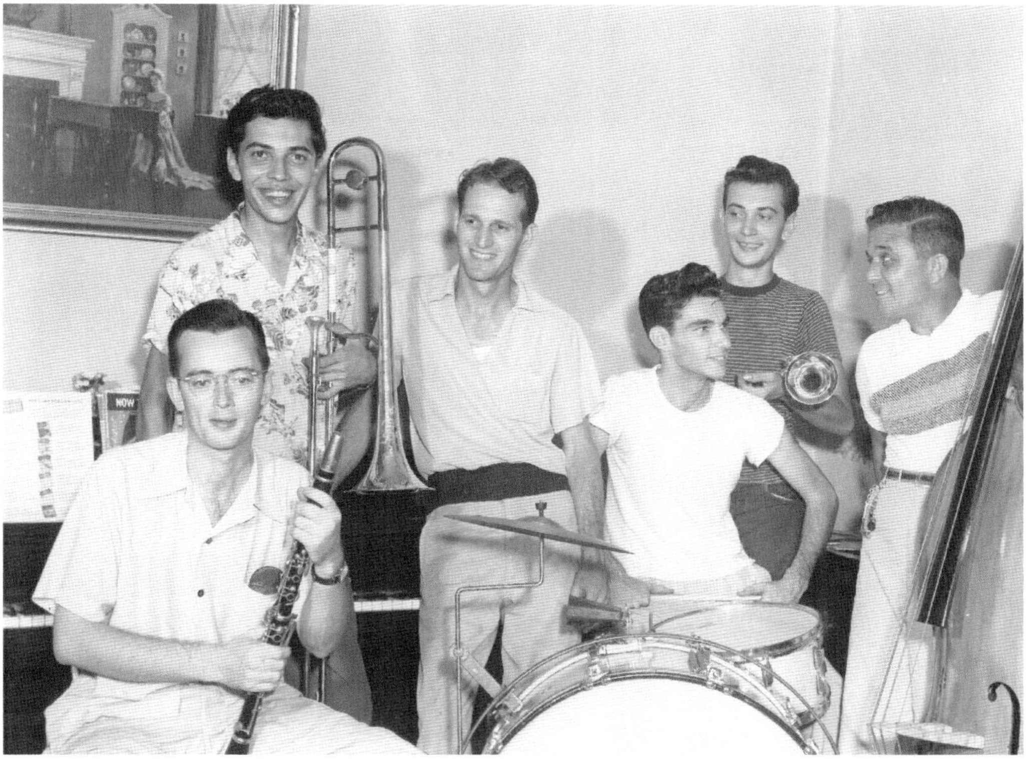

The Assuntos

In 1946, teenage brothers Frank and Fred Assunto began playing professionally, often with a young Pete Fountain, at Mama Lou's camp/restaurant on Lake Pontchartrain. The following year, they began (depending upon the number of musicians playing) to call themselves the Basin Street Four, Five, or Six.

Under the name The Junior Dixie Band, they performed each month at Doc Souchon's New Orleans Jazz Club meetings (Frank's son Deano is now the club's vice president) and in 1949 played at the New Orleans Jazz Festival, where they first used the name Dukes of Dixieland. In 1950, the Dukes began a three-and-a-half-year gig as the house band at Bourbon Street's Famous Door. Their first professional recording was "Cooking with Gas" (1951), which was used in a NOPSI commercial.

While still in high school, Fred met 14-year-old Betty "The Duchess" Owens, who became the band's singer and his wife. This 1955 postcard from drummer Roger Johnston mailed from Chicago gives a glimpse into their budding fame as a nationally known local band. It is addressed to "Dr. Edmond Souchon; 523 Betz Place; Metarie; Louisiana" and reads (on the back), "Hi Doc, We're really packing them in here. They really go for that good old New Orleans jazz. They don't want us to leave here; but Las Vegas wants us there. —Roger." Pictured from left to right in 1950 are Frank Assunto on the trumpet, Bill Shea on the clarinet, Fred Assunto on the trombone, and Artie Seelig Jr. on the piano during a rehearsal at the Assuntos' home.

Fred and Frank's father, Jacinto "Papa Jac" Assunto, joined the band when Betty took leave to start a new generation of the Assunto family. In 1956, the Dukes became the first jazz band to record in stereo on Audio Fidelity Records. They appeared on national television, toured internationally, performed and recorded with Louis Armstrong, and played at Carnegie Hall in 1959.

After Fred died in 1966 at age 36 in Las Vegas, Frank donated his brother's trombone to the New Orleans Jazz Museum. By 1969, the extended family moved back home to Metairie and the Dukes became regulars at Al Hirt's club. Frank passed away in 1974 at the age of 42. The Onward Brass Band, for the first time in their 90-year history, honored a white musician by playing at his funeral. Papa Jac passed away in 1985 at age 79. Betty followed in 2006. She was 72 years old. (LDL.)

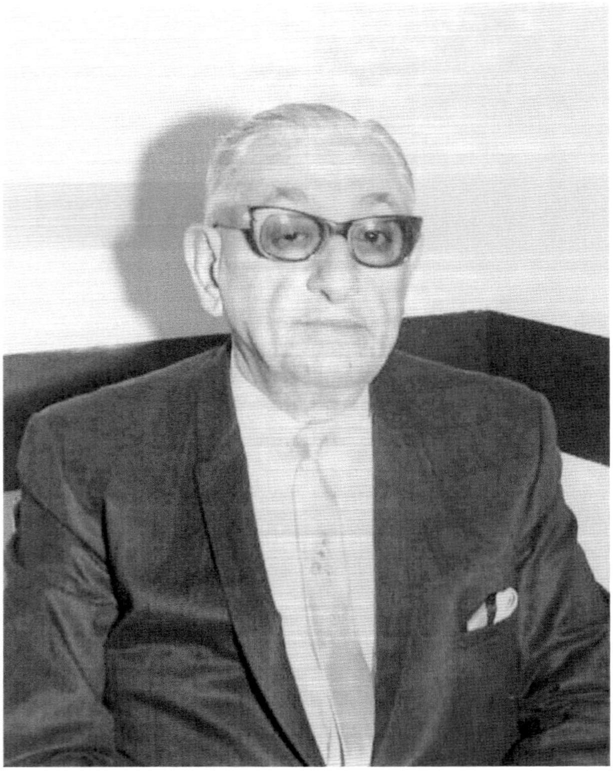

Felix Bonura

In 1954, Green Acres Civic Club opposed a planned harness racing course in their neighborhood, filed a suit, and parked cars to block access to the construction site—to no avail. Felix Bonura had leased 424 acres with a 10-year lease, and the Louisiana State Racing Commission granted him a permit for night racing at Magnolia Park. In 1959, it was converted into Jefferson Downs horse racing course at what is now Lafreniere Park.

Known as "Chicken Man," Bonura also owned Magnolia Broilers, the largest processor and distributor of non–federally inspected dressed chickens in the New Orleans area. The reputed mafia figure reported in 1959 that four sticks of dynamite were found in his broiler room. He was also owner of Magnolia Liquor wholesale distributor and Future Realty, which was the sole shareholder in Magnolia Park. During the 1960s, he was president of the French Market Corporation. Bonura passed away in 1975. (NOPL.)

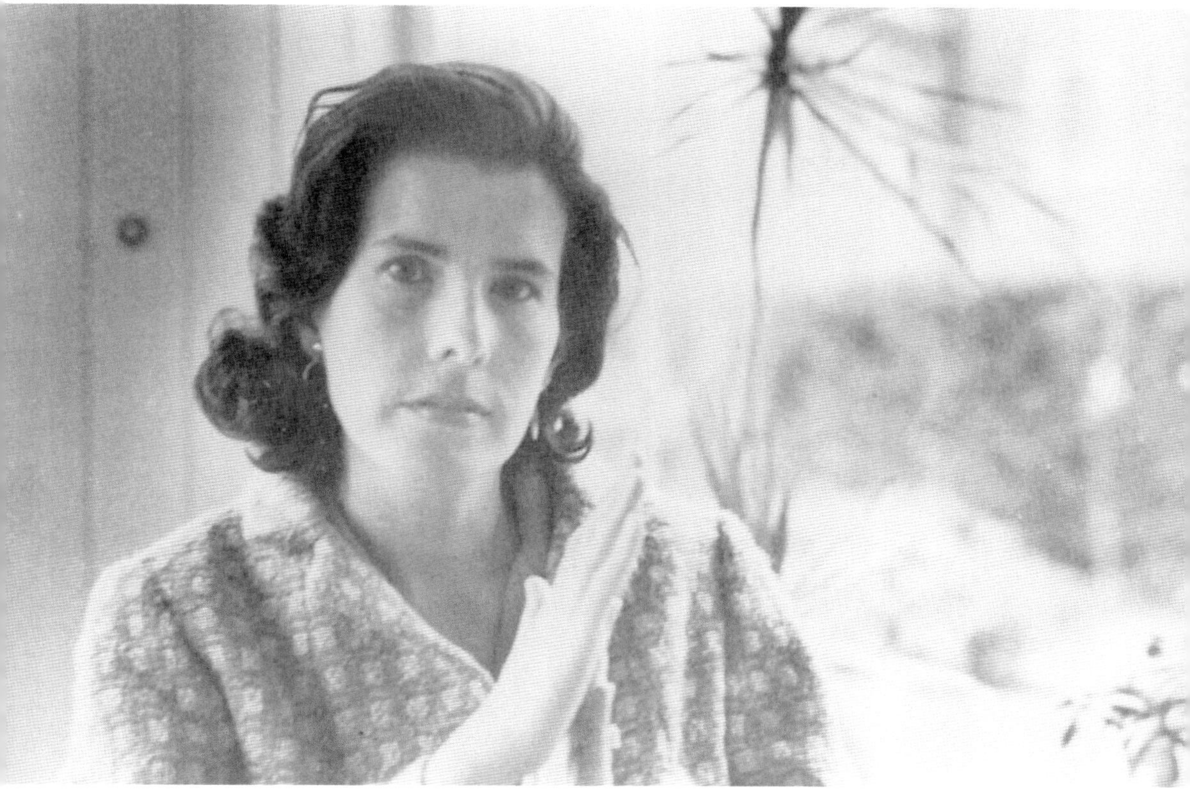

Shirley Ann Grau

When Interviewed by Mabel C. Simmons of the *Times-Picayune* in 1955, young author Shirley Ann Grau said she aspired to write an "even dozen" books. Simmons wrote, "Their author, like her characters, has the charm of originality. She is no imitator of Southern writers but is an individual, standing alone, devising and developing her own style. This reader wants to read the other 11 books she is going to write." Grau, a native New Orleanian, had graduated from Ursuline Academy and Sophie Newcomb Memorial College in 1950 with honors and a Phi Beta Kappa pin. The book was her first: *The Black Prince, and Other Short Stories*. One story, "Joshua," was included in the O. Henry Prize Stories in 1955 and appeared in the *New Yorker*. Ten years later, her novel *The Keepers of the House* was awarded the Pulitzer Prize for Fiction.

Grau lived in Old Metairie while raising her four children with her husband, Tulane professor and writer James Kern Feibleman. She served on the board of directors of St. Martin's Episcopal School, taught creative writing at the University of New Orleans, and contributed writings to *Atlantic*, *New Yorker*, *Redbook*, and *Mademoiselle* magazines. Her books include the novels *The Hard Blue Sky* (1958), *The House on Coliseum Street* (1961), *The Condor Passes* (1971), *Evidence of Love* (1977), *Roadwalkers* (1994), and the short story collections *The Wind Shifting West* (1973) and *Nine Women* (1985). (LDL.)

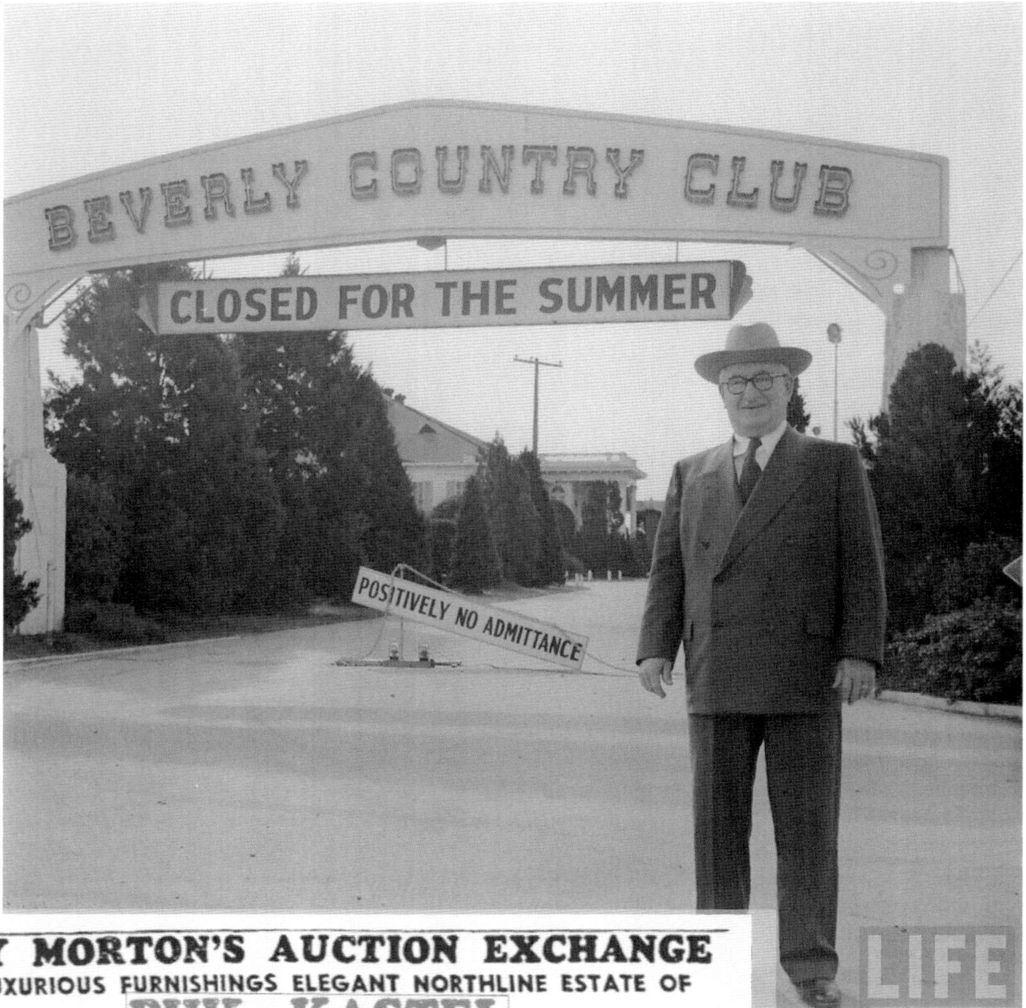

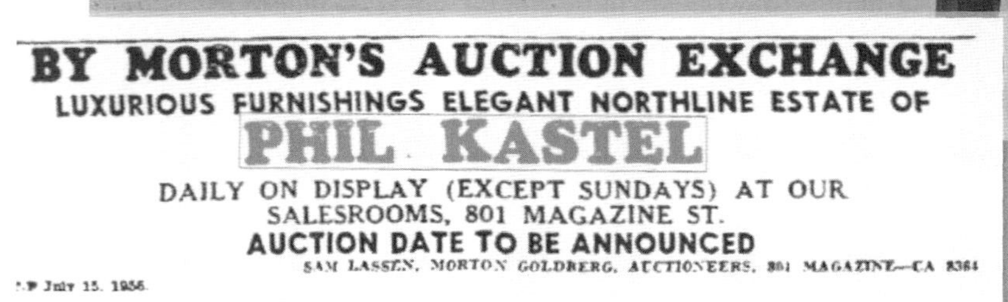
BY MORTON'S AUCTION EXCHANGE
LUXURIOUS FURNISHINGS ELEGANT NORTHLINE ESTATE OF
PHIL KASTEL
DAILY ON DISPLAY (EXCEPT SUNDAYS) AT OUR SALESROOMS, 801 MAGAZINE ST.
AUCTION DATE TO BE ANNOUNCED
SAM LASSEN, MORTON GOLDBERG, AUCTIONEERS, 801 MAGAZINE—CA 8364
July 15, 1956.

Sheriff Frank Clany and Phillip Kastel

"Things are tougher for gamblers in Jefferson Parish where Frank Costello and Phil Kastel once operated one of America's finest gambling clubs, The Beverly. Sheriff Frank Clancy [pictured above] who piously agreed with Senator Tobey at the Washington hearing that gambling was evil promised the committee he would close down his kingdom," reported *Life* magazine in the October 1, 1951, issue.

By 1956, Sheriff Clancy was serving his last year in office but also sold 855 acres of his property to Chateau Estates Incorporated for $382,500. Phillip "Dandy Phil" Kastel's long stint as one of Jefferson Parish's most noted gambling entrepreneurs had come to an end. He was busy preparing for the opening of the $15 million Tropicana casino in Las Vegas, and his fine Metairie home was up for auction. Kastel returned to New Orleans and was found dead in his Claiborne Towers apartment. The gunshot to his head was ruled an apparent suicide in 1962. (Time-Warner.)

CHAPTER THREE

Boomers and Risk Takers

The Jefferson Parish population doubled in the 1960s, then tripled, then tripled again by the 1970s. Shopping malls, restaurants, and new businesses sprang up along the highways and major arteries of Metairie's 150-square-mile footprint. Baby boomers were born in new Metairie hospitals. New schools, churches, and playgrounds were built.

Of the eight Metairie playgrounds, only half are named in honor of Metairie citizens. They are Bright Playground on Cleary Avenue, Girard Playground on Irving Street, Miley Playground and Stadium on West Metairie Avenue, and Pontiff Playground on Palm Street. Girard Playground (officially Louis Girard Memorial Field) was named for Louis C. "Noot" Girard, the Jefferson Parish superintendent of recreation and commissioner of the Dixie Youth Baseball program who passed suddenly at age 39 in 1963. Johnny Bright Playground was named in honor of the supervisor of Metairie Playground. When the playground on Cleary opened in 1965, he was honored for his dedication to the youth of Jefferson Parish. Mike Miley and Wally Pontiff Jr. are noted in this chapter.

During the 1960s, Lakeside Shopping Center opened as an open-air double strip mall. The Do Drive-In replaced the old greyhound track on the DeLimon Metairie Road property. The Joy Bowling Center on Airline was converted into the Joy Theatre. In 1963, Joseph Dorignac Jr. moved his city grocery to 710 Veterans Highway and Airline Bowling Center opened at 7401 Airline. In 1965, Interstate 10 was butting through central Metairie and Jefferson Downs closed to become Lafreniere Park. Ground was broken in 1977, and it opened in 1982. WestGate Drive-In showed its first films in 1966. The New Orleans Saints began practicing in Metairie on David Drive in 1967 and moved to their current facility on Airline Drive in 1995. Woolco Department Store opened its doors on Veterans in 1968 and the beautiful Metairie High School building was demolished. In 1969, the second span of the Causeway opened.

The Metairie Road Italian-American St. Patrick's Parade made its debut in 1971 after being organized by the clientele of Fulco's bar on North Turnbull. The 1970s brought a building boom along Causeway Boulevard and the new "town" Fat City developed by Ray Anselma, Joseph Peters, Joseph Marcello, and David Levy in 1972.

The boom was slowing by the 1980s, as most Metairie land was occupied. Restaurant Sclafani closed in 1985. The East Bank parish office building on Metairie Road was demolished during the 1990s. Schwegmann Brothers sold its 24-store chain in 1996. The Zephyrs debuted at UNO's Privateer Park in 1993 before moving to the $21 million "Shrine on Airline" in 1997. At Clearview Mall, the historic Maison Blanch department store was replaced by a Target store in 2002. The Jefferson Parish Public Library on West Napoleon Avenue replaced the Lobby Library in 2003.

In 1995, at age 21, Metairie's own 2nd Lt. Rebecca Elizabeth Marier became the first woman to graduate first in class at West Point, with a 3.95 GPA. She had also been captain of the women's tennis team at West Point. At Metairie Park Country Day School, she was senior class president and had lettered in volleyball, soccer, and tennis. From West Point, she went to Harvard Medical School and is now a surgeon.

Included in this chapter are Seafood City's Al Scramuzza, who coaches at Johnny Bright playground; St. Angela Merici Church pastor John Clement Favalora, who became the third archbishop of Miami;

scientist Verne Tripp, who pioneered use of the electron microscope and worked to unravel the mystery of cotton's properties to formulate Wash 'n Wear clothing; and World War II Coast Guard coxswain Marvin Perrett, who piloted Higgins-built LCVPs to the shores of Iwo Jima, Okinawa, and Normandy on D-Day.

Metairie educators featured here are Paul Hubell, Metairie High School principal and superintendent of schools; Jefferson Parish School Board president and realtor Emile Gennaro; Lobby Library organizer Maurice Walsh; Jay Harney, principal of John Q. Adams and J.D. Meisler middle schools; and teacher Hazel Romano, who also taught and choreographed Saturday Hop's Romano Dancers.

Pantera's lead singer Phil Anselmo, dancer Peter Gennaro (who choreographed the Broadway production of *West Side Story* and was awarded a Tony for his work on *Annie*), Louisiana Rock and Roll Hall of Fame inductees The Nobles, members of The Glory Rhodes ("I'm So Happy"), and Saturday Hop's John Pela all have lived in Metairie.

Business owners Charles Gennaro (restaurant owner, grocer, oyster dealer, and owner/manager of Gennaro Park baseball field), home-builder John Speir Treen, casket company owner Newton E. Shirer, Smoothie King's king and queen Stephen Kuhnau and Cindy Zimmer, Zack's Famous Frozen Yogurt creators Mike Williams and Sam Holt, cobbler and World War II veteran Chuck Azzarello, and fried chicken magnate Al Copeland all contributed to Metairie's quality of life and economic growth.

Public servants William J. Dwyer Jr. (first city marshal) and state legislator William J. Dwyer III, parish president John J. Holtgreve, parish assessors Vernon J. Wilty Sr. and Jr., Louisiana Public Service Commission members George J. Ackel and Jeanette Lentini Ackel, Jefferson Parish clerk of court Jon A. Gegenheimer, Sheriff Alwynn Cronvich, Gov. Dave Treen, state house of representatives member David Duke, and parish council members Donald T. Gillen, Vial J. Blanke, and Cullen C. Shouest served Metairie and Jefferson Parish through much of its history.

Dave Dixon, Bernard "Buddy" Saverio Diliberto, Tom Dempsey, Jim Mora, Dick Nolan, Wayne J. Francinques, and Otis Smith are sports figures who reside or lived in Metairie, as are writers Leon Soniat ("La Bouche Creole") and Sister Helen Prejean (*Dead Man Walking*). Crime figure Carlos Marcello had two homes and at least one legitimate business in Metairie. David Ferrie, Gordon Novel, Perry Raymond Russo, and Dean Andrews were involved in the Warren Commission's investigation into the assassination of Pres. John F. Kennedy, as well as Jim Garrison's trial of Clay Shaw. They all lived in Metairie.

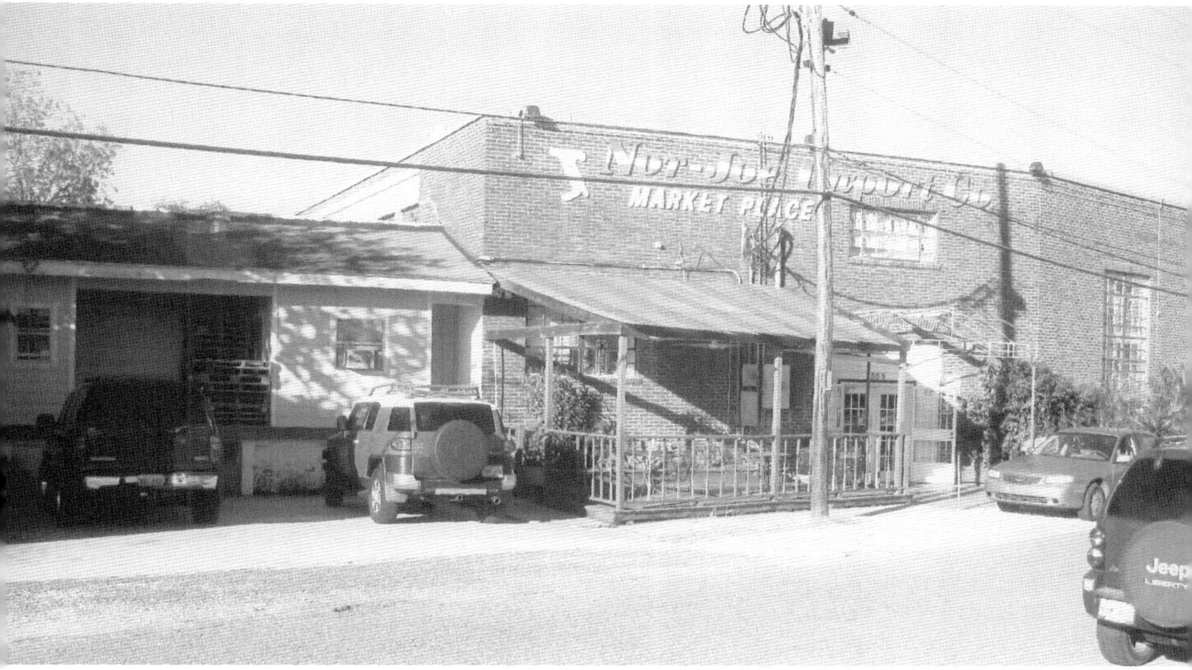

Nor-Joe Imports

Norma Webb's grandfather produced cheese on his dairy farm many decades ago and sold it in New York. Norma became a hobbyist who created her own recipe for mozzarella and, with her mother's encouragement, decided to begin selling it in 1982. She and her husband, Joseph Giglio, opened Nor-Joes at 505 Frisco Avenue a few years later in the building where Irbin Pailet (see page 51) had created Big Shot cola.

The business grew to supply local restaurants and grocery stores with imported Italian foods and then expanded to distribute Italian and other European gourmet products coast to coast. Nor-Joe now offers products from Argentina, Bulgaria, France, Denmark, Hungary, the Netherlands, England, Germany, Norway, Greece, Spain, and Switzerland. But locals know Nor-Joe best for its delicious muffulettas and St. Joseph Altar staples.

Their delivery trucks service restaurants, casinos, and hotels throughout the area. And in their old Metairie building, they still sell Norma's mozzarella but have also added Nor-Joe brand Granada Padano, marinated Ciglini, Parmesan, Reggiano, and Romano cheeses. The dock of the old Pailet icehouse is on the left in this photograph.

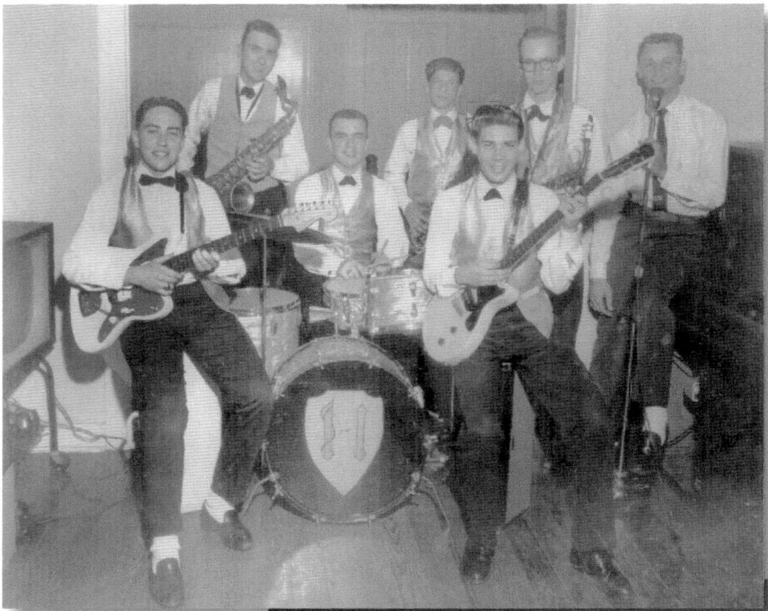

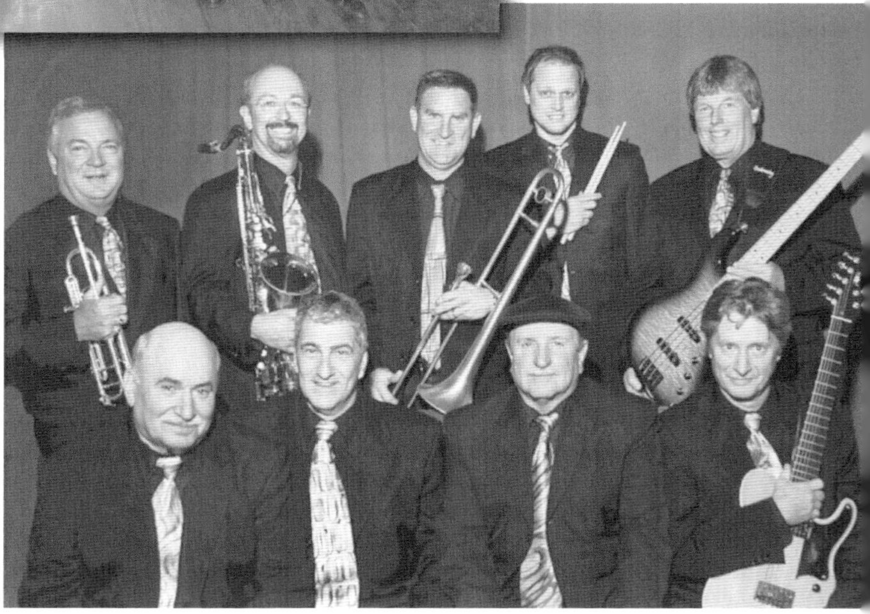

The Nobles

From 1959 until 2012, with over 70 different musicians comprising the band for more than 50 years, The Nobles entertained local audiences. In 1999, they were inducted into the Louisiana Rock and Roll Hall of Fame. Their last performance was on June 16, 2012, at Rock n' Bowl. Pictured in the top photo are the original members in their first publicity photograph. From left to right are Don Courtade, John Dauenhauer, Bill Murray, George Fried, Don Sixkiller, Roy Mark, and Melvin Navo.

Drummer Bill Murray led the band for 47 years before retiring in 2007, when Maurice Trosclair took the reins. Band members through the years included Eddie Freche Jr., Danny Hebert, Eddie "Gypsy Woman" Powers, "Good-Rockin' " Ronnie Lamarque, Tony Manale, Jerry Stalcup, Billy Haden, Maurice Trosclair, Ray Genovese, Steve Bacharach, Randy Hebert, Mike Wibel, Don de la Houssaye, Allan Linker Jr., Barklay Emmons, Bobby Ohler, and Bert Cotton. On the bottom is a 2012 photograph. (The City of Slidell.)

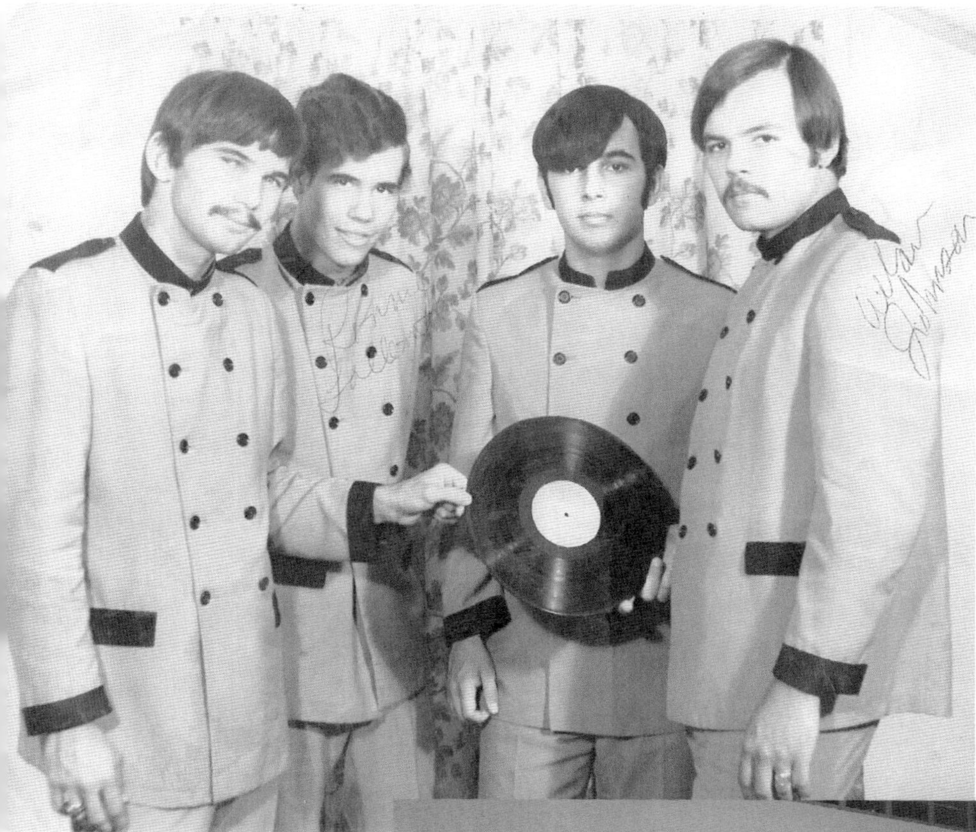

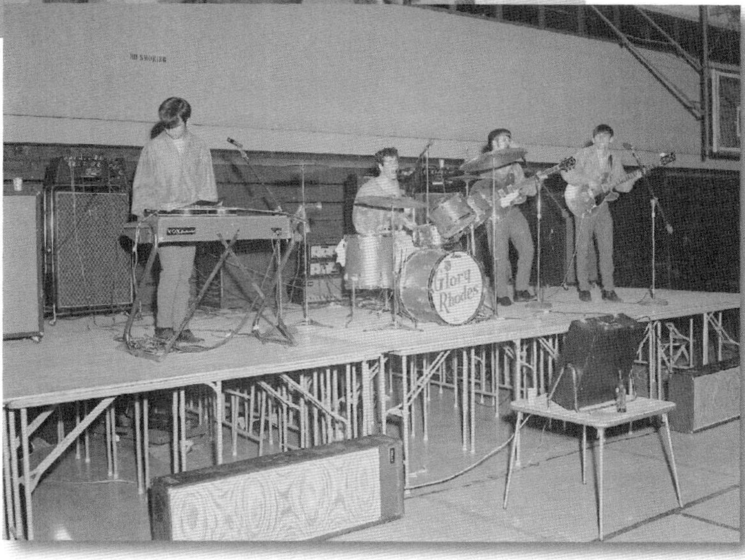

The Glory Rhodes

The Glory Rhodes were one of the most popular bands at local school dances and fairs during the 1960s and early 1970s. Their original members were Kenny Lyles (lead vocals), Frankie Spencer (lead guitar), Sal Serio (keyboards and rhythm guitar), John Laviolette (bass), and Greg Nobile (drums).

They recorded "Not that Kind of Guy"/"Gonna Be Somebody" by Nobile, Serio and Lyles, "I'm so Happy"/"Can We Go to the City?" "Old Laces"/"She's a Big Girl Now" (arranged by Allen Toussaint), and "I'm Gonna Change the World"/"Stay Out of My Way," written by Nobile, Serio, and Laviolette, which was featured in the 1967 film *Hot Thrills and Warm Chills*. In 1968, Ronnie Tallent became the lead vocalist and replaced Kenny Lyles as drummer. Later members included Allan Johnson on lead guitar and Kenny White on drums. Pictured in the top photo from left to right are John Laviolette, Ronnie Tallent, Sal Serio, and Allan Johnson. In the bottom photo from left to right are Sal Serio, Ronnie Tallent, Frank Spencer, and John Laviolette at Rummel High. (Laura Matherne Ditta.)

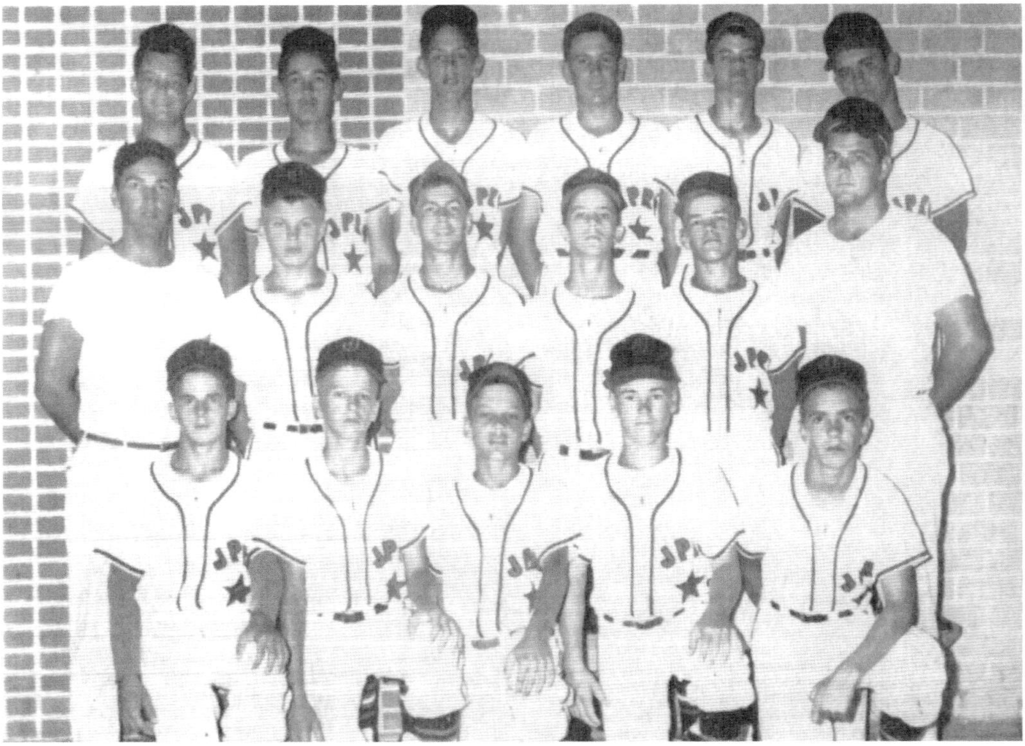

National Champs

Metairie Playground's 1961 Dixie Youth All Star team included Wayne J. Francinques, who grew up to play for the Baltimore Orioles (1966) and the Chicago White Sox (1969). Jay Harney was a star player at East Jefferson High who chose education for his career, having worked as a teacher, counselor, disciplinarian, assistant principal, and principal of John Q. Adams and J.D. Meisler middle schools. (JPYR.)

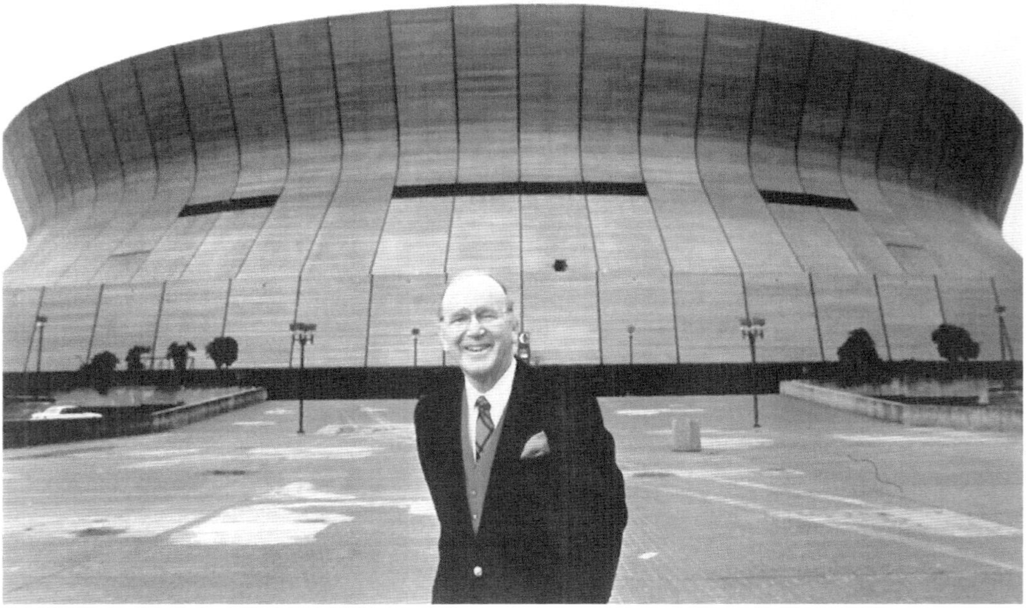

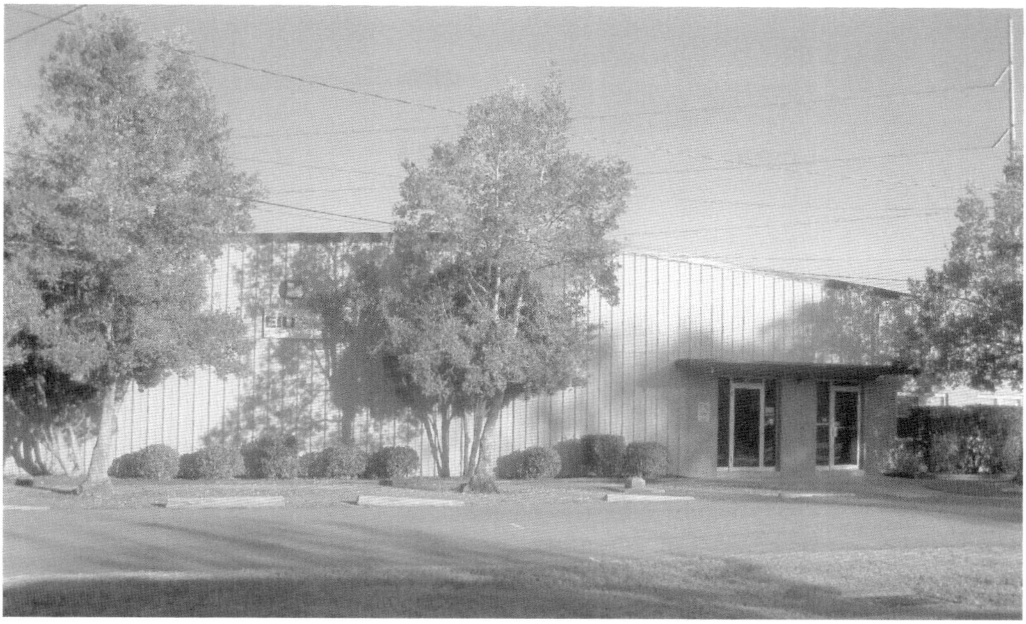

The Shirers, Casket Makers

In April 1963, residents of the Metairieville Improvement Association protested the planned construction of a coffin manufacturing business that was to be located between Pink Street and Lake Avenue along the Seventeenth Street Canal. Jefferson Parish Council chairman Cullen Schouest (see page 74) explained that although the area had been zoned Residential-2, in 1959 it had been changed to Commercial-2 and that the parish certificate approving business in that location had already been issued. He told the residents that if they could not abide with living near a coffin factory, they would have to "take it to court." The citizens' ardor died, and in the same year Shirer Casket Company moved to its new headquarters at 383 Lake Avenue (pictured here; now EIU Electrical & Instrumentation Unlimited). The company had a long history in New Orleans. In 1914, Newton E. Shirer invested $75,000 in his new business at 400 Canal Street. Originally from Zanesville, Ohio, he had moved to New Orleans in 1886 to oversee a local casket company and was eventually named its president. In 1952, Shirer moved to 830 Conti Street (now the Prince Conti Hotel) and used the advertising slogan "The only casket manufacturer in the French Quarter." After that building was sold, the company moved to St. Philip at North White Street. Irwin N. Shirer succeeded his father, who died in 1939, to become the company president. His brother Fred became the general manager. Every member of Irwin's immediate family worked in the business. His sons built and sold caskets. His wife and daughters crushed and sewed fabric. Fred noted that the Shirer family ran all operations, including office duties. In a 1976 *Times-Picayune* interview, Fred said that the company made three types of caskets: hardwood, metal, and cloth-covered (the biggest seller and the most affordable) with doeskin, velvet, felt, or printed material. Sizes included adult at 6 feet 6 inches by 22 inches wide (the largest), to 1 foot 9 inches by 8 inches across (infant), with custom sizes available by special order.

Shirer Casket Company's headquarters is now at 1025 Harimaw Court in Metairie between Airline Drive and the Earhart Expressway, just south of Metairie Country Club's golf course.

Dave Dixon (OPPOSITE PAGE)

The Father of the Superdome was also a super salesman who worked first to bring professional football to New Orleans with a sold-out 1962 AFL preseason game at City Park Stadium. After Dixon died in August 2010, Mayor Mitch Landrieu called him "one of the most visionary civic leaders in New Orleans' nearly 300-year history." He lived in Metairie. (TP.)

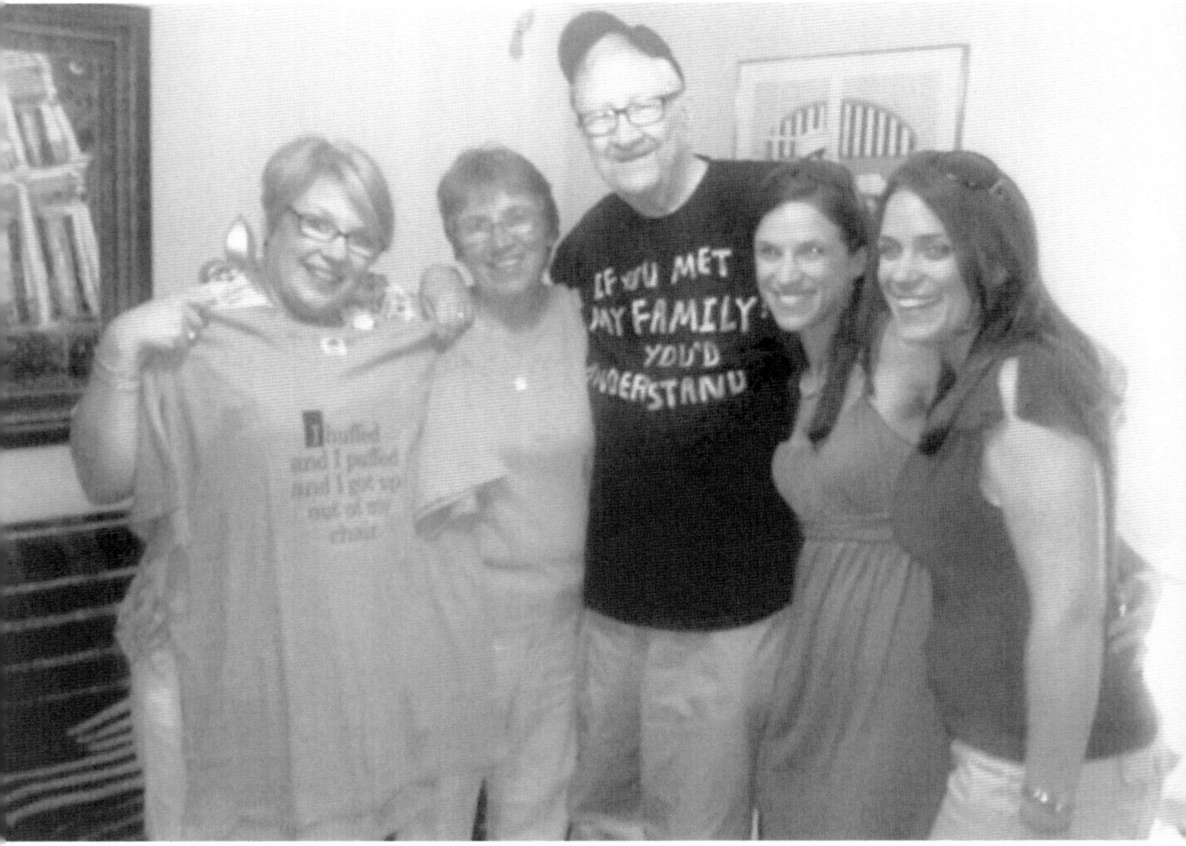

The Wash-and-Wear Wizard

"Use of the electron microscope in discovering hidden secrets of cotton fiber will be revealed at a meeting of Naval Research Company 8-1 Tuesday at 7:30 at Southern Research Laboratory, 2100 Robert E. Lee. Verne Tripp, cellulose chemist at the laboratory, will be the speaker at the meeting," read an announcement in the *Times-Picayune* on August 11, 1957. At that time, only four 1,200-pound $19,500 electron microscopes were in use in New Orleans—at Verne Tripp's lab, at Charity Hospital, and at the medical schools of Tulane University and Louisiana State University. Few people, other than Tripp, knew how to use them. He had given a presentation at Charity Hospital on "Medical Possibilities of the Electron Microscope" in 1951, so he was well versed in the field.

Verne Tripp graduated from Loyola University, where he was on the dean's list, in 1939. After completing a teaching fellowship at the University of Detroit, he began working at the lab in 1942. In 1949, with Rita Council (his wife), Leon Segal, and Carl M. Conrad, he wrote "Determination of Cellulose by Acid-Dichromate Oxidation." Some 10 years after local scientists began puzzling out the mysteries of cotton, the first advertisement for wash-and-wear (also known as permanent press) appeared in the *Times-Picayune* (1953). A decade after that (1964), Tripp received the highest citation of the US Department of Agriculture: the Distinguished Service Award in honor of "contributions to the development and improvement of wash-wear cotton fabrics and thus the welfare of the cotton industry." Fellow Southern Regional scientists Dr. Ruth R. Benerito and Lawrence W. Mazzeno Jr. shared the award. The USDA noted that an estimated 45 million yards of cotton fabrics were being produced weekly in the nation utilizing the laboratory's wash-and-wear developments either directly or indirectly.

Verne is pictured here with, from left to right, daughters Liddy Hanemann and Dolly Breaux and granddaughters Robin Breaux Lauga and Erin Breaux, all wearing wash-and-wear. Tripp died on November 24, 2012, at the age of 92. (Harry and Dolly Tripp Breaux.)

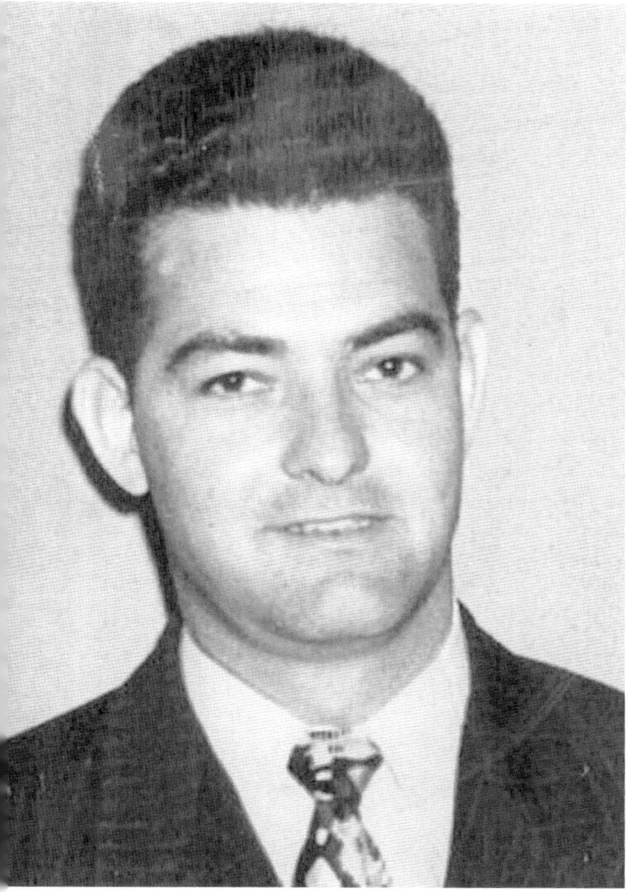

La Bouche Creole

Leon D. Soniat was a multitalented man whose career included early television and radio work as "John Kent," a seat on the Jefferson Parish school board (1960–1964), the state legislature (1968–1972), and teaching Creole cooking at UNO and St. Mary's Dominican College as well as producing and hosting a radio show on the same topic. He is best remembered for his popular 255-page cookbook *La Bouche Creole*. (Paul Yacich.)

Al Scramuzza

"Seafood City wasn't very pretty / Down on Broad and St. Bernard / But when Al Scramuzza says you'll never be a loser / Metairie playground kids applaud."

The kids applaud because Al Scramuzza volunteers his time to coach at Johnny Bright Playground near his Metairie home. After four decades in the seafood business, he closed Seafood City in 1993. Scramuzza says he was the first to industrialize and retail the sale of crawfish. (Krewe du Vieux.)

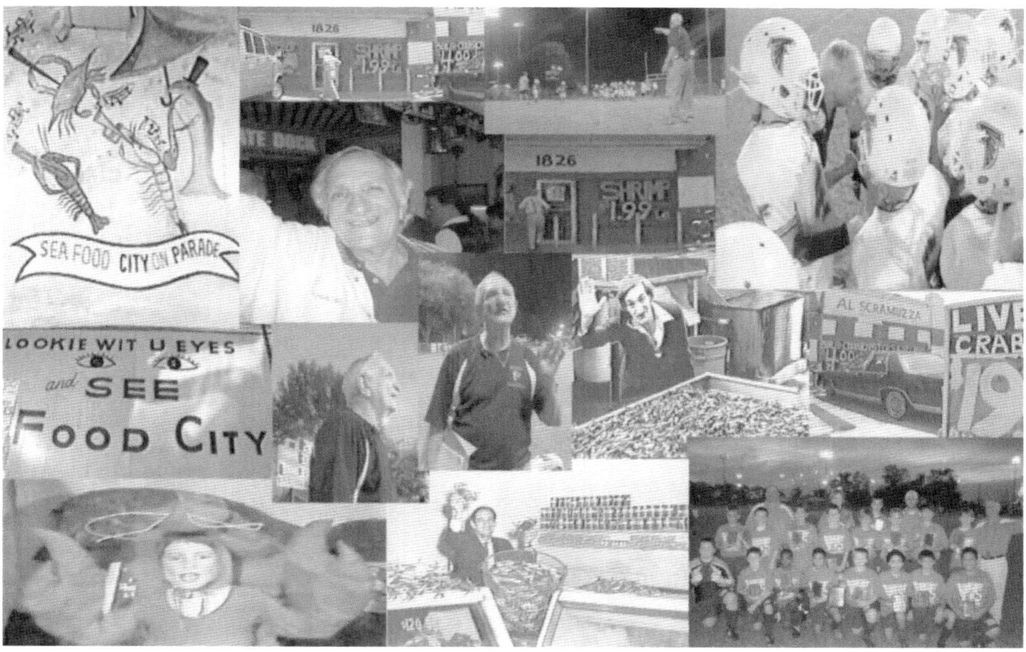

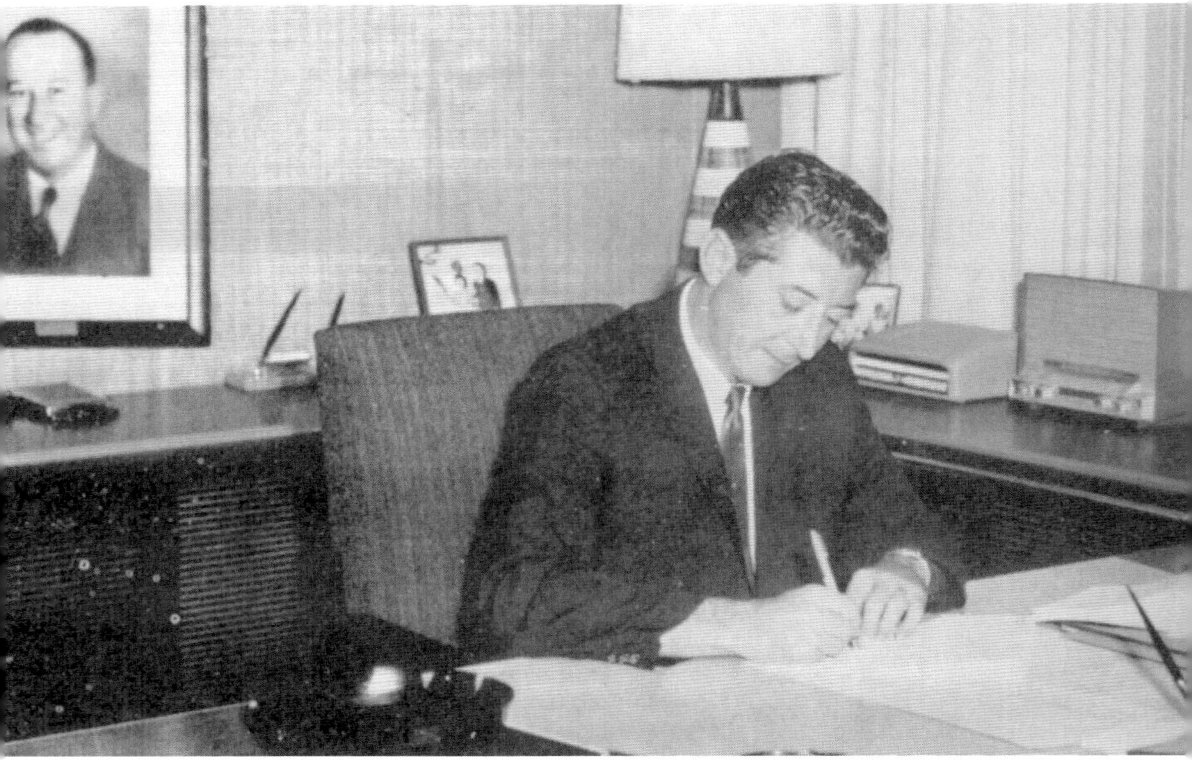

Like Father, Like Son

Pictured is Vernon J. Wilty Jr. in his office in 1962 with a portrait of his father over his shoulder. In 1940, when Wilty Sr. was parish assessor, $1,211,778 was collected from 50,000 residents and businesses. By 1961, the numbers were up to $12,841,429 and 215,000, respectively. The Jefferson Parish population had grown at such a tremendous rate that overseeing the office then required 35 employees. (JPYR.)

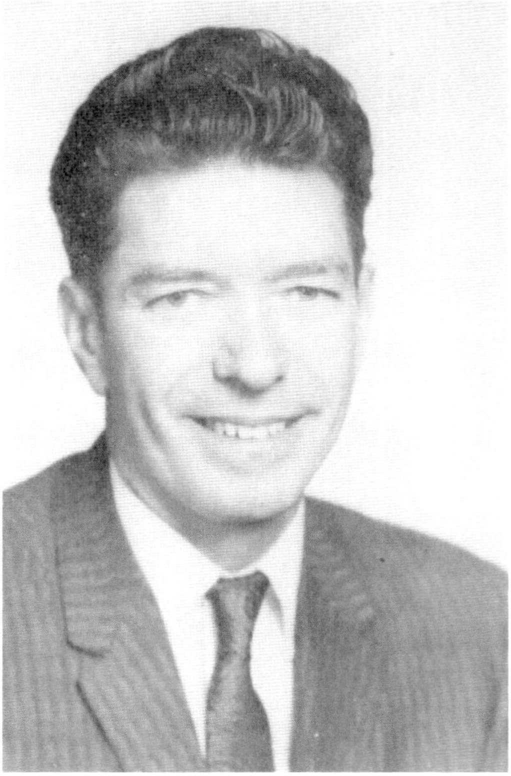

Donald T. Gillen

After Jefferson Parishioners voted to change their governing body from a police jury to a parish council in November 1952, they elected Gillen to serve on it (along with Harold A. Buchler, who would later form the Bissonet Plaza Corporation). At that time, Gillen was the manager of the PIG (Progressive Independent Grocers) Store No. 2 at 3750 Jefferson Highway near the parish waterworks. (JPYR.)

Vial J. Blanke

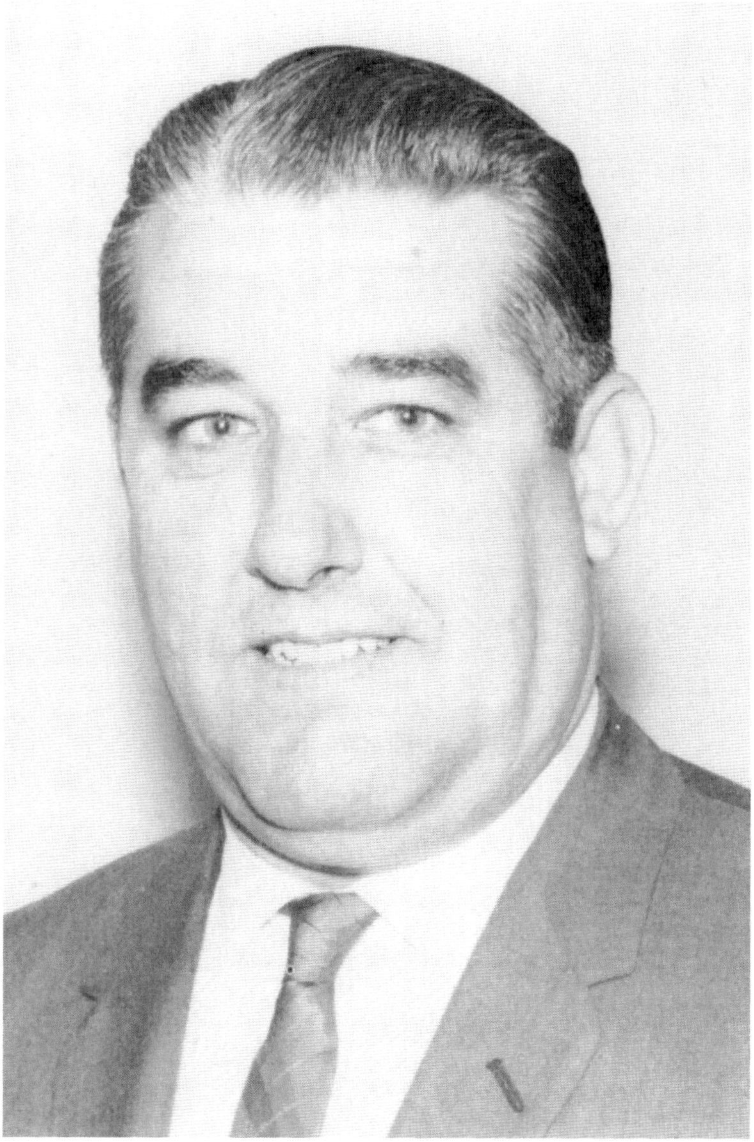

Blanke served on the parish council with Gillen, but his past was more colorful than his cohort's. As a parish constable for the Fifth Justice Court in 1957, he (along with a deputized citizen—both unarmed) made front-page news for raiding Vic Gallo's gaming house at 120 Chesterfield Street off Monticello Avenue along the New Orleans/ Jefferson Parish line. Blanke had claimed that Sheriff William S. Coci was soft on gambling and did not enforce the laws. A photographer from the local press apparently just happened to be there at the time, as the photograph and story of the bust ran in the paper. By February, Gallo was acquitted for insufficient evidence and Blanke lost his soft-drink route at Zet's Seven-Up Bottling Company. He wrote in a November 1959 letter to the editor of the *Times-Picayune*, "I was dismissed on the grounds that I was causing the company loss of sales due to the pressure brought against all employees of the company by the sheriff and business establishments . . . [which] refused to do business with said company with a resultant drop in sales and my being fired." Blanke was infuriated, because the newspaper failed to endorse his antigambling candidacy for a parish council seat. (He won the election.) In July 1957, fire had gutted Gallo's establishment in the darkness of early morning, though no fire had been reported and no calls to police had been made. The state fire marshal determined that an overloaded electrical circuit had been the cause. Gallo repaired his place and continued his business, while Blanke's future in local politics was relatively uneventful until September 8, 1967, when *Life* magazine included a photograph of him consorting with Joseph Armenio (described by *Life* as "a convicted murderer," alleged associate of Carlos Marcello, and Blanke's ally) at The Mist Restaurant and Lounge in Waggaman. *Life* reported that the two were discussing contributions to Vincent H. Ebeier Jr.'s unsuccessful campaign for sheriff against antiracketeering incumbent Alwynn Cronvich. Ebeier went on to become commander of Louisiana State Police Troop B (1964–1967). Blanke's political career was over. (JPYR.)

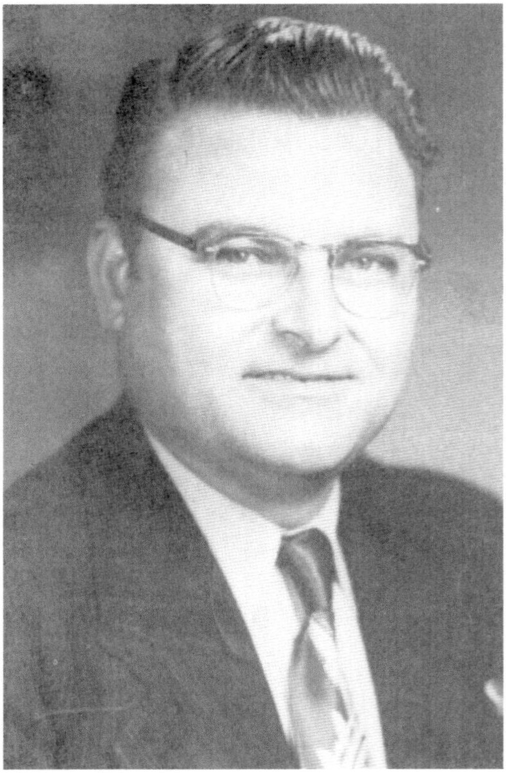

Cullen C. Schouest

Schouest served along with Gillen and Blanke in 1962. With Paul V. Lambert, he owned and operated Sterling Ice Cream Company Inc., located on Lafitte Avenue before moving to 340 Brooklyn near Jefferson Highway in 1950. In 1956, he was appointed to serve on the Parish Charter Commission to form a parish council. In 1957, he contracted with Jefferson Parish to serve dairy products with school lunches. (JPYR.)

Streets Named for Them

A look at this map of a section of Bissonet Plaza subdivision reveals that the streets running east to west south of West Esplanade were named for Assessor Wilty (see page 72) and 1962 Jefferson Parish Councilmen Schouest, Blanke (see page 73), and Gillen (see page 72). The subdivision was chartered on April 5, 1956, initially built by contractors King and Sheets, and included 106 homes at a cost of $1,376,400.

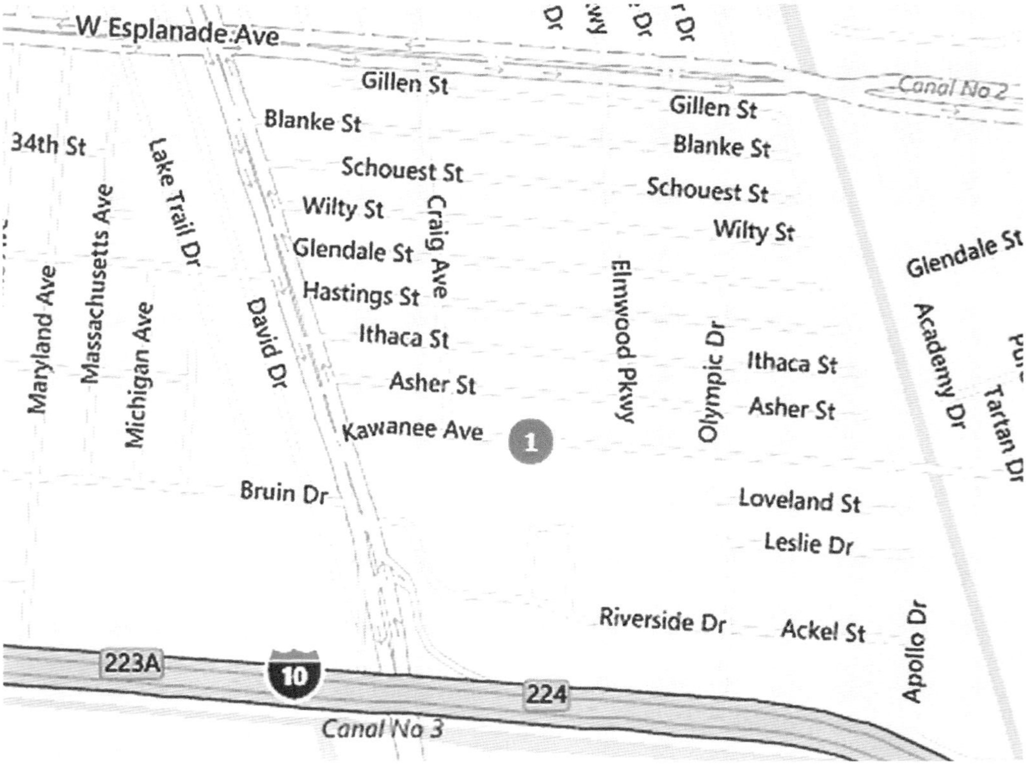

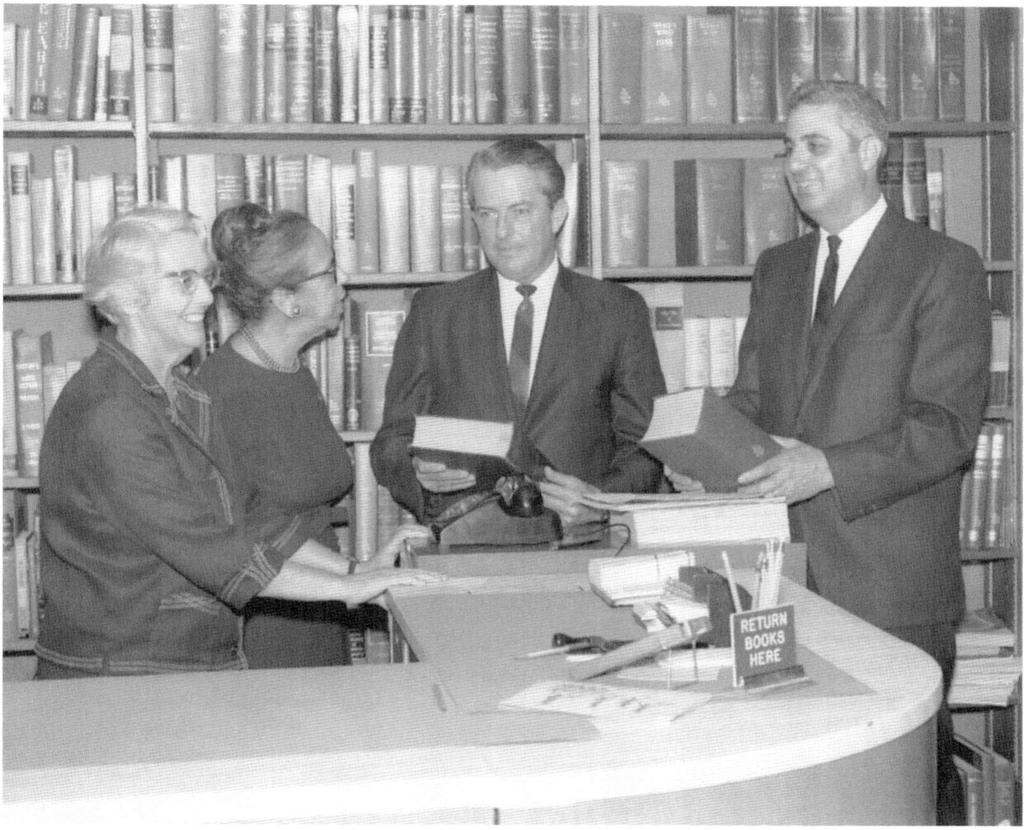

George J. Ackel

Ackel (far right) served in public office for 28 years—as a parish councilman for 17 years and as a member of the Louisiana Public Service Commission from 1976 until his death in 1988. He was an insurance executive, horse breeder, and real estate developer. He is seen here (right) at the 1966 dedication of the Kenner branch of the Jefferson Parish library with Mrs. Marion Stewart, branch manager; Debora R. Abramson, assistant state librarian; and Merlin Hudson. Ackel Street can be seen in the lower right corner of the map opposite.

After Ackel's death, Gov. Buddy Roemer appointed Ackel's wife, Jeanette Lentini Ackel, to serve his unexpired term on the public service commission. She was the first woman to serve on the state utilities regulating group and did so for eight months. Jeanette was the sister of Kenner police chief Sal Lentini. (LDL.)

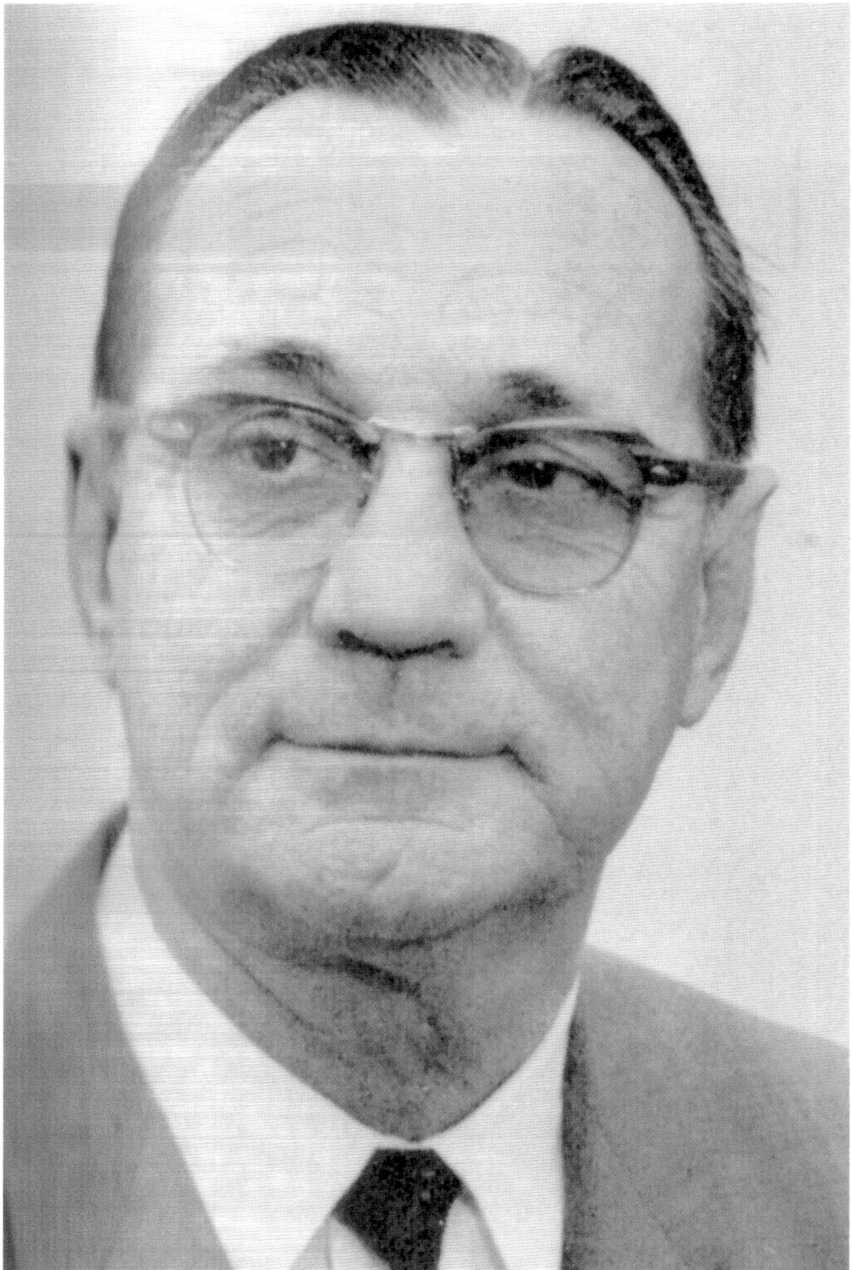

Paul Hubbell

Hubbell spent his entire career in education, beginning in 1930 when he coached and taught at Metairie High School, where the Yellow Jackets won many titles under his direction. He was appointed principal in 1940 and moved to East Jefferson High in 1958 as assistant principal. From 1959 until 1968, he held various administrative jobs for Jefferson Parish Schools, including assistant superintendent in 1965 and 1966, then superintendent in 1967. He became supervisor of teachers at Archbishop Chapelle until his retirement in 1976. Hubbell died in 1985 at age 77 after working for 46 years in public and Catholic schools. (JPYR.)

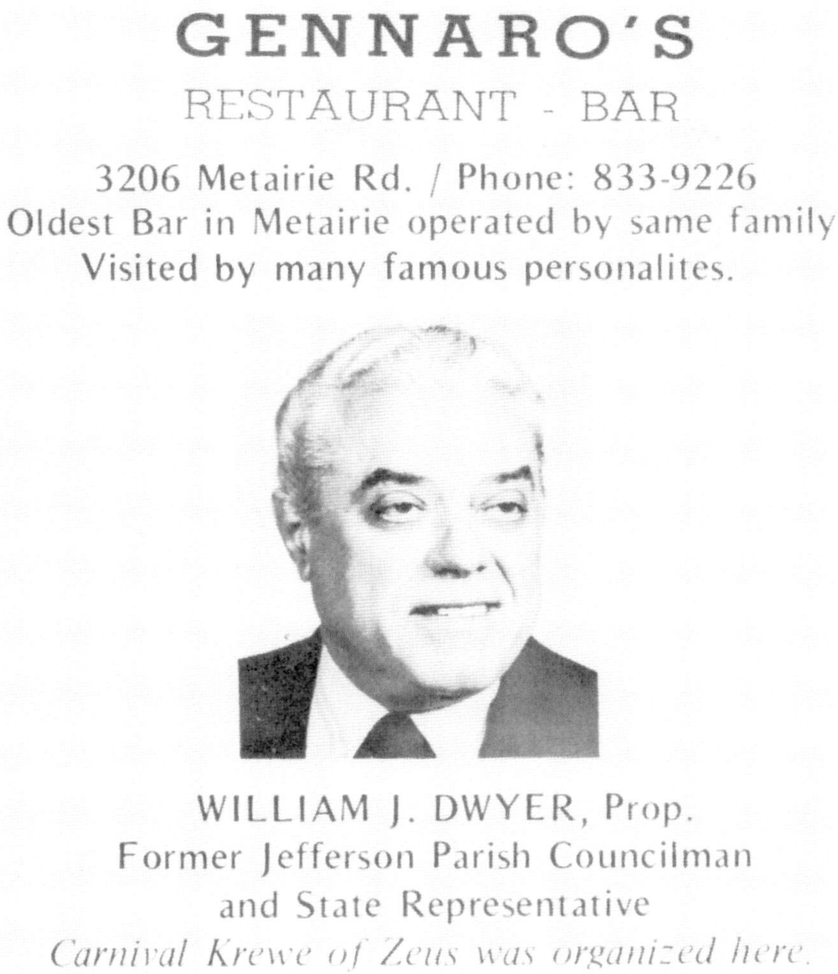

The Gennaros and the Dwyers

The Dwyers and the Gennaros have long resided in Metairie. William J. Dwyer Jr. was the first city marshal in 1927. His son William J. Dwyer III (pictured) was a parish commissioner in 1955, chairman of the railroad commission and president of the Metairie Business Association in 1957, a parish jurist/councilman from 1956 through 1960, and a state legislator from 1960 through 1964. He was a charter member and first king of the Krewe of Zeus in 1958—Dwyer said that their first parades were organized at Gennaro's bar. He was also grand marshal of the Metairie Road St. Patrick's Day parades and president of the Air-Line Lions Club. A World War II veteran, he was married to Antoinette Gennaro and had managed Gennaro's Inn (where his family lived on the second floor) on Metairie Road at Causeway for 40 years before he died in 1987 at the age of 68.

Gennaro's was first opened by Charles Gennaro in 1937. New owners celebrated its 75th anniversary in August 2012, still using the old slogan William Dwyer coined years ago: "The Oldest Bar in Metairie." During the 1940s and 1950s, orchestras played to a finely turned-out clientele that occasionally included well-known celebrities. Gennaro was also a grocer, oyster dealer, and manager of Gennaro Park—a baseball field he opened in the late 1920s, located at what is now Airline Drive at Causeway, where local high school teams played as well as others. A one-block street, Gennaro Place, is located across Metairie Road from the bar. It was here, at house number 126, that Charles and his family lived. (JPYR.)

Peter Gennaro

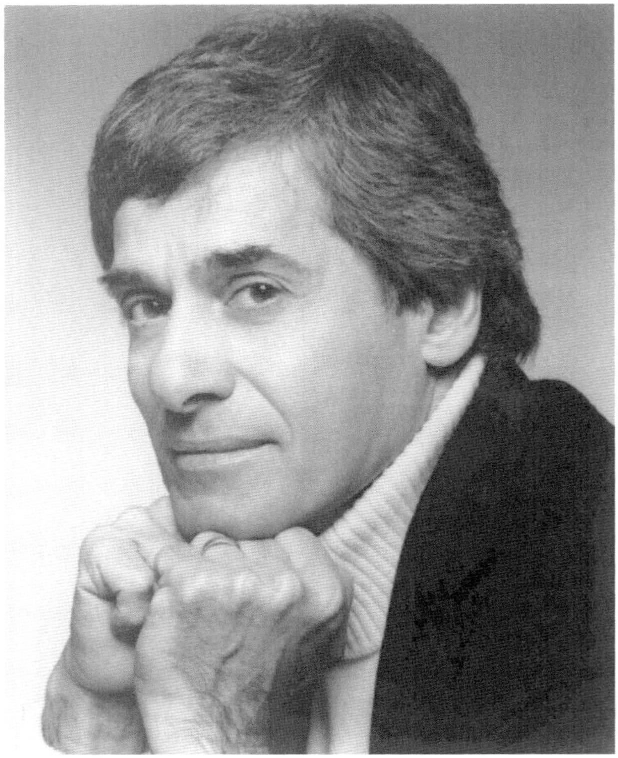

Charles and Conchetta's son made a name for himself on Broadway during the 1950s. With Jerome Robbins, he choreographed *West Side Story* in 1957. He danced and choreographed his own troupe and coached guests who appeared on Perry Como's *Kraft Music Hall* from 1960 through 1963. In 1977, he was awarded a Tony for choreography of the smash hit *Annie*. Peter Gennaro died in September 2000 at the age of 80. (LDL.)

Emile Gennaro

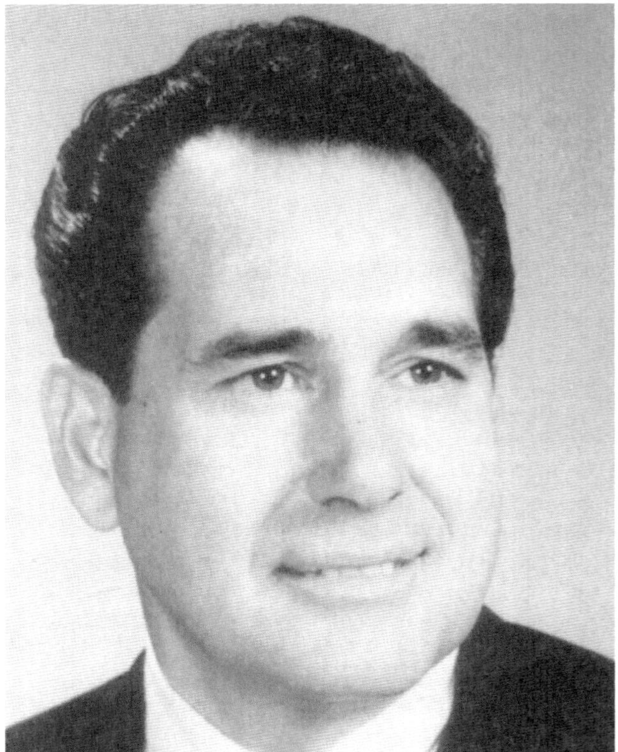

Peter's brother Emile was a standout baseball player at Metairie High. The *Times-Picayune* nicknamed him the "Mighty Met." He often played games at his dad's ballpark. He worked at the restaurant before becoming a realtor selling property and homes during the 1950s in booming Jefferson Parish. He was elected to the Jefferson Parish School Board in 1959, became its vice president in 1961, and was elected its president in 1963. (JPYR.)

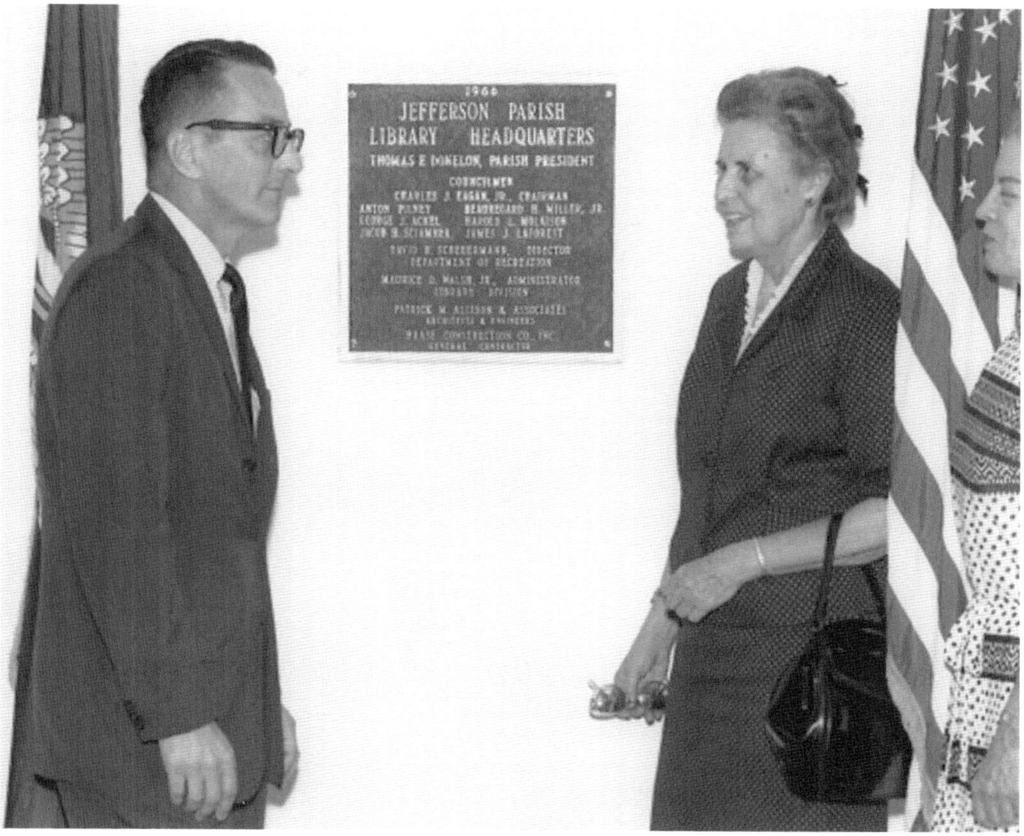

Maurice Walsh and the Lobby Library

The mystery of what went on behind the closed doors at the Lobby Library was so compelling that local public television station WYES auctioned the privilege at yearly fundraisers. Columnist James Gill wrote in a 1991 *Times-Picayune* article, "People appreciate the kindness of parish officials in making this treat available and for the privilege of inspecting the dusty tomes. The interior of Buckingham Palace can scarcely be any less accessible."

Built in 1966 as the Jefferson Parish Library Headquarters, the 30,000-square-foot building at 3420 North Causeway Boulevard was constructed as a warehouse for books for circulation to local branches. By the 1970s, patrons from local branches began demanding direct access to the main collection, which contained over 300,000 books. In 1978, a unique system was devised by Parish Library administrator Maurice D. Walsh Jr. (pictured here in 1966 with Sallie J. Farrell and an unidentified fellow librarian). Visitors entered a room in the rear of the building to tell the librarian which books they wanted, and staff workers would retrieve books (from behind closed doors). The warehouse shelving contained sliding drawers that were considered unsafe for the public to use. Deemed "the Lobby Library" because of this arrangement, it was one of the few public libraries in the country that did not allow users free interaction with its books.

In 1997, the Lobby Library's books were moved to the new 140,000-square-foot East Bank Regional Library at 4747 West Napoleon Avenue. "These books were the books no one could get to except for the staff, who had to dig their way through the stacks," Joan Adams, Jefferson Parish library director while the move was in progress, told the *Times-Picayune*. "Now, when library patrons come in, the books are right there on the shelves, not stacked away somewhere because of lack of space. Someone asked me how many of these books were at the lobby branch. I don't know the exact number, but I figure it was enough books to cover five miles." (JPYR.)

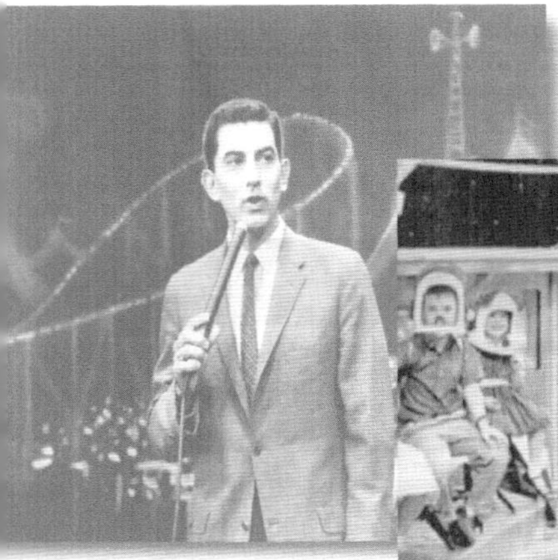

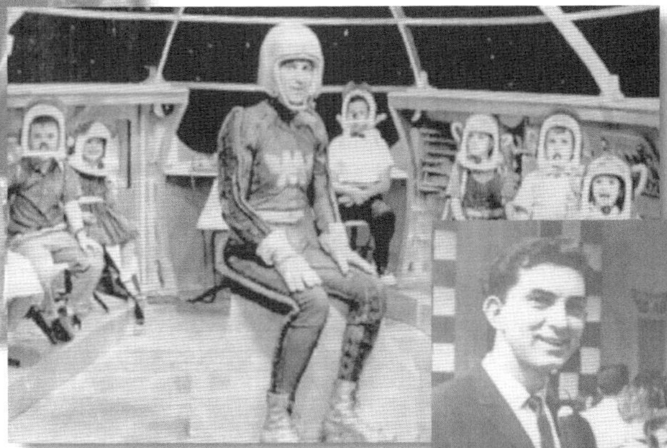

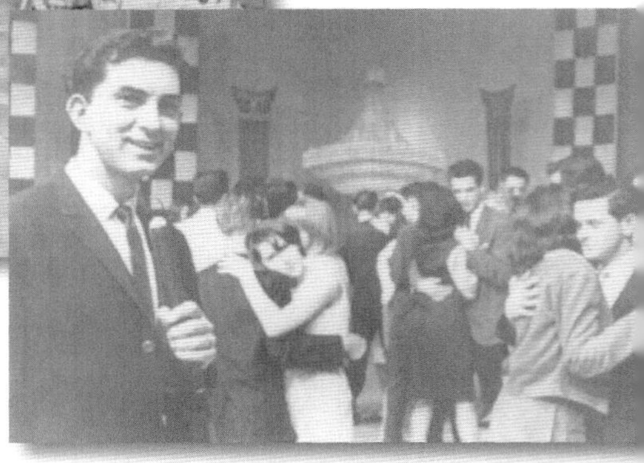

John Pela and Hazel Romano

WWL television staff announcer John Pela wore many hats during his career. He donned a sailor cap and suit to replace "Uncle Henry" Dupre after he retired from *Popeye and Pals*. He was also Captain Mercury on Channel 4. Some of the children seen here (above, center) might have later danced on his weekly *Saturday Hop/John Pela Show* (1961–1972). In 2011, Pela celebrated the 50th anniversary of the show, which featured the Tony Bevinetto and Hazel Romano Dancers and was one of the first to racially integrate—without any hoopla, because, as Pela said, "It was all about the music and dancing." Former Romano Dancers celebrated a 50th anniversary in 2008 (below right). Helen Loyacano Romano (below left) is also loved and remembered by generations of children who attended St. Philip Neri School in Metairie, where she taught kindergarten for many years. (Courtesy of Paul Yacich.)

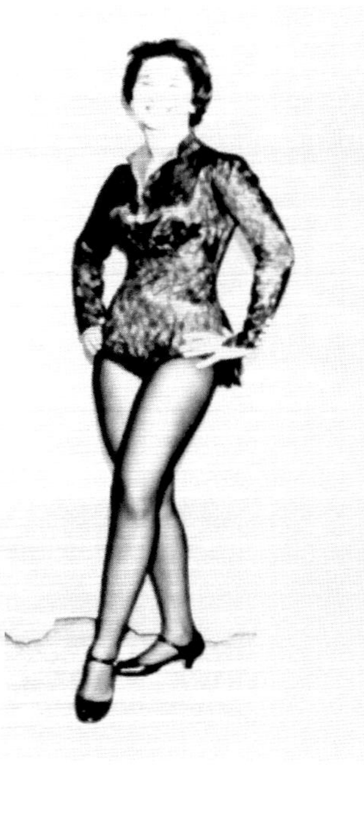

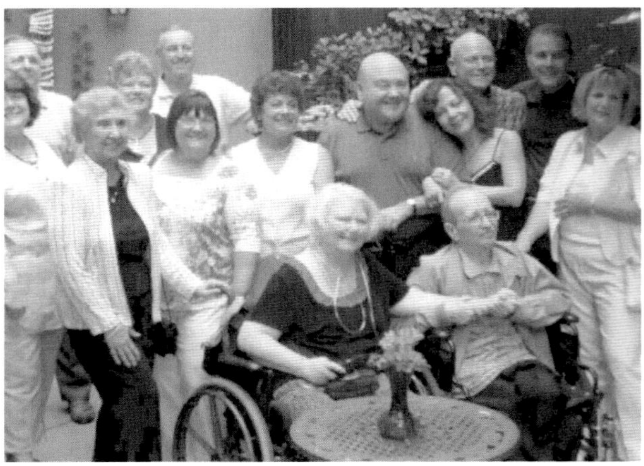

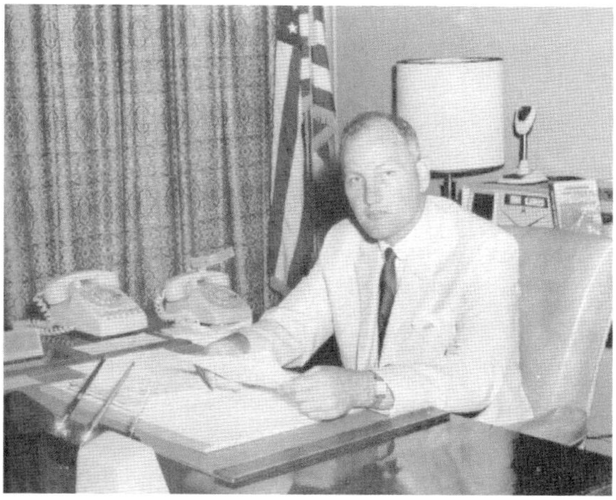

Sheriff Cronvich
While *Life* magazine exposed Blanke, it noted that Sheriff Alwynn Cronvich, who was in office from 1964 to 1979, "has frequently raided Marcello joints." His accomplishments included creating vice and narcotics squads, a crime laboratory, an officer training program, a rescue unit, and a neighborhood watch. He also updated equipment and reorganized departments under his command. After 15 years in office, he was defeated by Harry Lee. (LDL.)

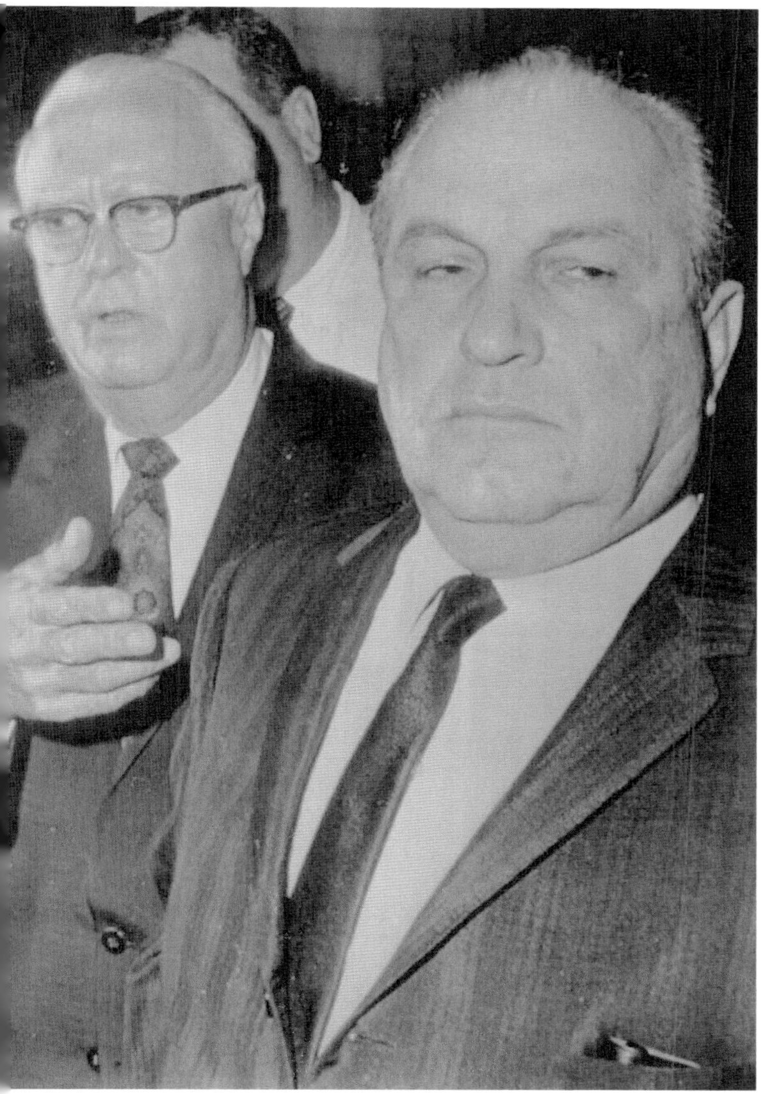

Carlos Marcello
Former Old Metairie resident (of 577 Woodvine), Carlos Marcello told *Times-Picayune* reporter Iris Kelso in 1981, "I hadda move out of there. They aristocrats and think they somebody. . . . A lot of times, they puttin' on because they don't have money." His take on Metairie Country Club, which was just a few doors from his home, was as follows: "You gotta die before you can get in there." He died in Metairie in 1993 at the age of 83. He had moved back after being released from prison in 1989 on conspiracy, racketeering, and mail and wire fraud charges. Allegedly linked to the Kennedy assassination, this Sicilian-born "Little Man" (because he stood at five feet, two inches) claimed to be a tomato salesman but was reputed to have been the mafia boss of Louisiana and the Gulf Coast beginning in the 1940s. Marcello is pictured here in 1970 with his attorney, G. Wray Gill. (UPI.)

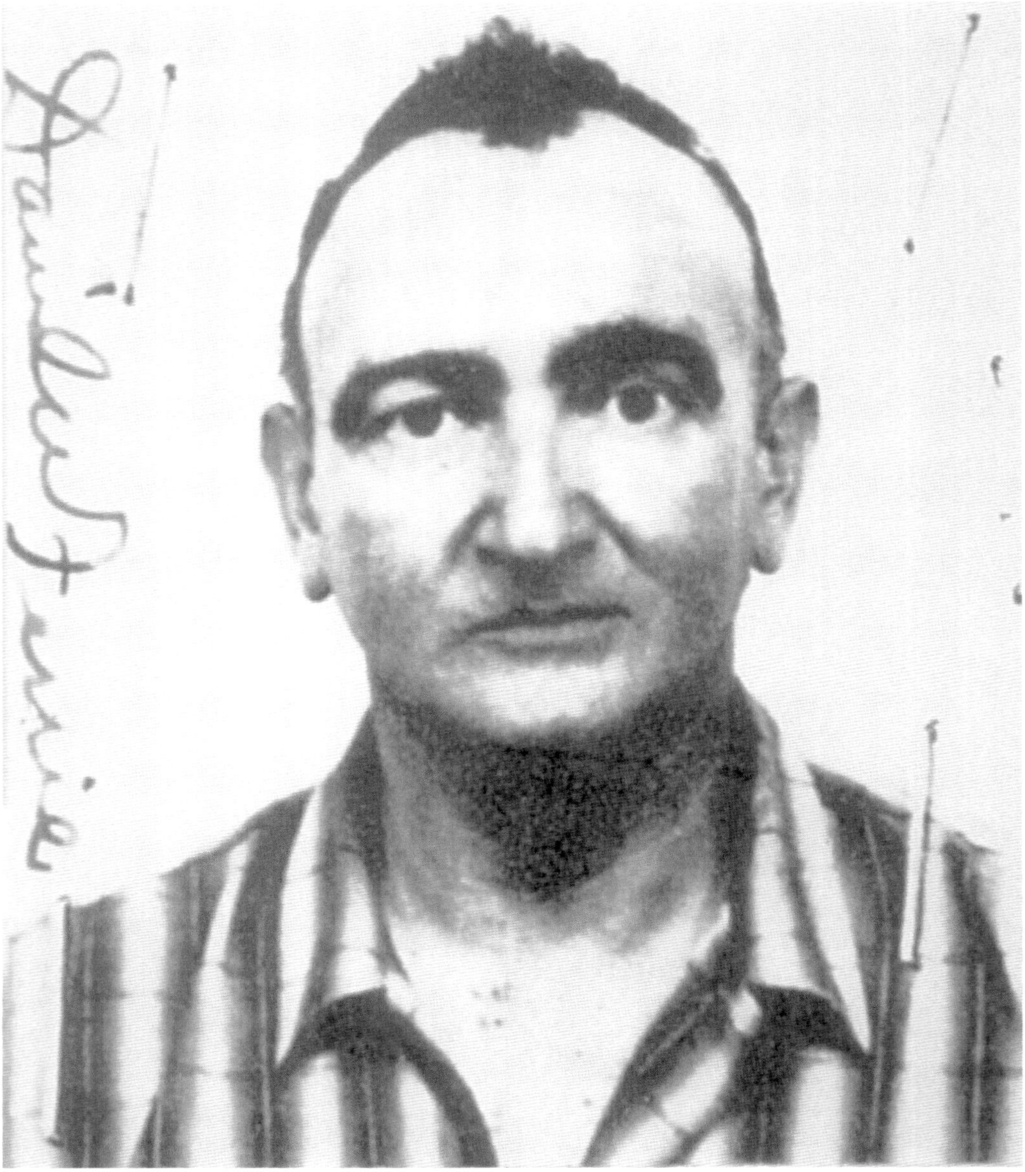

David Ferrie and Gordon Novel

In a 1963 interview with the FBI, David William Ferrie, who was alleged to have been involved in a conspiracy to assassinate Pres. John F. Kennedy, stated that he was employed by Carlos Marcello's attorney G. Wray Gill as an investigator. A former pilot, he lived at 331 Atherton Drive in Old Metairie and formed an unofficial Civil Air Patrol group he named Metairie Falcon Squad, in which Lee Harvey Oswald had been a member. From that same address, he was charged in August 1961 with extortion, intimidation, threats, and five counts of indecent behavior with juveniles.

In 1961, Gordon Novel and his wife drove from their residence at 124 Lake Avenue to David Ferrie's home, from which they drove to Houma, stole ammunition, explosives, and aerial devices and then returned—storing most of it at Ferrie's house, allegedly for use to aid anti-Castro Cubans. He later caused a stir when he admitted to a night launching of an 18-foot fluorescent balloon over the area—apparently one of the stolen goods. (UPI.)

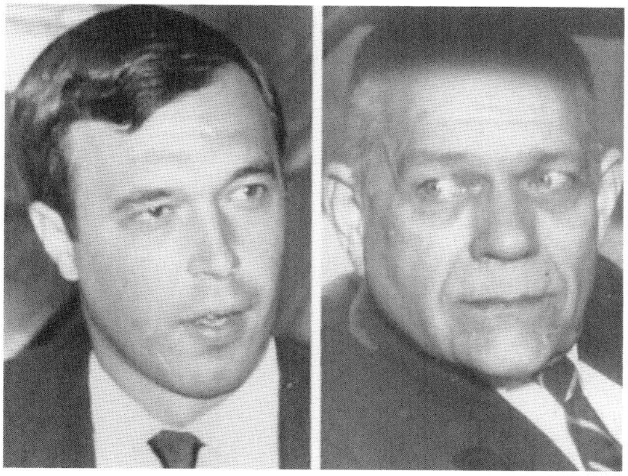

Perry Raymond Russo

Taxi driver Perry Raymond Russo (left) lived at 214 Canal Street in Metairie during the 1970s. He is notorious for having claimed during the Clay Shaw (right) trial that he attended a party also attended by Shaw, Ferrie, and Lee Harvey Oswald, who were discussing assassinating President Kennedy. The following day, he changed his story, saying that only Ferrie had vowed to kill the president. (AP.)

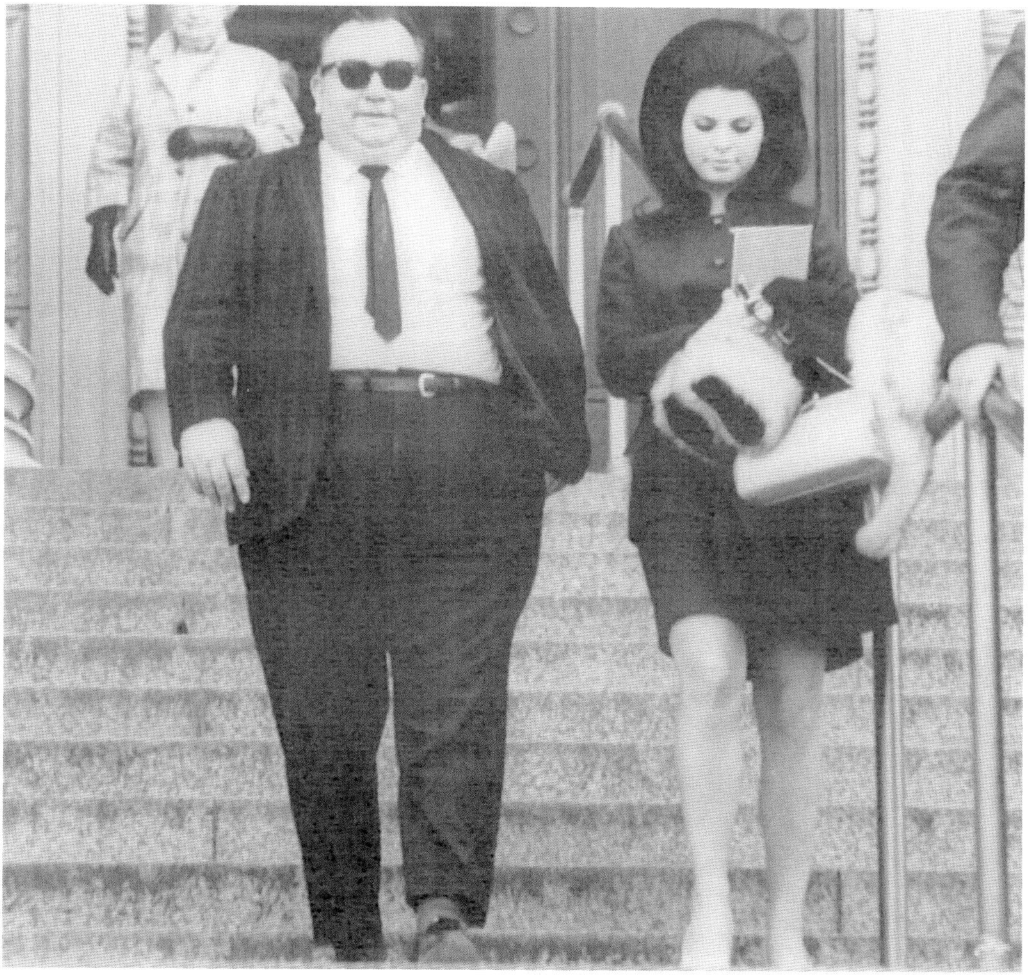

Dean Andrews

Metairie resident Dean Adams Andrews Jr. was a Jefferson Parish assistant to the sheriff, criminal deputy, and assistant district attorney before being convicted of perjury in the Shaw trial for claiming, then denying, that Clay Shaw used the alias "Clay Bertrand." He is pictured here during the trial with his unidentified secretary. (UPI.)

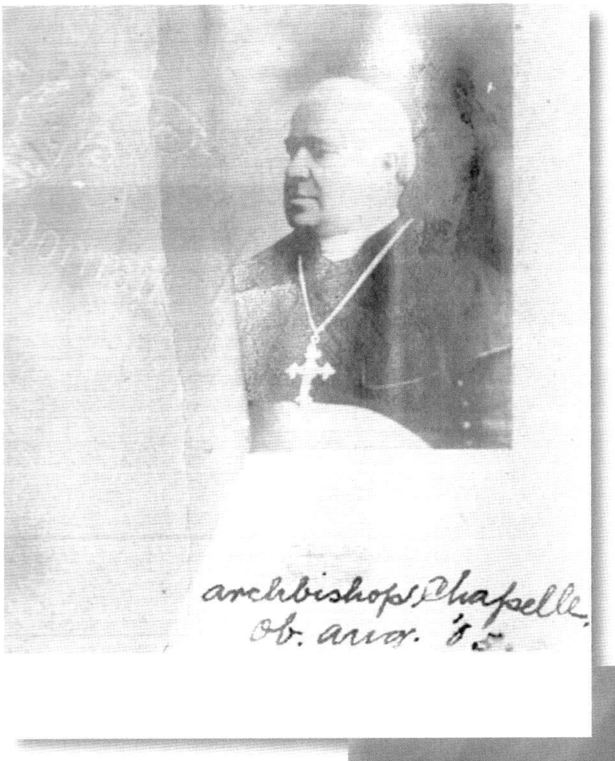

Archbishop Chapelle

Frenchman Placide Louise Chapelle was appointed archbishop of New Orleans in 1897. The following year, he was sent to France while negotiations were conducted for the 1898 Treaty of Paris, which ended the Spanish American War. He was responsible for the inclusion of a confirmation that the church would continue to posses all properties it had owned under the Spanish government. In 1905, Chapelle died during the last outbreak of yellow fever in New Orleans. In 1962, Archbishop Chapelle High School was named for him. (LDL.)

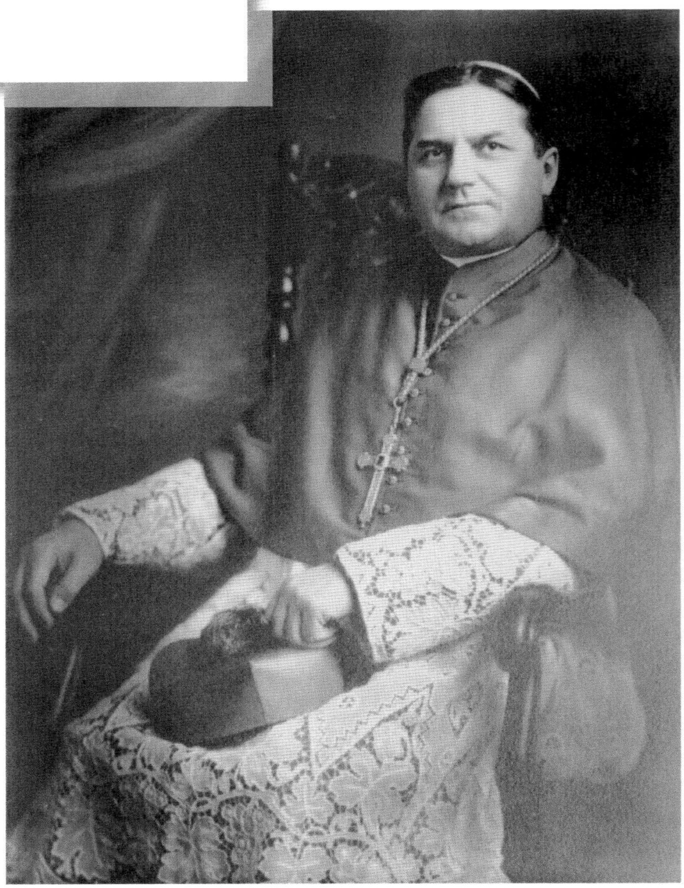

Archbishop Rummel

German-born Joseph Francis Rummel became the ninth archbishop of New Orleans in 1935. During his tenure, the Catholic population doubled and the number of Catholic school students rose from 40,000 to over 85,000. Rummel opened 44 new church parishes and 70 new schools, including Archbishop Chapelle and his namesake Archbishop Rummel high schools that opened in 1962. The archbishop attended both the ground breaking (September 1961) and the dedication ceremony (September 1962) for Rummel High. (LDL.)

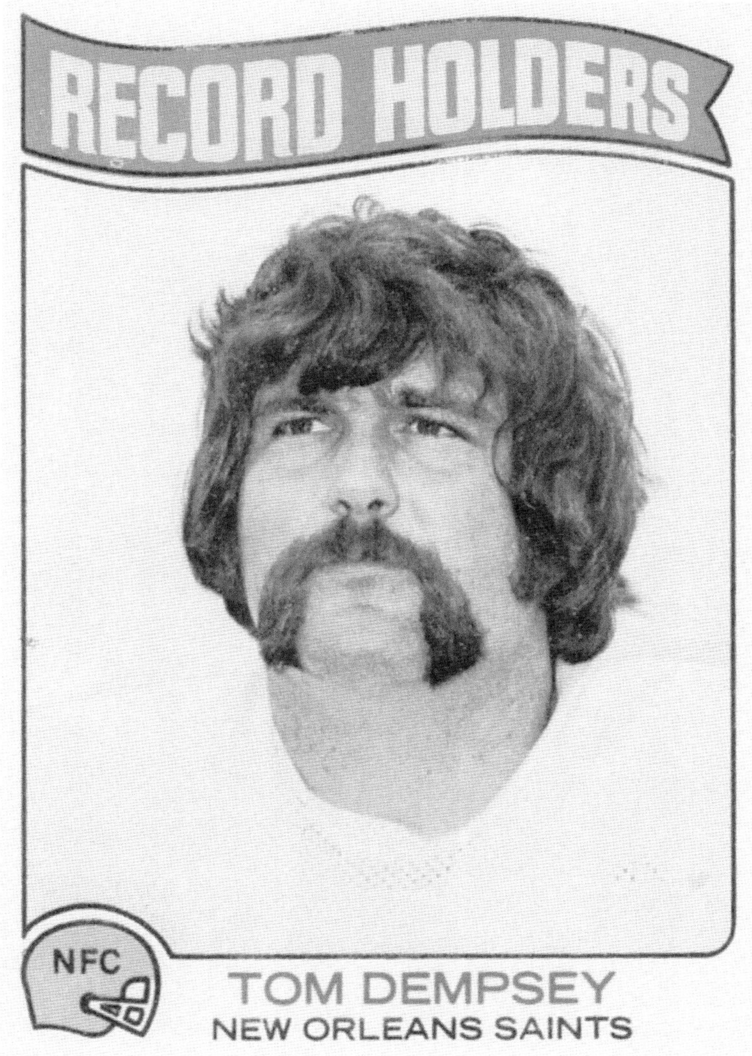

Tom Dempsey
On November 8, 1970, with two seconds left in a Saints home game at Tulane Stadium against the Detroit Lions and the Saints behind with a score of 17-16, Thomas John Dempsey broke an NFL field goal record with a 63-yard kick, beating the record of 56 yards set by Bert Rechichar two decades before. The Saints won the game, and Dempsey won fame as well as a record that has yet to be broken. It was known as "the kick heard 'round the world."

Born without a right hand and only half a right foot, he wore a custom-made shoe, which caused some controversy as to whether it afforded him an advantage over other kickers. In 1977, the "Tom Dempsey Rule" was adopted by the NFL, mandating that "any shoe that is worn by a player with an artificial limb on his kicking leg must have a kicking surface that conforms to that of a normal kicking shoe."

As a Saint, he played in the Pro Bowl in 1969—his first year as a professional. It was in his second season that he blasted the "kick heard 'round the world." He went on to play with Philadelphia, Los Angeles, Houston, and Buffalo before retiring in 1979 after an 11-year career. He then went back to his adopted home in Metairie to raise his family. He was inducted into the New Orleans Saints Hall of Fame in 1989 and the American Football Kicking Hall of Fame in 2010. (Author's collection.)

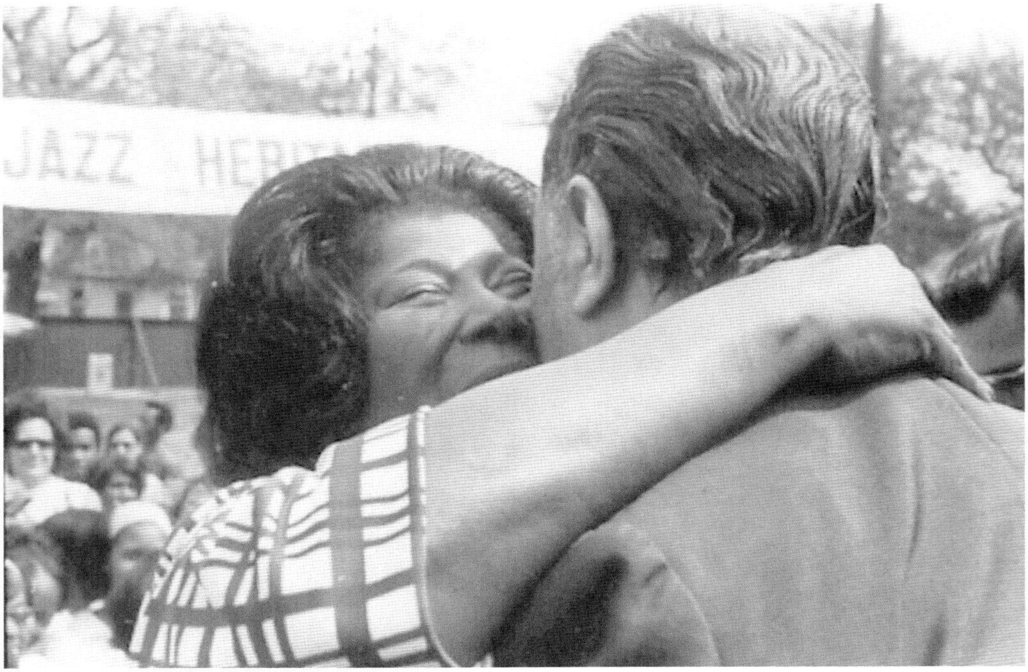

Mahala

"I sing God's music because it makes me feel free," said Mahalia Jackson. "It gives me hope. With the blues, when you finish, you still have the blues." But she did rattle many preachers who disdained her infusion of a bluesy style into her gospel singing. Pictured here at the first Jazz Fest in 1970 with Duke Ellington, "Halie" (born Mahala) traveled the world but rests in Metairie's Providence Memorial Park. (AP.)

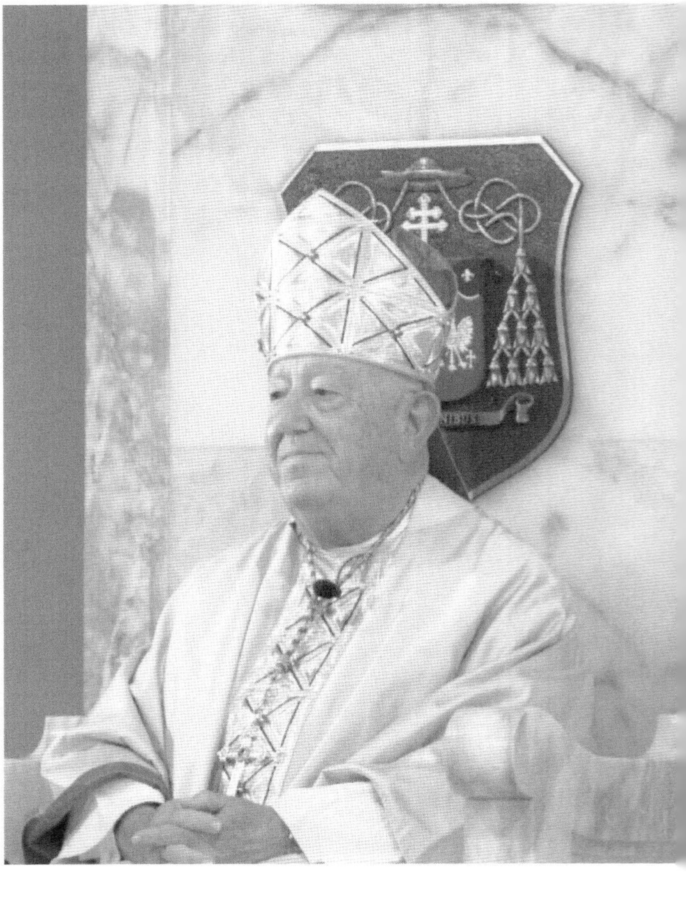

Archbishop of Miami

Father Favalora was the pastor of St. Angela Merici parish from 1973 to 1979. Born in Metairie in 1935 and trained at Notre Dame Seminary in New Orleans, John Clement Favalora became the third Archbishop of Miami in 1994. His province included all of Florida (over a million Catholics). He served until 2010. (Ana Rodriguez-Soto.)

SMOOTHIE KING®

Nutritional Lifestyle Centers™

Smoothie King and Queen

"It's like a roux . . . you've got to add other ingredients to make a good stew or gumbo," said Cindy Zimmer in 1991, describing the creation of her business partner and future husband, Stephen Kuhnau, who began selling Muscle Punch at his tiny Town & Country health food store at 2725 Mississippi Avenue in 1973. Cindy realized that franchising could be successful, designed the operations and training systems, and in 1989 oversaw the second of 600 Smoothie King stores opened on Baronne Street.

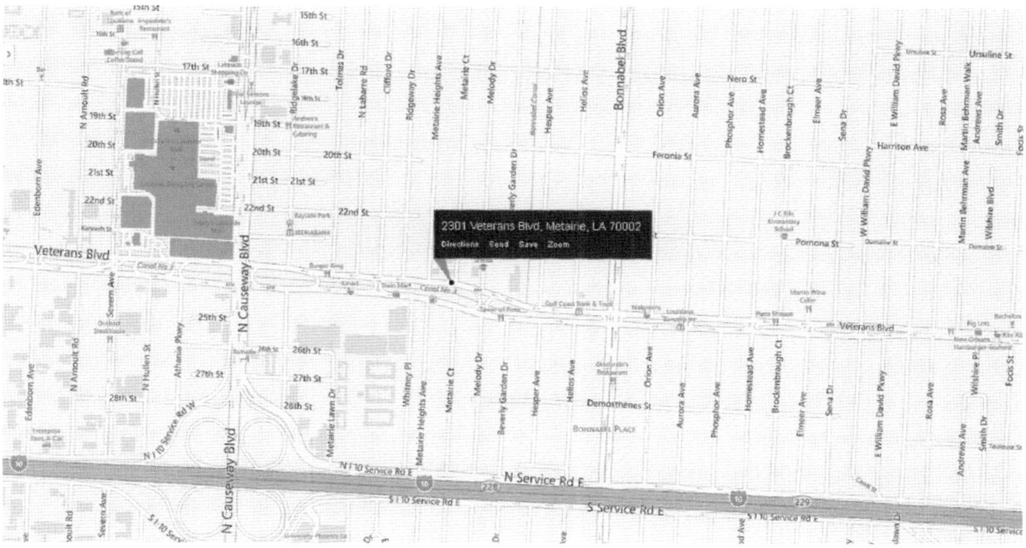

The Little Yogurt Shop on Veterans

During the early years of the fitness and jogging craze, Mike Williams and Sam Holt owned a racquet club in Metairie. Their next venture also focused on healthful lifestyles. In 1977, they opened a little store at 2301 Veterans Boulevard and named it Zack's Famous Frozen Yogurt. From it grew an empire of franchises across the United States, headquartered at 3850 Causeway Boulevard. In 1990, Zack's stores sprung up in Japan.

Al Copeland

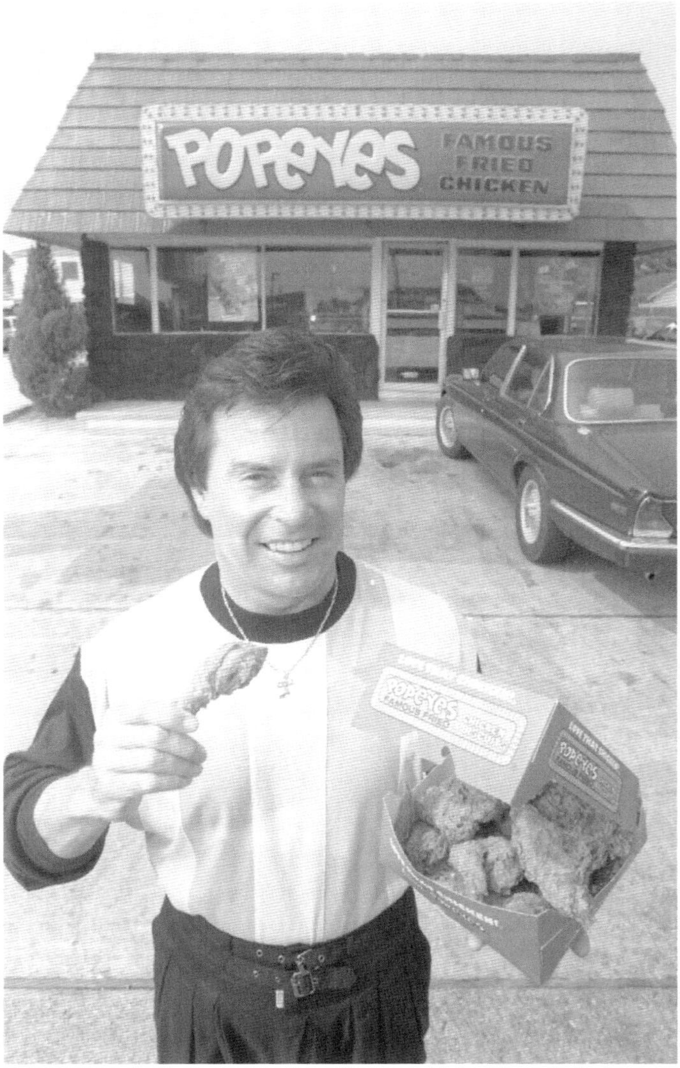

As a boy, Al Copeland and his family had lived for a time in the St. Thomas public housing project. He dropped out of high school at 16 and, after drifting through low-paying jobs, worked at a doughnut shop of which his brother Gil had an ownership interest. Al bought his own shop in 1962 at age 18. In 1971, he opened Chicken on the Run, serving mild-flavored fried chicken and losing money. Copeland changed the name and the recipe – serving spicy chicken at Popeyes Mighty Good Fried Chicken (he named it for Gene Hackman's *French Connection* character, Popeye Doyle). Renaming it again to Popeyes Famous Fried Chicken, he began franchising the restaurants. By 1976, a total of 800 Popeyes locations were operating in the United States and abroad. Some 500 outlets were added over the next 10 years, followed by 200 more.

By 1989 (when this photograph was taken), Popeyes was the third-largest chicken chain in the United States. During that same year, June 28 was declared "Al Copeland Day" in both the city of New Orleans and the state of Louisiana. The International Franchise Association named him the 1989 Entrepreneur of the Year. Other awards followed. The Louisiana Restaurant Association honored Al Copeland with their first Service to Humanity Award, he was entered into their Hall of Fame in recognition of his many contributions to the community, and he received the organization's Lifetime Achievement Award.

As Copeland's wealth and fame increased, so did his flamboyant lifestyle. He became an award-winning powerboat racer and displayed his boats in a windowed showroom for all of Metairie to see as they drove past along the Interstate. In 1997, during a feud with *Interview with the Vampire* author Anne Rice over his renovation of a St. Charles Avenue car dealership into a Copeland's restaurant, he threw garlic from his converted boat/float during Mardi Gras parades. A 2001 brawl at a local steakhouse with Robert Guidry (who he had bid unsuccessfully against for a gambling license in 1993) landed Copeland and his wife in the hospital and Guidry and his cohorts in jail. His extravagant weddings and controversial divorce were well publicized and topics of conversation all over the area.

His life was exceedingly successful and colorful, but not long. Copeland died at the age of 64 after a battle with Merkel cell carcinoma, on Easter Sunday, March 23, 2008, near Munich, Germany, where he had gone to receive treatment for the rare but fatal condition. (TP.)

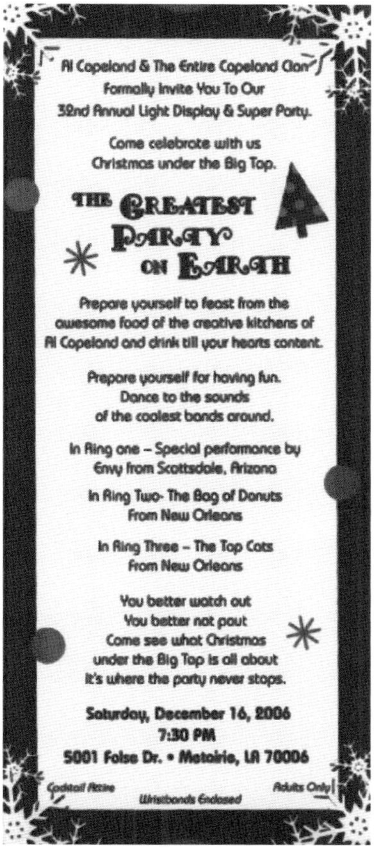

Al Copeland & The Entire Copeland Clan
Formally Invite You To Our
32nd Annual Light Display & Super Party.

Come celebrate with us
Christmas under the Big Top.

THE GREATEST PARTY ON EARTH

Prepare yourself to feast from the awesome food of the creative kitchens of Al Copeland and drink till your hearts content.

Prepare yourself for having fun.
Dance to the sounds
of the coolest bands around.

In Ring one – Special performance by
Envy from Scottsdale, Arizona

In Ring Two- The Bag of Donuts
From New Orleans

In Ring Three – The Top Cats
From New Orleans

You better watch out
You better not pout
Come see what Christmas
under the Big Top is all about
It's where the party never stops.

Saturday, December 16, 2006
7:30 PM
5001 Folse Dr. • Metairie, LA 70006

Cocktail Attire
Wristbands Enclosed
Adults Only!

Secret Santa

While most local residents knew of Copeland's lavish Christmas light displays at his huge home on Folse Drive, only a few were so lucky as to receive a personal invitation to his yearly Christmas party. According to his family, Copeland also funded and personally oversaw a Secret Santa program through which 1,000 children of poor families were visited on Christmas Eve to receive personally tagged gifts from a huge sack carried by Santa.

Copeland's Lights

His spirit lives on through the $1 million Alvin C. Copeland Endowed Chair of Franchising at Louisiana State University that he established in 1989, as well as the Chefs Apprentice Program at Delgado Community College and the National Food Service Institute—both funded by Al Copeland. Metairie children still enjoy his Christmas lights (pictured), which now glow each year at Lafreniere Park. (Eric Miller/Al Copeland Foundation.)

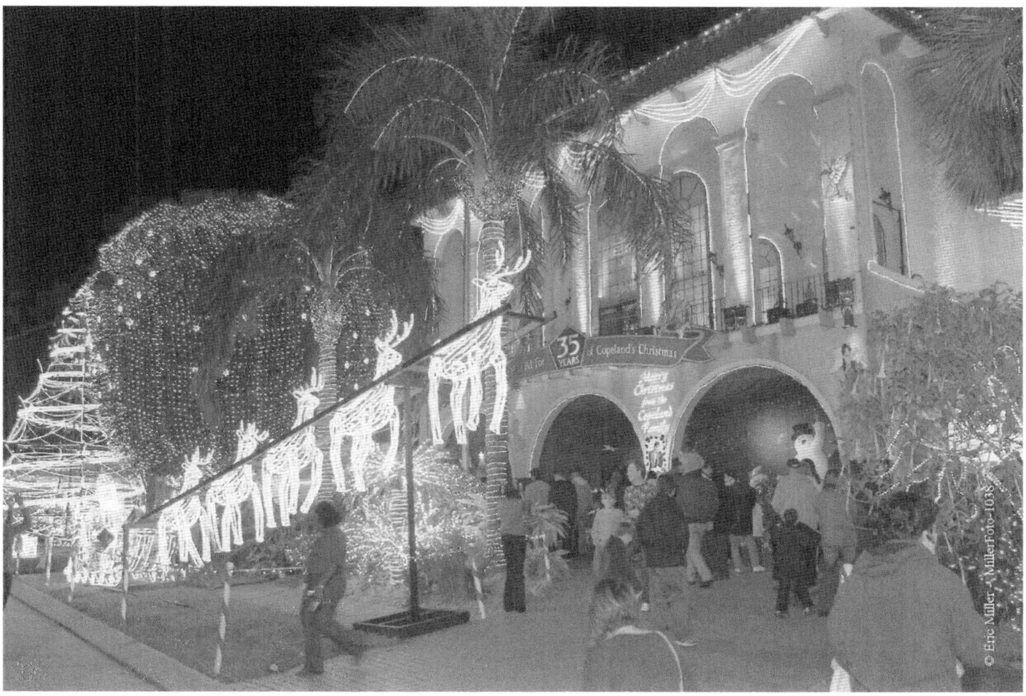

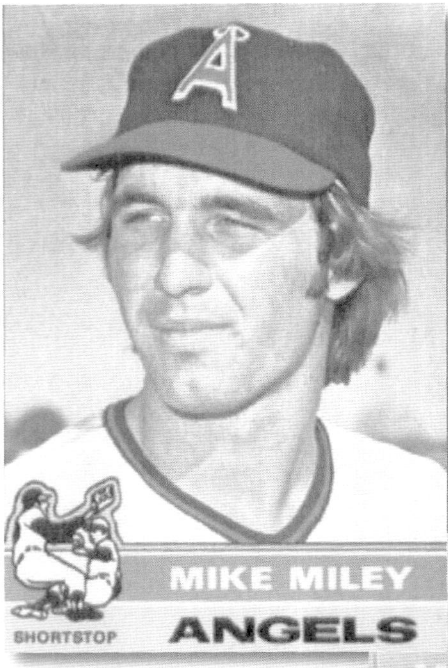

Miracle Mike

Born in Yazoo, Mississippi, Michael W. Miley graduated from East Jefferson in 1972 as an outstanding quarterback and shortstop. While playing the same positions at LSU in 1974, he was drafted in the first round to play professional baseball for the California Angels. On January 6, 1977, at the age of 23, "Miracle Mike" died in an automobile accident on Highland Road in Baton Rouge. Airline Park Playground was renamed in his honor.

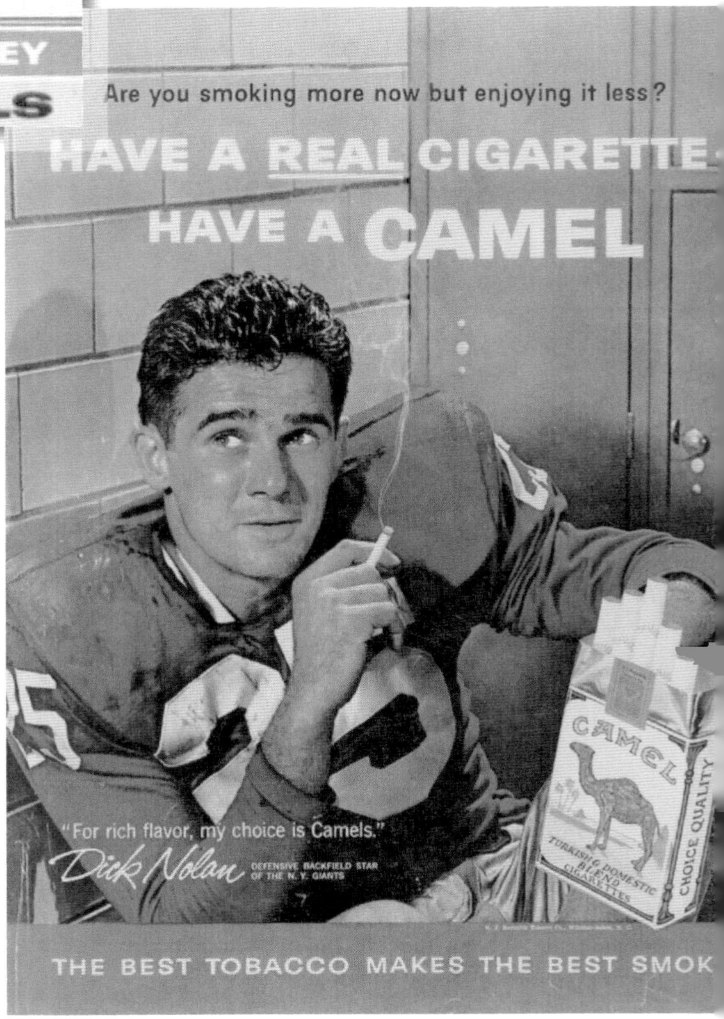

Dick Nolan

Saints head coach (1978–1980) Dick Nolan was the first to win six, seven, and eight games in a single season. He wore business suits on the sidelines—this was before the National Football League contracted with Reebok for a $250-million deal that allowed only official Reebok-issued clothing to be worn. The NFL had no qualms about allowing him to endorse cigarettes.

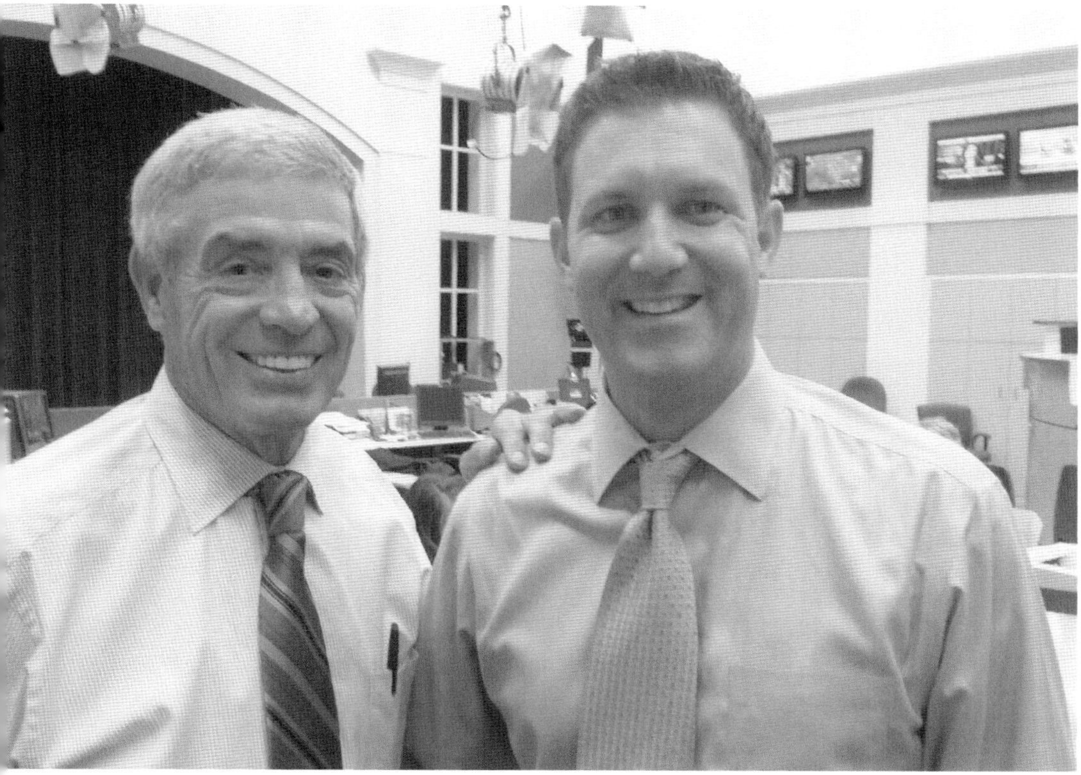

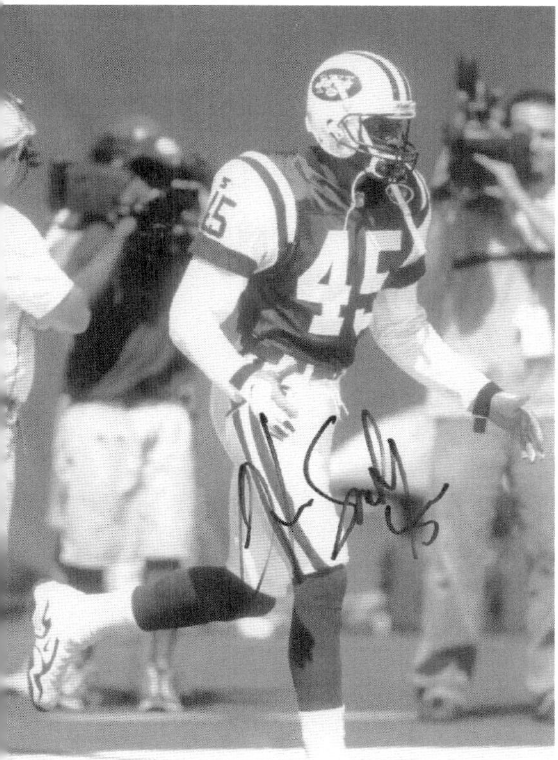

Jim Mora

Ten-year (1986–1996) New Orleans Saints coach Jim Mora was the first to end a season with a winning record and a playoff game (1987) and first to earn a division title (1991). After a 24-22 loss to the San Francisco 49ers in 1987, he said, "I'm tired of saying 'Could've, should've, would've.' . . . I'm pissed off right now. You bet your ass I am. I'm sick of coulda, woulda, shoulda, coming close, if only." Then he went home to his house in Metairie. (Scott Walker.)

East Jefferson High's Otis Smith

A 1984 All-State graduate of East Jefferson High, Otis Smith played in two National Football League championship games for the New England Patriots, earning a ring for Super Bowl XXXVI. His professional career began as a free agent with Philadelphia in 1990. Smith played 13 seasons in the NFL, with Philadelphia (1990–1994), the New York Jets (1995–1996, 1997–1999), New England (1996 and 2000–2002), and Detroit (2003). Smith went on to coach for Kansas City and Philadelphia. (AP.)

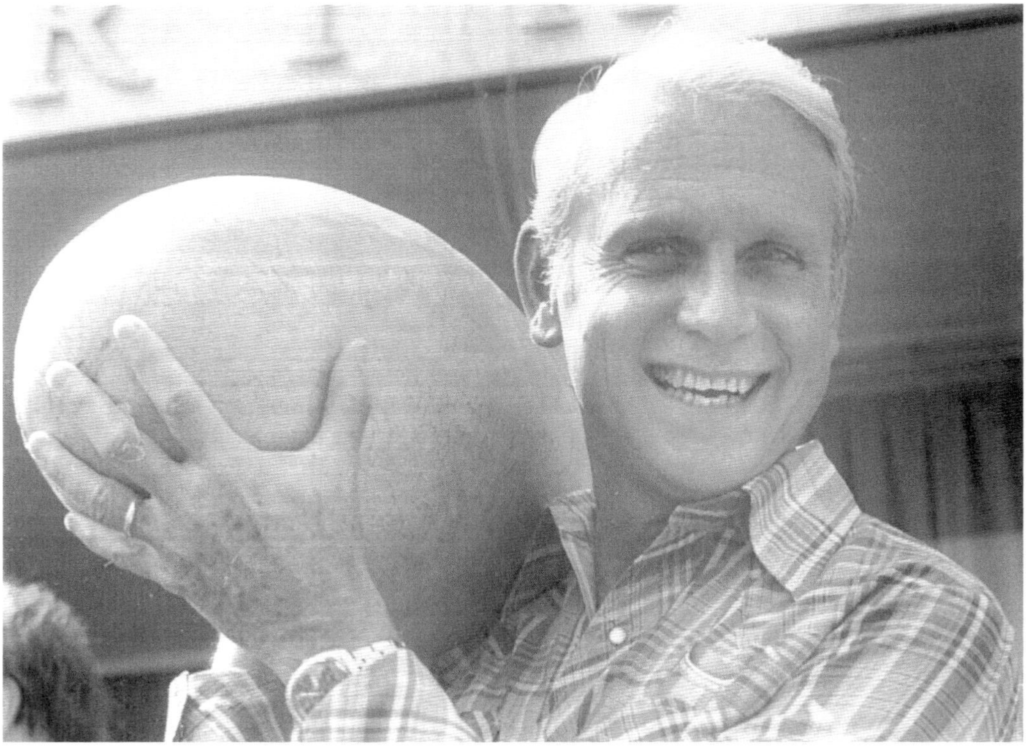

Governor Treen

While in office, Gov. David Connor Treen lived at 430 Dorrington Boulevard in Old Metairie. The first Republican governor since Reconstruction, he appointed more blacks to office than any other previous governor. During his administration (1980–1984) Louisiana's revenue from oil and gas plummeted when the "boom" went "bust," but he overcame that huge setback to establish the Louisiana School for Math, Science, and the Arts and to strengthen much-needed teacher certification requirements. (John Andrew Prime.)

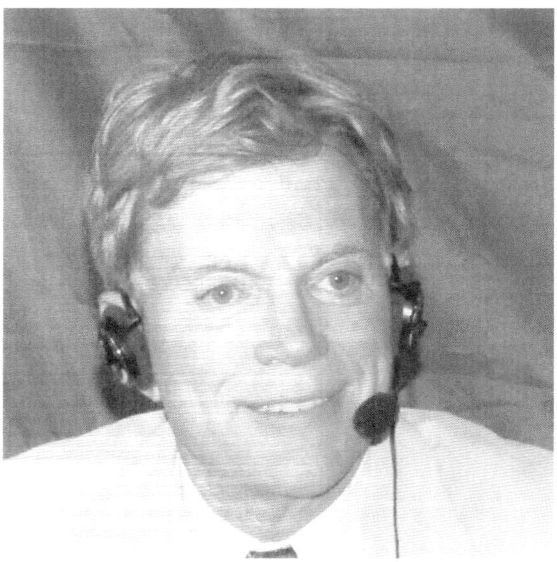

Duke and John Treen

Governor Treen's brother, homebuilder John Speir Treen, lost the 1989 special election for the Metairie district Louisiana House of Representatives to former Ku Klux Klansman David Duke. Duke's 8,459 votes (50.7 percent) edged out Treen's 8,232 votes (49.3 percent). John Treen is perhaps best known for coining the expression "All things being equal, Cajuns vote for Cajuns." Duke served in the House from 1990 until 1992—his first and only public office. (Emmanuel d'Aubignosc.)

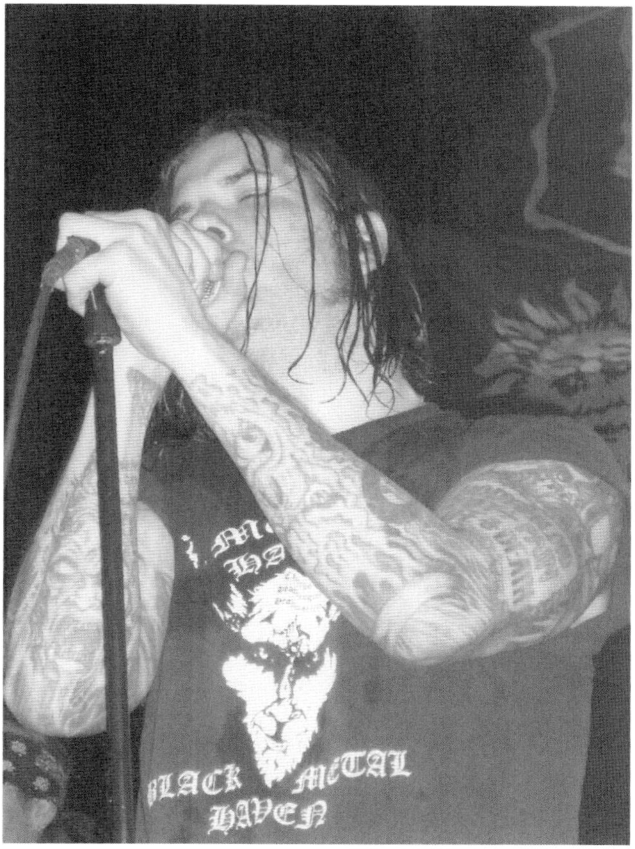

Phil Anselmo
Grace King High School alumnus Philip Hansen "Phil" Anselmo was Pantera's lead singer and is the owner of Housecore Records. Son of a restaurateur, Anselmo joined Pantera at age 19 in 1987. The band broke up in 2003. He is a partner in ownership of the House of Shock. (Mario.)

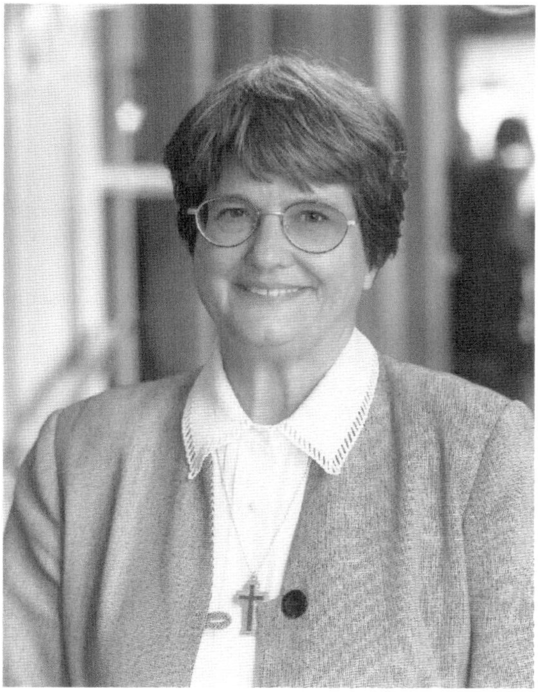

Change
Helen Prejean has advocated and acted upon social issues since the 1970s, when she was coordinator of religious education for St. Francis Cabrini Parish. "The work of one individual, steady and constant, is the way things are changed," she said in 1974. Sister Prejean lived in Metairie, on Bonnabel Boulevard, when *Dead Man Walking* was published in 1993. (Grant Guerrero.)

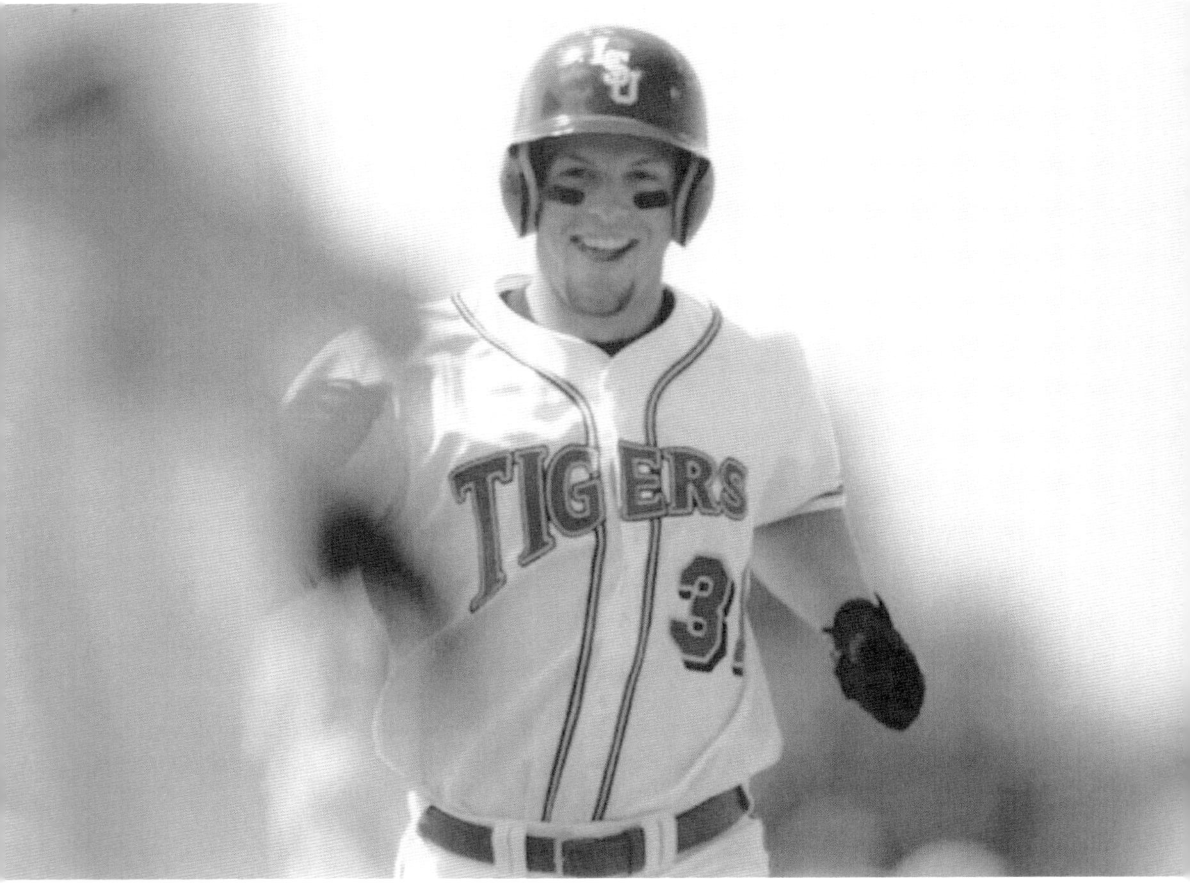

Wally Pontiff

Wally Pontiff Jr. was an outstanding 21-year-old LSU pre-med student and star baseball player (captain of the 2000 National Championship team, 2000 Southeastern Conference Tournament Most Outstanding Player, 2001 Southeastern Conference Academic Honor Roll) with a prospect to play professionally for the Oakland A's when he suddenly died at his home of undiagnosed hypertrophic cardiomyopathy, a genetic disease that results in a thickening of the heart muscle. The community honored his memory in 2003 by officially renaming his boyhood playground (the oldest playground in Metairie) Wally Pontiff Junior Playground.

His parents established the Wally Pontiff Jr. Foundation to funnel gifts and donations to charities and nonprofit organizations in the community. They also work in partnership with the Hypertrophic Cardiomyopathy Association (HCMA) to raise awareness of the condition as the most common cause of sudden cardiac arrest (SCA) in young people and to support awareness of measures available for early diagnosis and treatment. The foundation educates cardiologists in Metairie and the greater New Orleans area. "No parent should ever have to lose a child," said Terry Pontiff. "We want to get the word out that by simply improving pre-participation screening forms and conducting ECGs on properly selected children and athletes we can reduce cardiac death." (Wally Pontiff Jr. Foundation.)

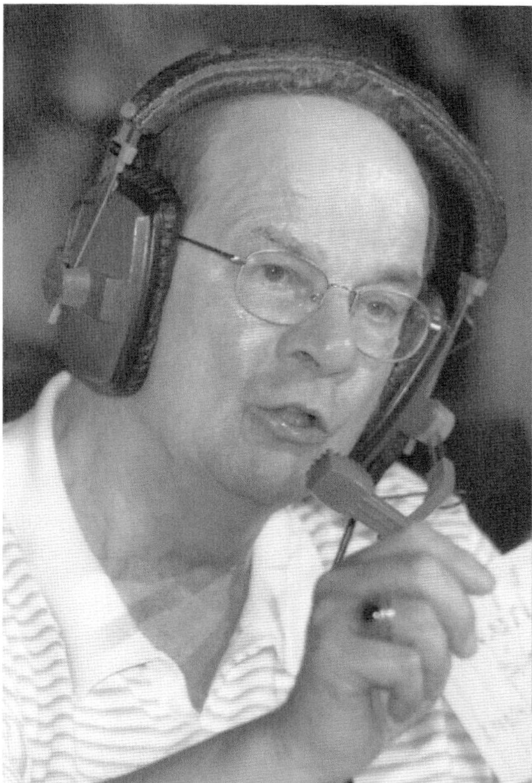

Buddy D

Upon learning of sportscaster Bernard "Buddy" Saverio Diliberto's death in 2005 at his home in Metairie at the age of 73 during the Saints' 38th season, Tom Benson wrote, "Buddy's passion for the Saints was as true as you can get. Although he could be our harshest critic, he was our most ardent supporter. There will always be a link, a connection between our team and Buddy, even with his passing, his legacy will live on." (TP.)

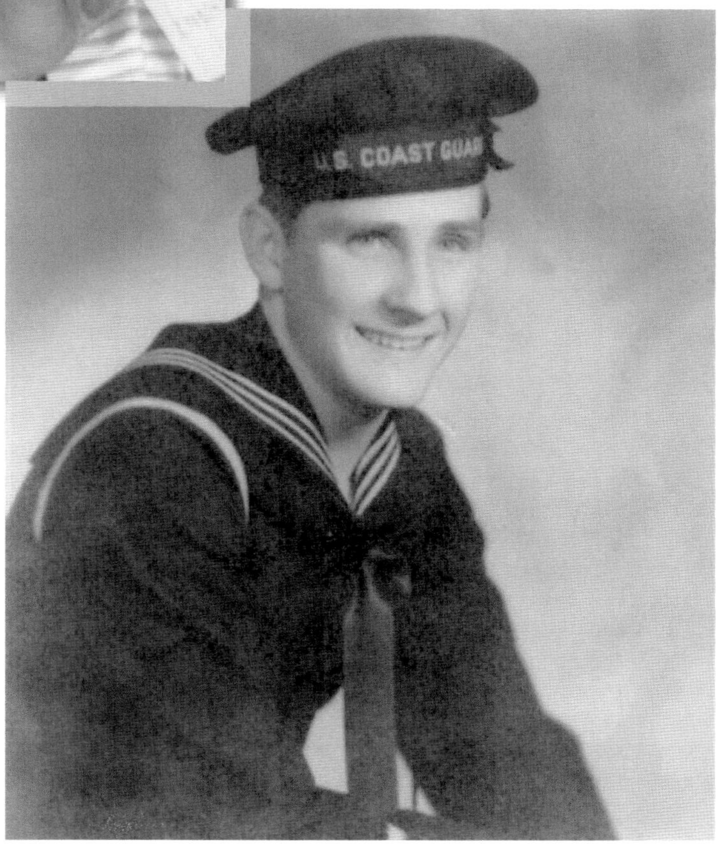

Marvin Perrett

Marvin Perrett enlisted in the US Coast Guard in 1943 and became a coxswain who piloted Higgins-built LCVPs (troop landing boats) to the shores of Normandy on D-Day, to Iwo Jima, and to Okinawa. In later years, he realized the need to share his wartime experiences and became a lecturer, most famously at the National World War II Museum. Perrett passed away in 2007 at the age of 81. In 2009, Vietnam-era LCVP PD4-3 was named in his honor. (USCG.)

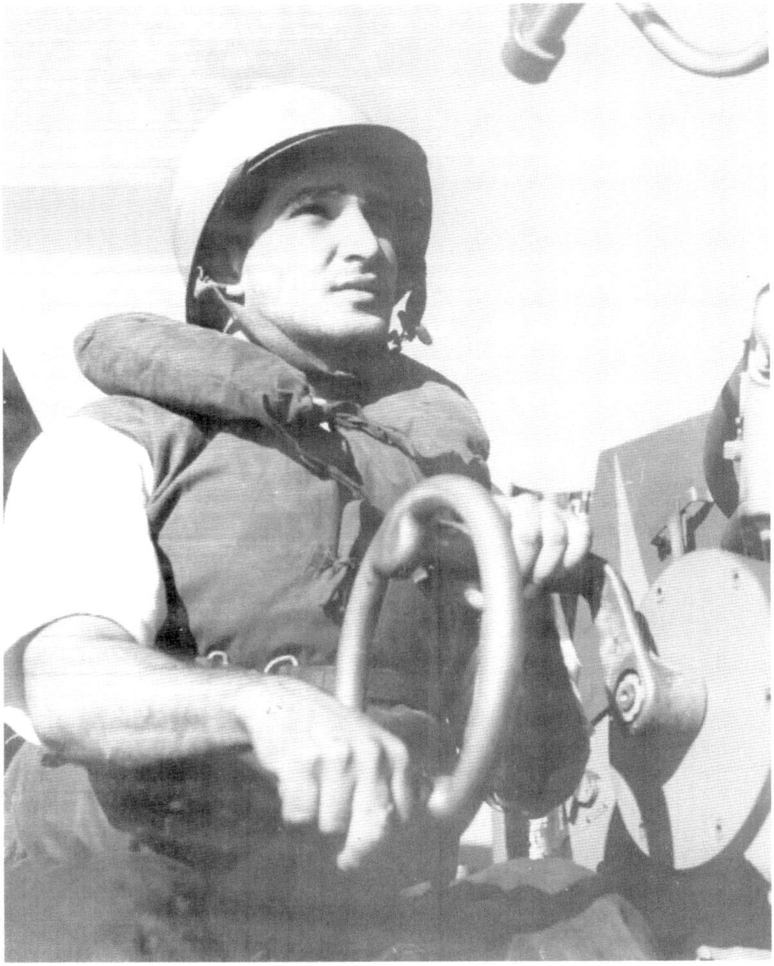

Chuck Azzarello

He was one of the last of an ancient breed—a cobbler who took great pride in his fine work. But he was most proud of serving his country during World War II on Landing Ship Tank (LST) No. 886. His LST transported vehicles, artillery, supplies, and troops directly onto shores in the Pacific Theater. The LST was also known as a "Large Slow Target," and the importance of his dangerous mission was arguably best illustrated by Winston Churchill, who said, "The destinies of two great empires . . . seemed to be tied by some goddamned things called LSTs."

His Sicilian born father, Frank, opened a shoe-repair shop on Royal Street during the 1920s. Chuck learned the family business in 1938 while attending Warren Easton High and made it his career.

The shop moved to 219 Bourbon Street in 1951. He mended shoes for strippers and added prescribed modifications for babies whose shoes required orthopedic corrections. He drank coffee in the neighboring Galatoire's kitchen and watched Earl Long's limousine come and go to the Sho-Bar Club, where Fannie Belle Fleming (known as stripper Blaze Starr) worked. He witnessed the change of the street from a venue where local musicians made a living playing uniquely New Orleans jazz to a tourist strip lined with T-shirt shops and lap dancers.

Chuck was as "New Orleans" as it gets and, like many of his generation, chose to live in Metairie for the last 40 of his 89 years. There, he knew the great love of his grandchildren and celebrated 59 years of marriage to his beloved wife, Audrey, until she passed away in 2006. He became a great-grandfather in 2010. Andrew August "Chuck" Azzarello passed away on January 28, 2011.

CHAPTER FOUR

Optimists

The grass-roots organization Levees.org, founded by Sandy Rosenthal and her son Stanford (while exiled in Lafayette after Hurricane Katrina) is devoted to educating America on the facts associated with the 2005 catastrophic flooding of the New Orleans region. On August 23, 2010, the group installed a Louisiana State Historic Marker that reads: "On August 29, 2005, a federal floodwall atop a levee on the 17th Street Canal, the largest and most important drainage canal for the city, gave way here causing flooding that killed hundreds. This breach was one of 50 ruptures in the Federal Flood Protection System on that day. In 2008, the US District Court placed responsibility for this floodwall's collapse squarely on the US Army Corps of Engineers; however, the agency is protected from financial liability in the Flood Control Act of 1928."

All residents of Metairie were touched by the failure of the federal levee system. This chapter highlights just a few of the 146,000 residents who returned home, endured, and optimistically brought their community back to life. Some featured here are unidentified but shared the same difficulties as all.

No strangers to storms, the people of Metairie have survived and thrived through years of bad weather, most notably the 1947 Fort Lauderdale hurricane that left much of the area covered by six feet of water; 1965's Hurricane Betsy, which brought damaging winds and moderate flooding; and major floods through the years. Katrina was different, not in its ability to defeat them but in the extent of the losses endured. Seventy-five percent of Metairie was flooded. An estimated $5 billion in insured damage occurred. Twenty-nine Katrina/flood-related deaths were reported.

Before Hurricane Katrina swept through Metairie, the community was placed under a first-ever mandatory evacuation on August 28, 2005. Most residents sought refuge just far enough away to return home quickly after the storm passed. After Katrina had its way with Metairie, no large-scale damage had been done. The author of this book and her family were in a Baton Rouge hotel packed with other New Orleans residents. All rejoiced together that a bullet had been dodged.

The storm was passing through Baton Rouge the day after it swept past homes in Metairie, roads were still closed, and the evacuation order had not yet been revoked, so another night in a hotel was the only option available. The evening found us out to dinner in a restaurant also packed with people from our area. A good time was being had by all—a celebration of joy and relief that we would soon be able to return home. And then the restaurant televisions began rolling footage of our inundated communities. Slowly, the heady celebration turned into a hush of silence as more and more people became aware of the horror on the screens. The sound had been muted, but what was heard were gasps of recognition of rooftops: "That's the school . . . I think that's my house . . . Oh, my God!"

The following morning, Jefferson Parish president Aaron Broussard announced that residents could not go home, possibly for six months. So we all took off for places of semipermanent settlement, often far from home. We landed in the home of relatives in Tennessee. Others were scattered all around the country. The kindness of families and strangers was profound as they offered to take us in, share what they had, and contribute what they could.

Some Metairie residents returned home permanently within weeks to relatively undamaged homes and businesses. Many were flooded, requiring much work. Slowly, the community returned to a semblance of normalcy, but within a few months Metairie was back in business, so to speak. Schools reopened. and Archbishop Rummel High opened its doors to students from the entire greater New Orleans area. St. Philip Neri Catholic School provided space for St. Ann students. Veterinarian Patrick Sweeney first cared for pets left behind by their owners, then took in the doctors, staff, and pets from Lakeview Veterinary Hospital. WWL television news and weather reporters Jill Hezeau, Laura Buchtel, and Scott Walker returned to the air, as did radio "Oldie King" Bob Walker, who returned to WTIX. Ellen Degeneres supported her hometown via her television show and in many other ways. T.H. Harris and East Jefferson High graduate Bunny Matthews created his arguably best work, *Nin't Wardica*. The Doerr-Mutter family stored new donated home furnishings in their warehouses, then delivered them in their trucks to people who had lost theirs to the floods.

Phil deGruy of Phil's Grill began organizing his Burgerpalooza to benefit the Miracle League of Greater New Orleans. Mike Azzarello and his little dog Olive Oyl began visiting area healthcare facilities as volunteers in the Visiting Pet Program. The Metairie Women's Club continued to support the community with their slogan "Think, Act, Resolve."

Business owners who returned to continue their work include Don and Joan Radosta, who reopened their po-boy restaurant six weeks after Katrina, Steven Bel of Sal's Sno-Balls, and Rufus Raider's namesake CPA/financial adviser Rufus Cressend. Merlin Schaefer of Schaefer & Rusich Seafood, Jerry Hendrick of Short Stop Po-Boys, Frank Sclafani of Sclafani Cooking School, Chef Anthony Spizale, and the Radostas not only endured Katrina but also the Deep Water Horizon oil spill in the Gulf of Mexico, which greatly affected their livelihoods. Shaefer drove 10-hour days to secure fresh safe shrimp for his customers.

Girard playground and Rummel High standouts Daniel Graff, Scott Buisson, and brothers Craig and Keith Steltz continued their dreams of playing football. Metairie Academy students brought handmade gifts to project Head Start children. Leigh "Li'l Queenie" Harris and Becky Allen continued to entertain. Becky's mother, Myrtis Butzman, survived and thrived after the storm but died at age 97 at Harrah's Casino. Longtime residents Vince Campanella and Eddie Krass returned home and now enjoy retirement in the community they have lived in for more than half a century.

Post-Katrina

NBC anchor Brian Williams, who sat on *Time* magazine's panel tasked with suggesting nominees for the 2005 Person of the Year, nominated Hurricane Katrina. "It has laid bare so many cracks and fissures in our system," he said. Fellow panelist Anderson Cooper agreed: "It was government that failed. It was people who stood up." An unnamed Metairie resident (above) walks her dog along the side of the Seventeenth Street Canal flood wall, about 11 weeks after Katrina. The water level is over her head and in the center one can see ongoing repair-work on the breaches on the New Orleans side of the canal. Levees.org installed a Louisiana State Historic Marker there. Below, young girls scale the wall for a peek at the water. (Mario Tama.)

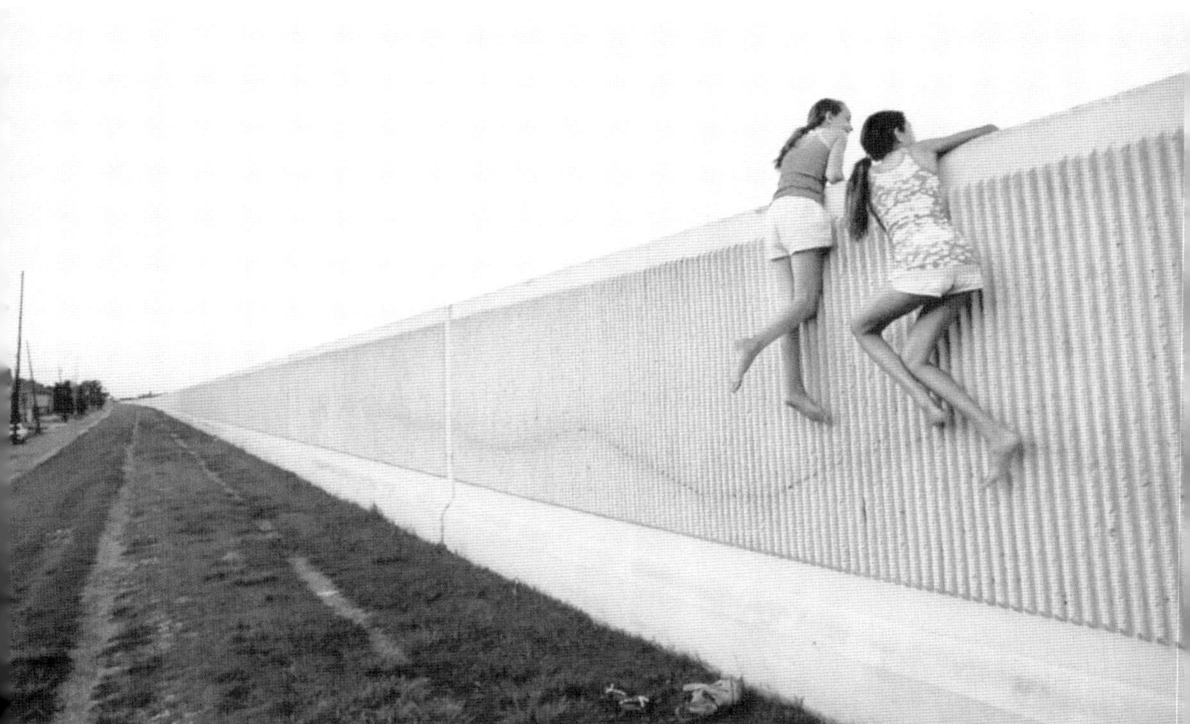

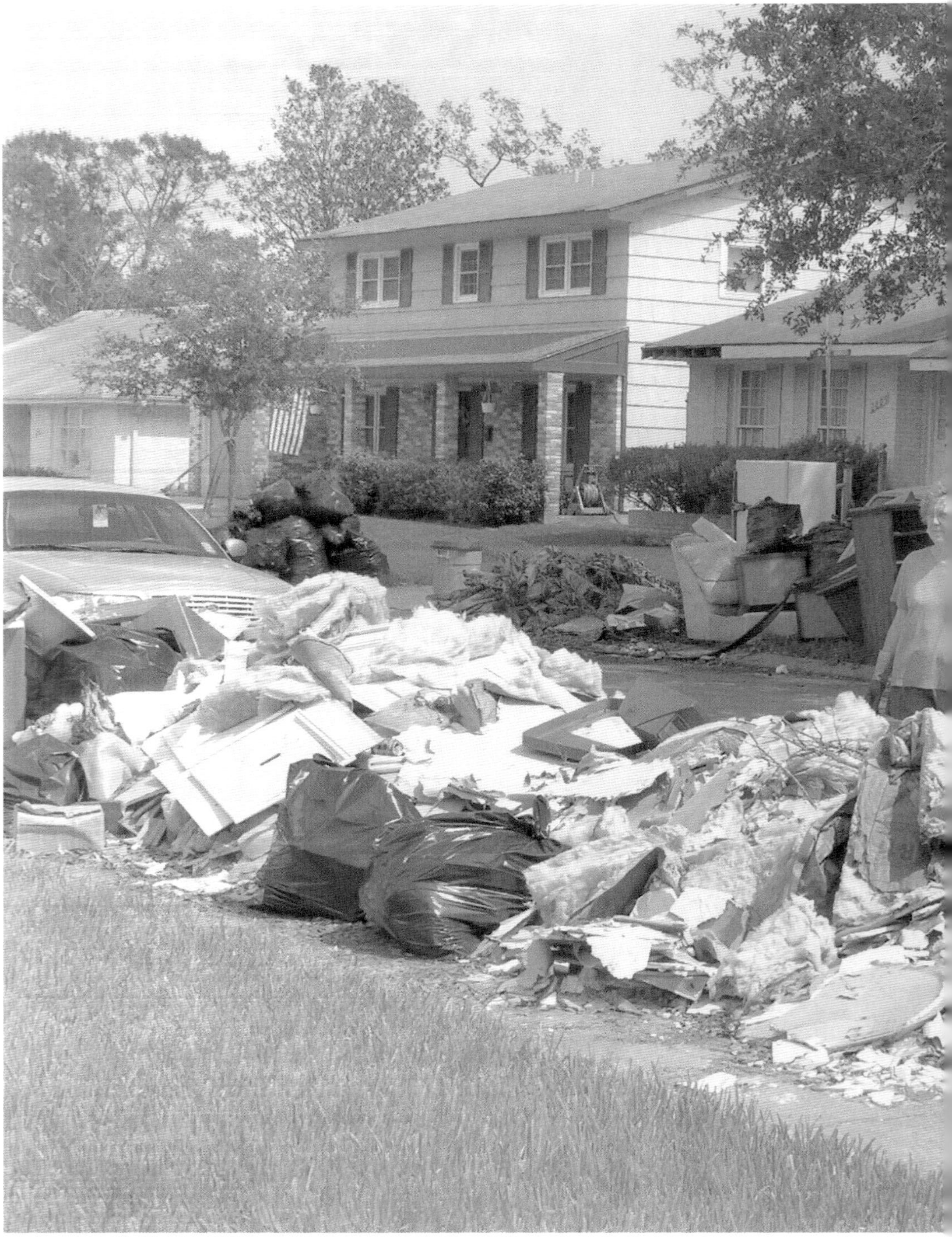

Picking Up the Pieces

An unidentified woman was captured ridding her home of waterlogged possessions by a Federal Emergency Management Assistance agency photographer in 2005. Like the vast majority of her fellow Metairie

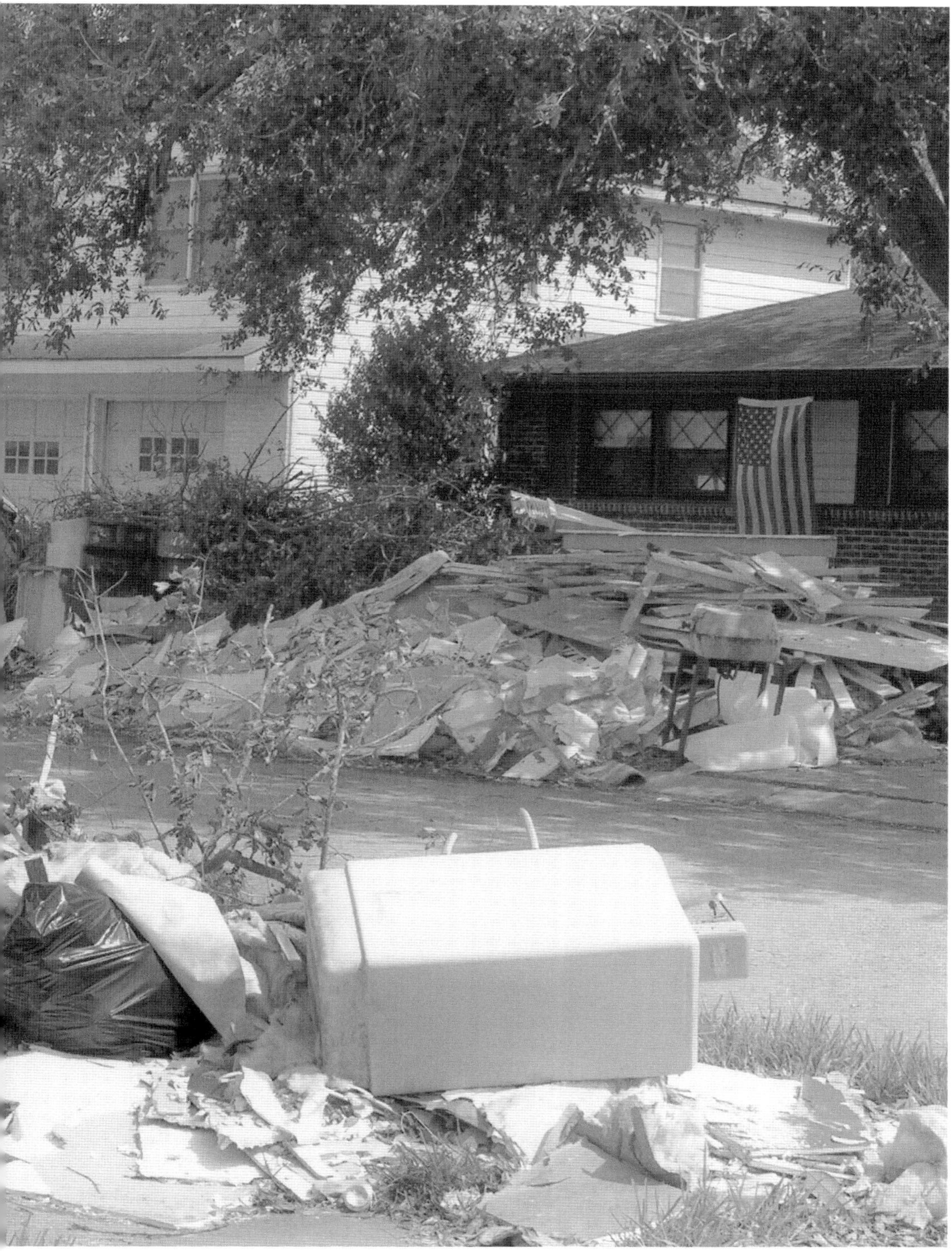

residents, she literally picked up the pieces and rebuilt a home—and her life forever changed. (Win Henderson/FEMA.)

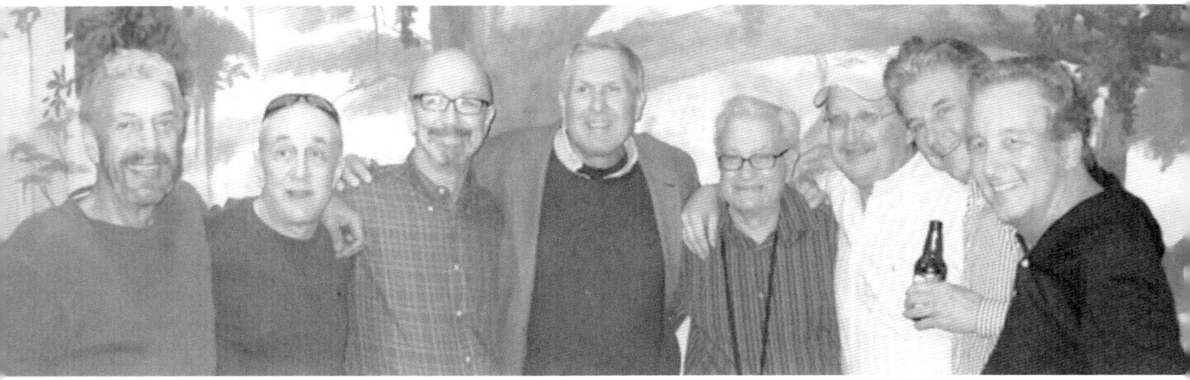

The Oldie King

Before you saw Frankie, Johnny, or The Special Man on the television commercial that was blasted into your home in 1989, you heard a familiar voice while a photograph of the furniture store was displayed. That was Bob Walker, the legendary "Oldies King" of radio fame.

On November 15, 1965, he played the first song ("Seventh Son" by Baton Rouge's own Johnny Rivers) on the first broadcast of student operated WLSU radio. He called his show *Bob Walker's Wax Museum* and played oldies, even back then. After 45 years in radio, Bob said, when speaking of his affinity for "the oldies," "It'll probably follow me to my grave."

Walker began his professional career in radio in 1965 at WNNR, spent a year at WSMB, and moved to WTIX-AM 690 in 1967. By 1968, the 22-year-old's *Afternoon Drive* show was one of the top five in the nation. In 1979, at age 32, while working for WTIX, he said, "My nickname around here is the Oldies King."

Robert Mitchell became program director in 1968, and the station had over 100 gold 45s and LPs on the wall for groups and singers who "broke" like Dr. John, Tony Orlando and Dawn, Sonny & Cher, Roberta Flack, and the Fifth Dimension by the 1980s.

Bob says that in 1973 WTIX introduced Malcolm John "Mac" Rebennack Jr. to the world as "Dr. John the Night Tripper" with "Right Place, Wrong Time" and that in 1975 he broke the three-year-old version of "Second Line" by Stop Inc. (1972) during the Mardi Gras remote broadcast. "The crowds around our station van went wild. The Second Line had been re-born." During the Carnival Day broadcast that same year, Bob premiered "They All Ask'd For You" by the Meters from the Fat City parking lot.

Pictured here at a reunion of local radio figures, from left to right are Bobby Reno, Bob Mitchell, Don Delahoussaye, WTIX general manager Bill Engel, Joe Culotta, "Pal Al" Nassar, Skip Broussard, and Bob Walker. (Bob Walker.)

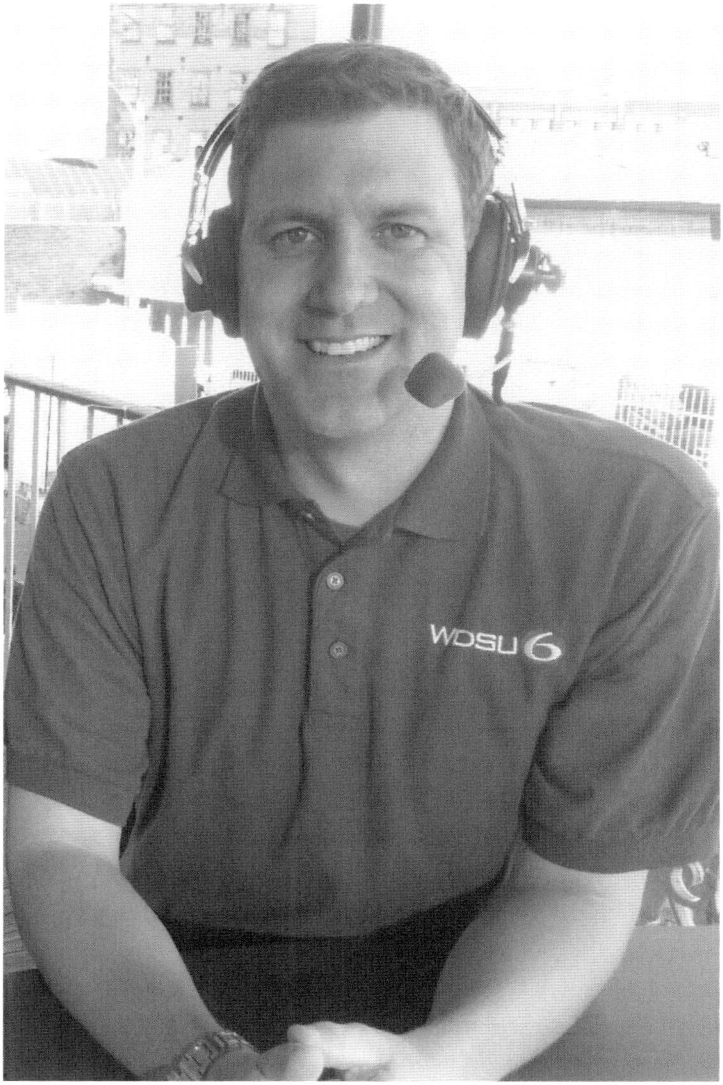

Second Generation On the Air

Walker said that in 1980, when he began hosting WTIX Original Oldie Hour at noon daily, "All the legendary '60s local singers were 'dead' (figuratively) and long forgotten." So he devoted every Thursday to feature the great ones. "WTIX and the *Oldies Hour* were personally responsible for restarting the careers of Irma Thomas, Ernie K-Doe, Benny Spellman, Tommy Ridgley, Oliver Morgan, the Dixie Cups, John Fred, and the Nevilles [individually and as a group]. Mardi Gras Mambo by Art Neville & the Hawketts was literally forgotten. We were so successful, as written up in the trade mags like *Billboard* and *Cashbox*, that every major market and most minor markets popped up with an oldies station."

In 1986, when WTIX dropped most local programming by hooking into *Solid Gold*, produced by Dallas-based Satellite Music Network, Bob's dissatisfaction with that decision led him to leave the station. That year he moved to 990AM-WYAT, which billed itself as "The Oldies Channel." After a post-Katrina return to WTIX, he retired from radio in 2006.

You can catch him now on television (*Treme*) and movies (with Will Ferrell, Dan Ackroyd, Brooke Shields, Virginia Madsen, Daryl Hannah, Wanda Sykes, Jeremy Irons, Emma Thompson, Tim Robbins, and Brad Pitt, to name a few).

To help make ends meet while his children were growing up, Bob took on a variety of DJ gigs at weddings, parties, and reunions. His son Scott, as a young teen, helped carry and set up the then bulky audio equipment He too, got the bug to speak before an audience. By age 15, Scott was doing his own gigs while also working as a weekend DJ on Oldies 106.7. Scott attended the University of Southern Mississippi, majored in broadcast journalism, and began a career in television—working while still a student at a Hattiesburg station. After a variety of moves to several Southern stations, the sports announcer turned to news. He is now as familiar a face in the greater New Orleans area as his dad is a familiar voice. Metairie-born Scott Walker is the Emmy-nominated news anchor for WDSU News. (Scott Walker.)

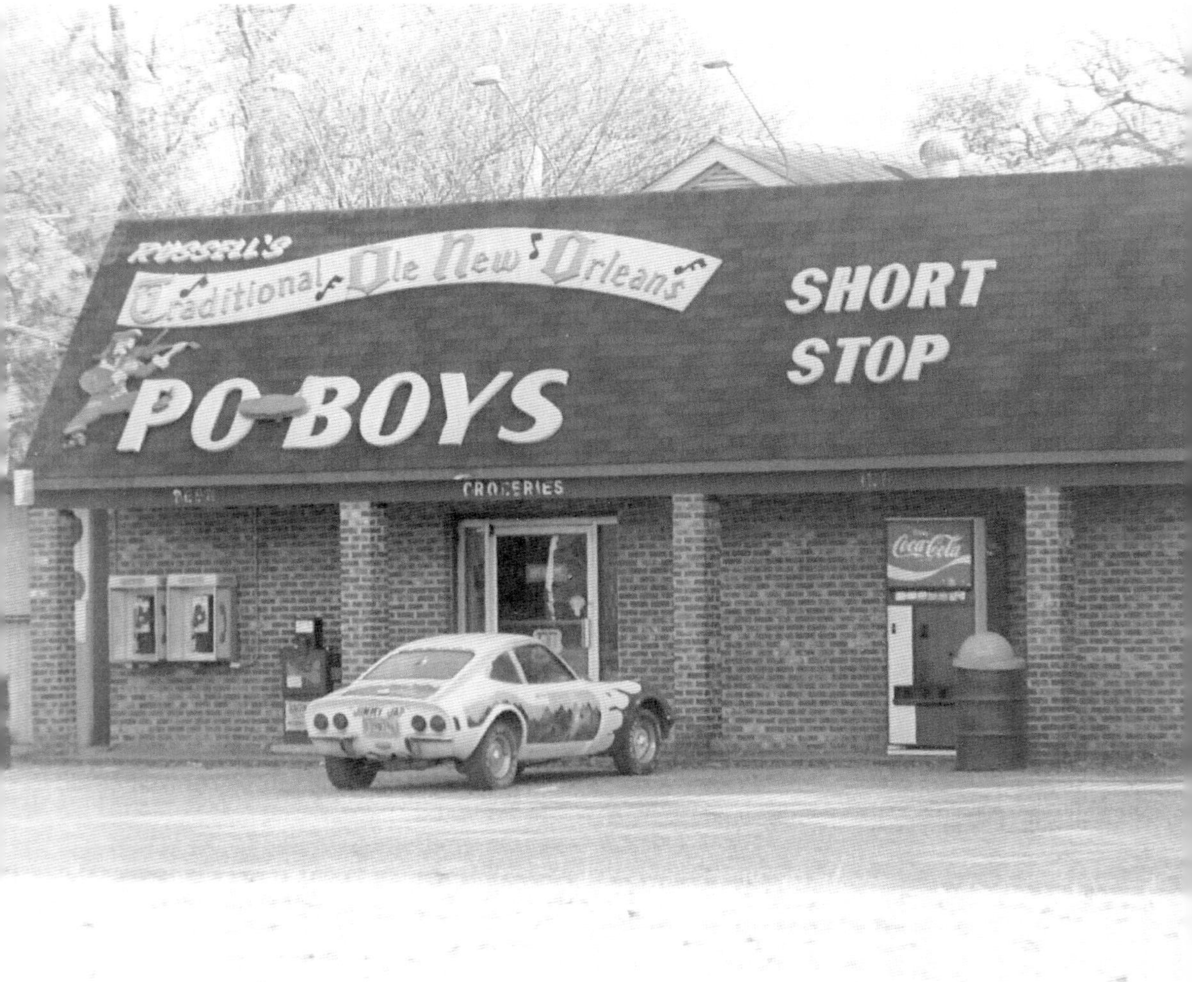

Short Stop Po-Boys

Russell F. Hendrick bought a corner grocery store and meat market on Transcontinental Drive near the corner of Airline Highway in 1966. He added a snowball stand, and his father, uncle, cousin, and children all lent a hand in making the business successful. Along with Russell's family, Metairie was growing and West Metairie Avenue was being expanded. Road workers and people from surrounding businesses dropped by the store to buy freshly sliced cold cuts and French bread for their lunches. Soon, they requested that the bread be sliced. Then they asked for the bread to be "dressed." It was apparent that the customers wanted po-boys, which Short Stop Superette began selling. Then a Crock-Pot of roast beef was cooked each day for sandwiches, and the rest is history.

Russell retired from working in the shop in 1992. His son Russell G. "Jerry" Hendrick became president of the corporation and continued to run the business as head of operations. In 2010, he bought the business. Almost 50 years after his dad opened the little store, Jerry says, "Short Stop hasn't changed much. I want people who know Short Stop to be able to return in a week, a year or 10 years and experience the same quality po-boys and fast service they knew."

From humble beginnings serving roast beef from a Crock-Pot, Short Stop now serves over 100 pounds of roast beef daily, as well as a wide variety of po-boys, deli meat, seafood, sausage, meatball, old-time french fries with gravy, gumbo, Zapp's chips, Barq's in a bottle, and ice cold beer on tap or in bottles. (Jerry Hendrick.)

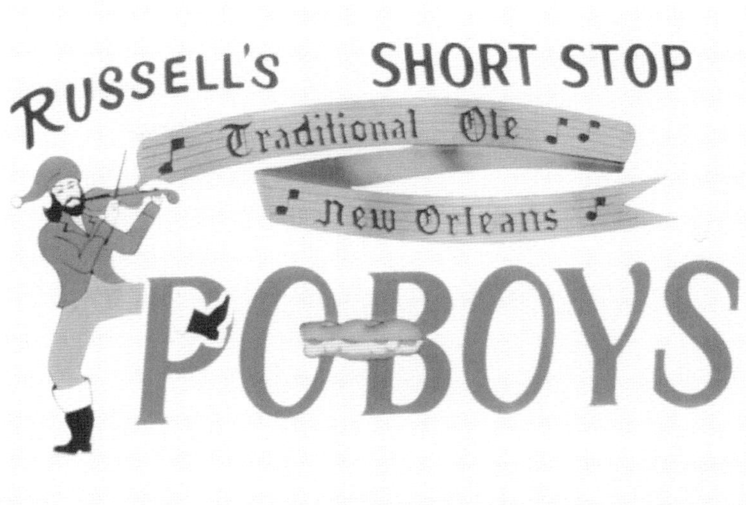

Fiddler on the Roof
Short Stop's logo came to be because Russell's favorite musical production is *Fiddler on the Roof.*

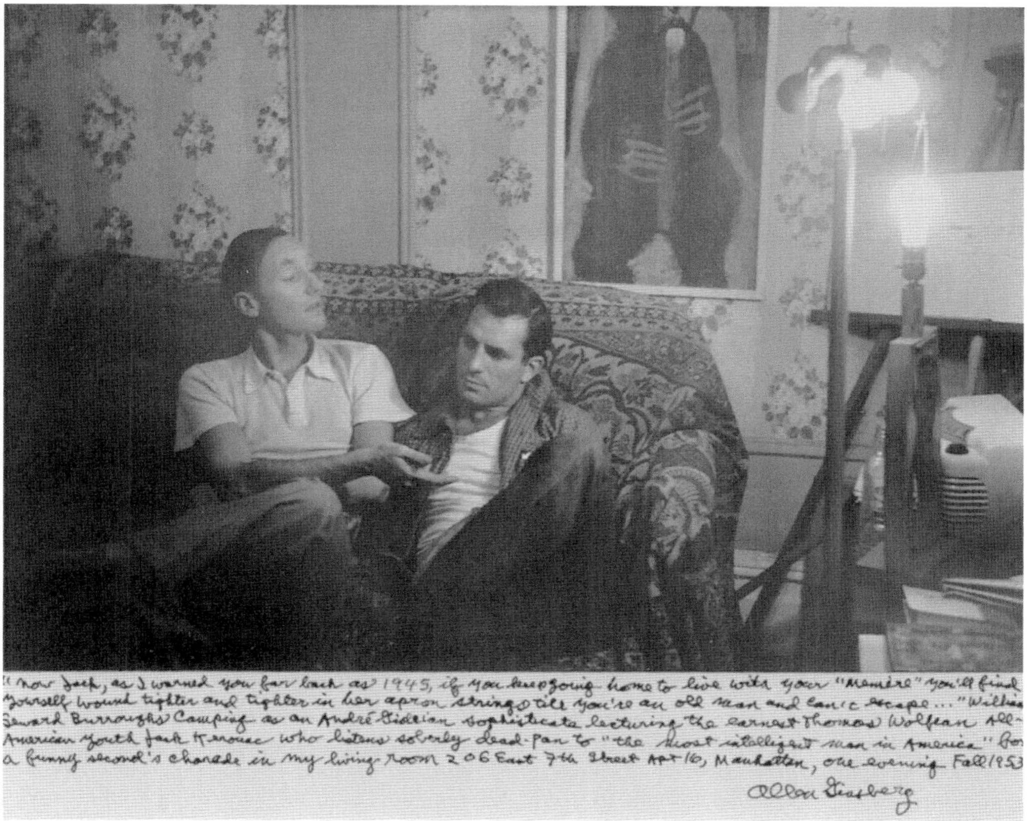

Naked Lunch
When one of the Beat Generation's founding fathers—novelist, short story writer, essayist, painter, and spoken-word performer William S. Burroughs—decided to move to New Orleans in 1948, his first home was a rental at 111 Transcontinental Drive. In 1958, he wrote the novel *Naked Lunch.* Ironically, some 12 years later he could have had a fully dressed po-boy at Short Stop, right next door. Pictured are Burroughs (left) and Jack Kerouac in 1953. (National Gallery of Art.)

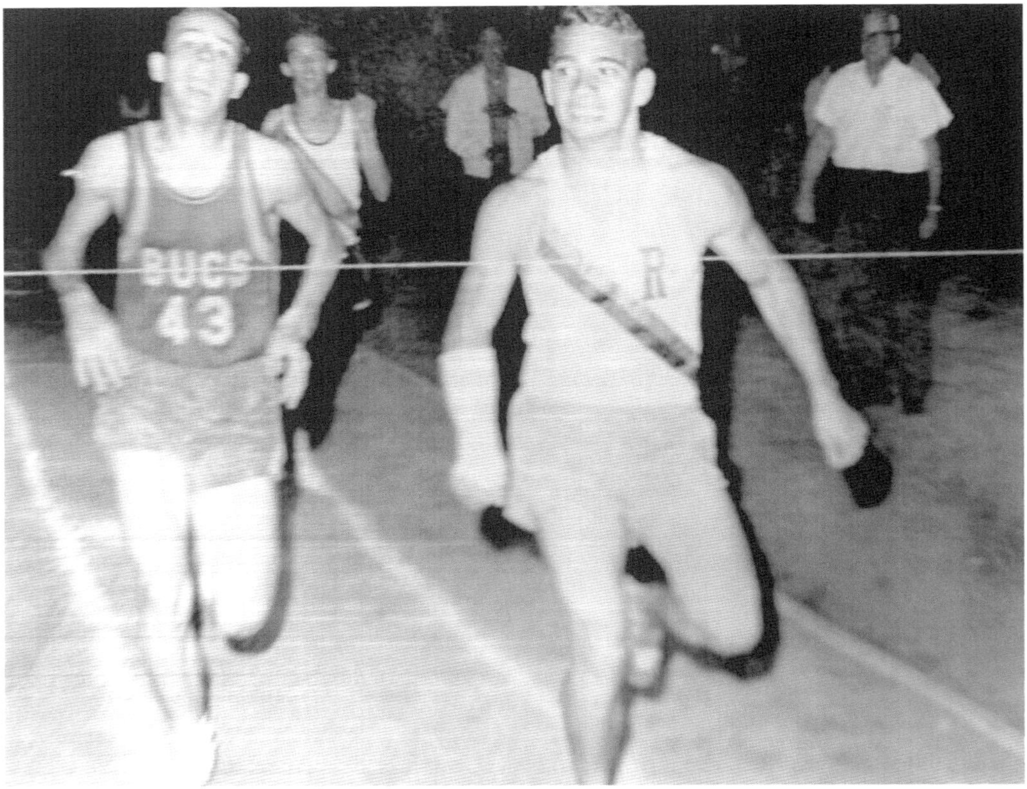

Rufus Raider

In May 1966, the *Times-Picayune* reported that "a diminutive senior from Archbishop Rummel led all the way, and captured the mile run" in the 5-AAA district championship track-and-field event. Rufus Cressend won the race at 4:48:5 and not only earned the trophy but also left his alma mater with a lasting legacy.

Before the race, Mrs. John Baptiste Cressend (Amelie-Francis Prados), mother of the senior team member, letterman, and captain, suggested her son's name as a more appropriate one for the school mascot that John Chase had created, then simply called "The Raider." The principal, Brother John Fairfax, told Mrs. Cressend that if her son won his upcoming mile race, it would be done. And so it was.

In honor of earning the first District Championship title in the school's history, the following day (Monday, May 10, 1966) was proclaimed "Rufus Cressend Day." The announcement was made that The Raider would forevermore be named Rufus.

Born and raised in Metairie, Rufus Cressend attended St. Francis Xavier elementary school before attending Rummel, where he also lettered in football while playing quarterback. He went on to graduate from the University of Southwestern Louisiana (now University of Louisiana in Lafayette) in 1970 (where he was on the dean's list) with a major in accounting. He attended Officer Candidate School in Quantico, Virginia, where he was commissioned as an officer in the US Marine Corps during the war in Vietnam. In 1976, he established his Metairie-based business, Rufus P. Cressend, CPA.

Still active in his career, Rufus is a commissioned special agent of the Jefferson Parish Sheriffs Office, an avid tennis player (having reached level 5.0), a world traveler, and a wine collector who is a member and leading officer of several local and international wine and dining organizations. He proudly serves as bailli provincial of the southwest of the Chaine des Rotisseurs.

Rufus Prados Cressend carries his name proudly. Since the 1800s, each generation of the Cressend or Prados family has named a son Rufus. And for generations to come, no Rummel student will ever forget the name Rufus Raider. (Rufus and Yvette Cressend.)

Rufus Cressend

Chaine des Rotisseurs is the world's oldest international gastronomic society, founded in Paris in 1248. While focusing on fine dining and hospitality, it also provides scholarships to students of the hospitality industry. As bailli provincial of the southwest region, Rufus leads membership chapters in Arkansas, Colorado, Kansas, Louisiana, Oklahoma, and Texas. Yvette D. Cressend, his wife, is the New Orleans bailli. (Rufus and Yvette Cressend.)

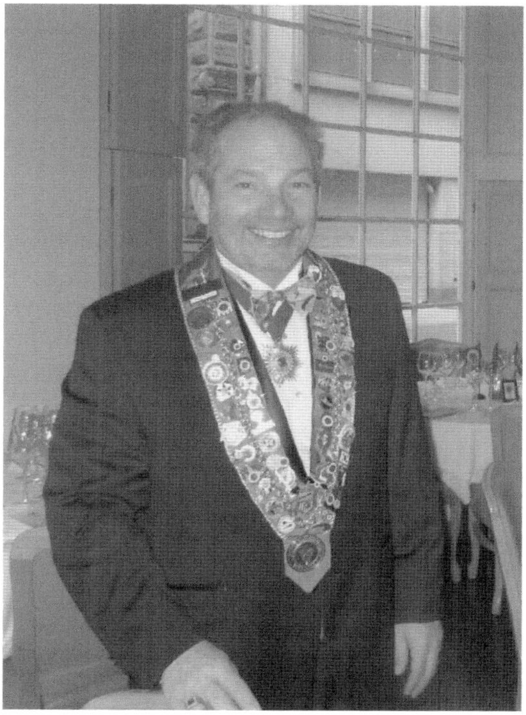

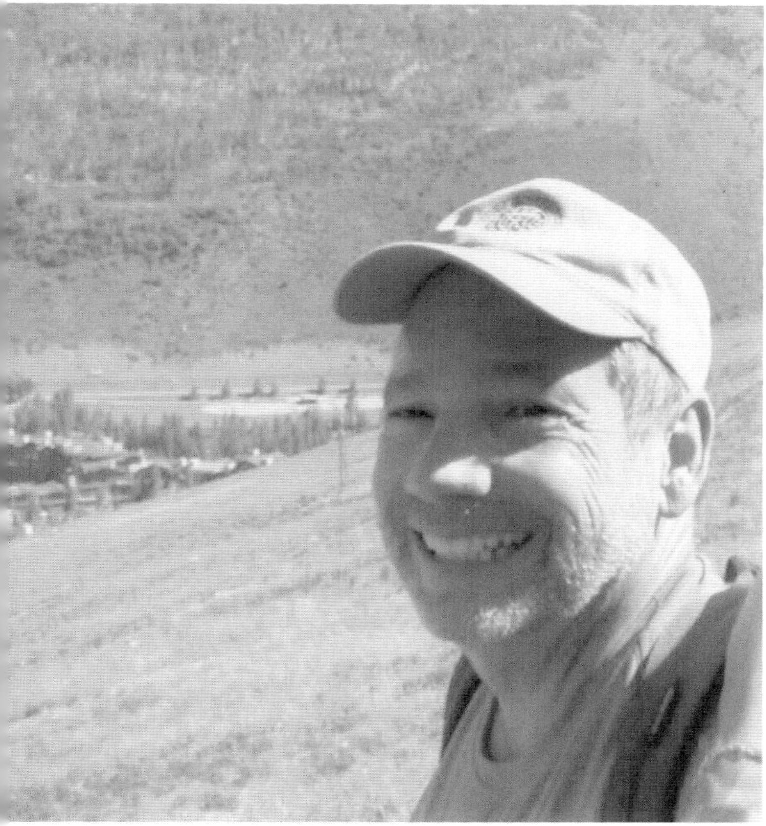

Hurricane Isaac Damages the Cressend Residence

During Hurricane Isaac, the interior of the Cressends' Metairie home was soaked though all three floors after winds badly damaged their roof. Yvette and Rufus spent the duration of the extremely slow-moving storm on 24-hour shift duty trying to save as many of their cherished possessions as they possibly could. Needless to say, they needed a vacation after that ordeal. Yvette captured Rufus here on one such occasion. (Rufus and Yvette Cressend.)

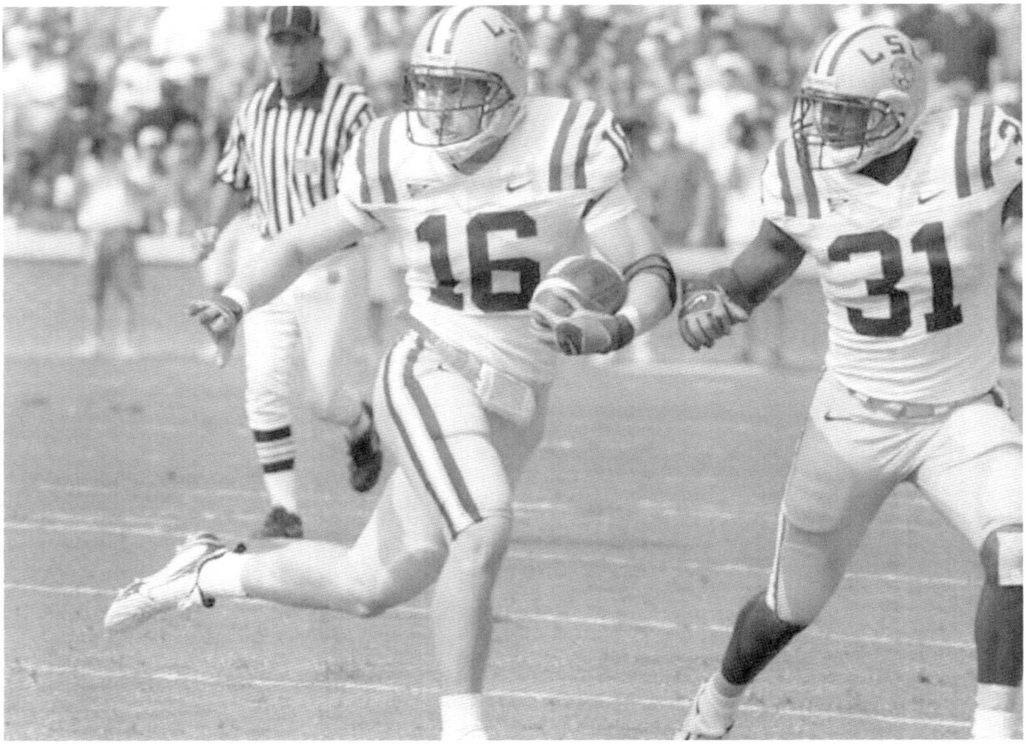

Four Outstanding Girard Boys

Kevin and Craig Steltz (pictured here), Daniel Graff, and Scott Buisson were born within five years of one another (1983–1988), and all played football as youths at Gerard Playground and Rummel High School. An All-American at LSU, Craig now plays for the Chicago Bears. (Dennis Hodges.)

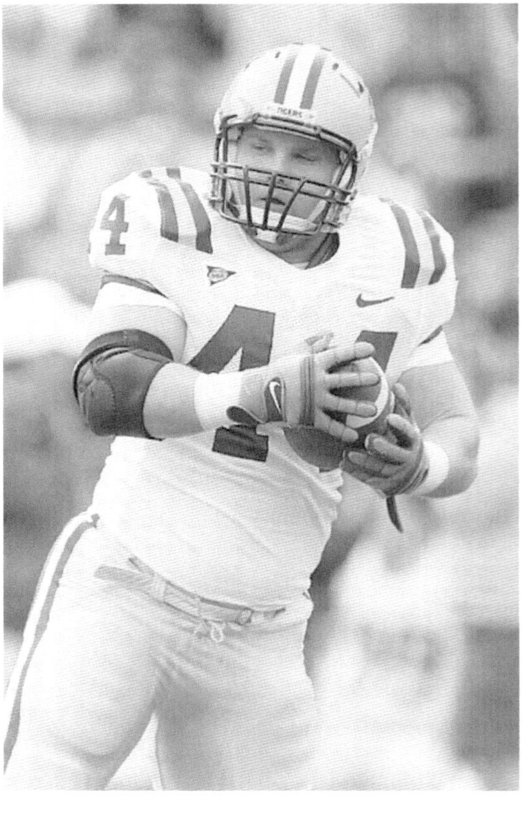

Kevin Steltz

Kevin Steltz, the oldest among the four young men above, holds Rummel's lifting record in the bench press at 470 pounds and in the incline at 415 pounds. He was a walk-on at LSU, where he played fullback and became the first former Girard Viking to win a national championship in the Bowl Championship Series in 2003. (John David Mercer/US Presswire.)

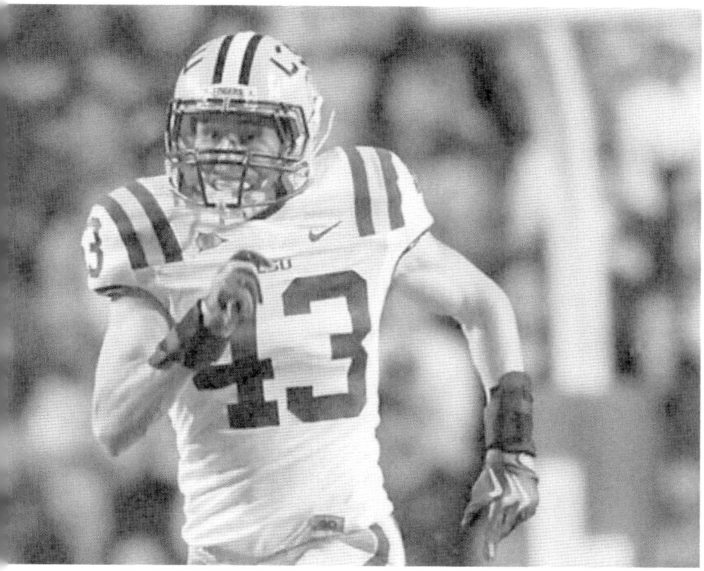

Daniel Graff

Walk-on safety Daniel Graff was a player-coach at LSU. He was awarded the university's Butch Duhe Award, which honors a player who demonstrates character, unselfishness, and commitment. He was nominated by Les Miles for the Rudy Award. Miles wrote in the nomination, "Daniel Graff is the epitome of a team player— unselfish, full of positive spirit, and a '100 percent every play' competitor." (Steve Franz.)

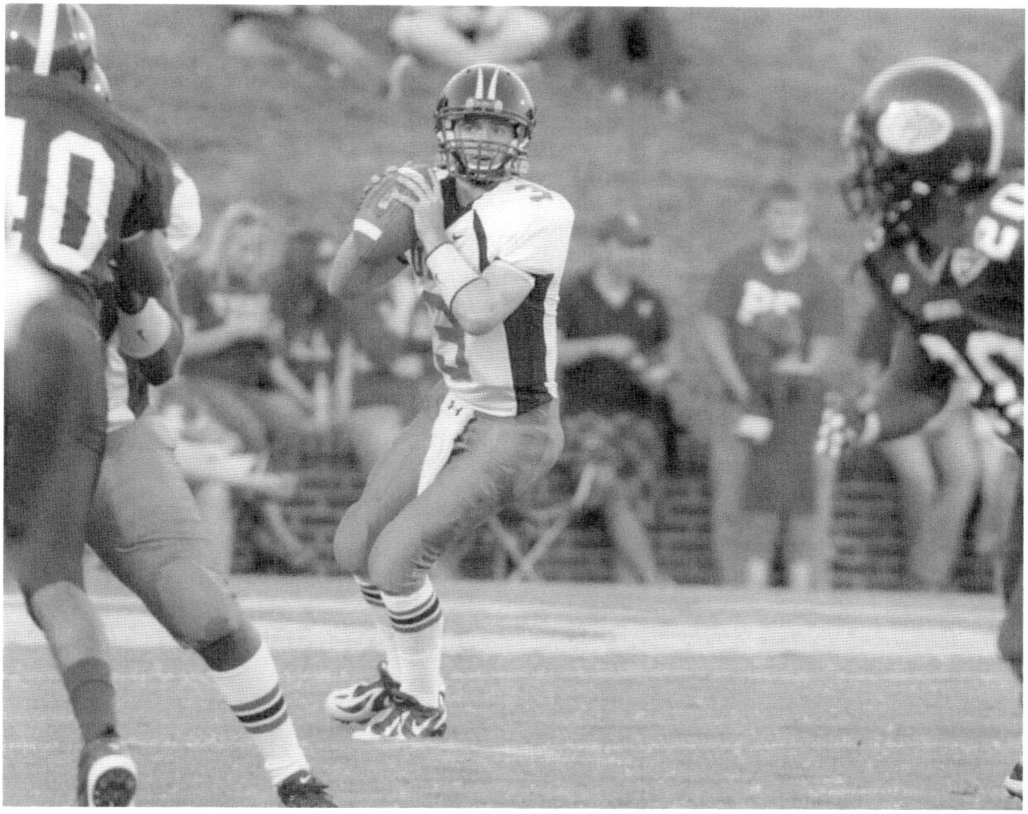

Scott Buisson

The youngest of the quartet, Rummel quarterback Scott Buisson played the same position at the University of Arkansas-Monticello, where he was the first player in NCAA history at any level to pass for more than 400 yards and rush for 200 yards in a single game. He is now the starting quarterback for the New Orleans Voodoo. (AP.)

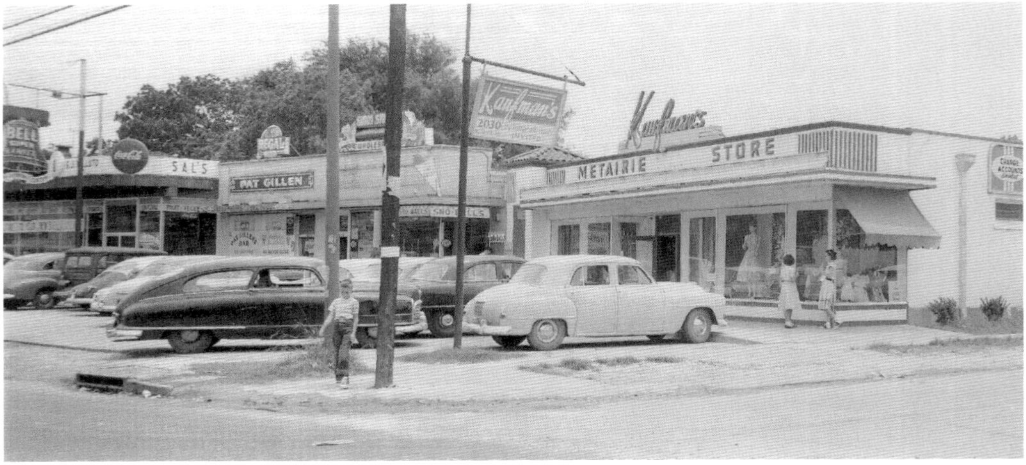

Sal's Sno Balls

Mr. and Mrs. Sal J. Talluto's Bell Supermarket is seen here in a 1950s photograph of Metairie Shopping Center in the 2000 block of Metairie Road. When the 40-foot-front, 100-foot-deep store opened on September 18, 1953, it replaced their smaller store next door: Sal's Fruit Market. The entire strip has been demolished to make way for a Regions Bank branch, but Talluto's name lives on across the road at Sal's Sno-Balls. (LDL.)

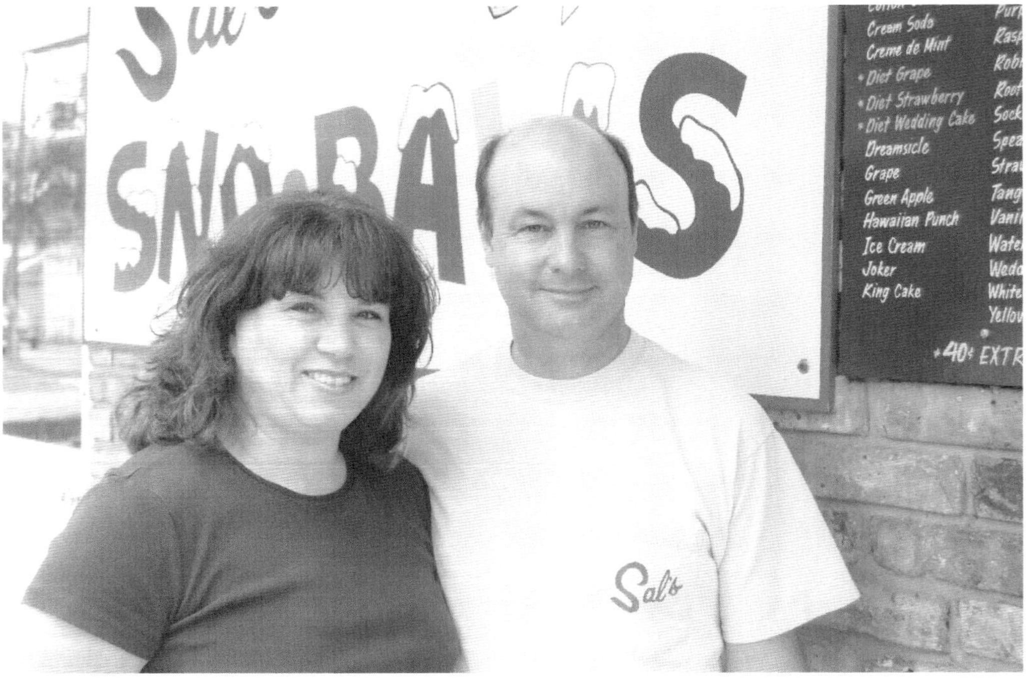

Steven Bel

After closing the grocery due to health issues, Sal built a small stand near his home at 1823 Metairie Avenue and began selling sno-balls in 1959. Neighborhood boy Steven Bel began working there at age 8 and at age 28 bought the business, which he continues to run today with his wife, Gretchen (they met while working there at 11 years old). Just 21 days after Katrina, they freely served their refreshing treats to military and police during the sweltering heat of September 2005. (Sarah Rohen.)

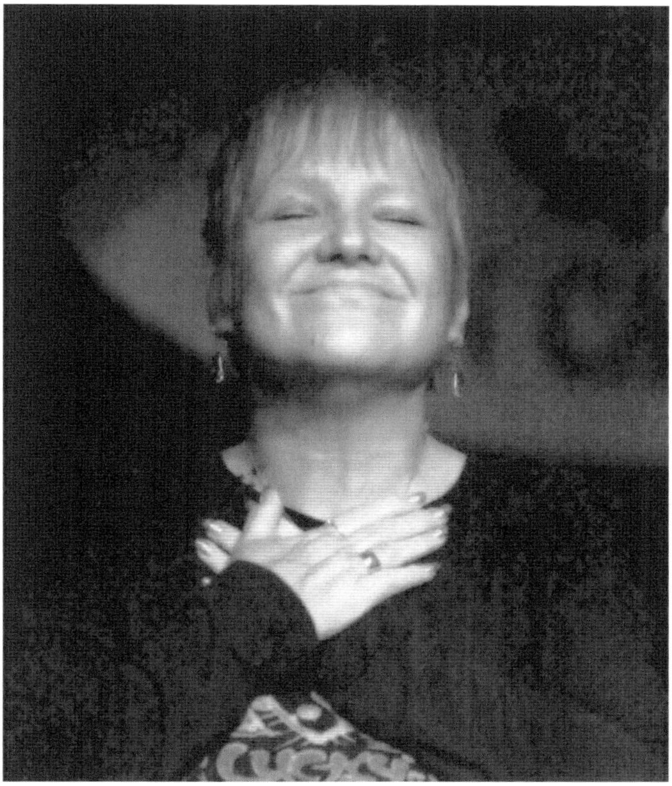

Leigh "Li'l Queenie" Harris

"She's proof that you can come from Old Metairie and have soul," said Bunny Matthews. *New York Times* critic John Rockwell wrote that she is "a short dynamic Southern woman with a tough, earthy, bluesy voice that can rise ecstatically to gospel abandon." While in her teens, Quint Davis, New Orleans Jazz Festival producer, suggested that she collaborate with keyboardist John Magnie. Together, they formed Li'l Queenie and the Percolators, one of the most popular local bands during the late 1970s and early 1980s. "Percolators" was taken from Milton Mezzrow's jazz memoir *Really the Blues*. His 1923 band was named Mezz Mezzrow and His Percolatin' Fools. "Little Queenie" was a nickname originally bestowed by a former boyfriend and shortened to "Li'l" by local music journalists, but when "Li'l" caused confusion in non-English-speaking countries, "Little" was quickly readopted. She is shown here performing at Chickie Wah Wah in New Orleans.

The daughter of clarinetist and musical arranger Allan J. Harris Jr. (who played in Jay Zainey's orchestra) and a product of Ridgewood Prep and St. Martin's Episcopal schools, Leigh has appeared with B.B. King, Elvis Costello, Harry Connick Jr., Pete Seeger, Taj Mahal, and Buckwheat Zydeco, to name just a few. She has performed locally with many familiar artists, including the Dixie Cups, the Pfister Sisters, Charmaine Neville, and Amasa Miller. A concert with the New Orleans Philharmonic Orchestra included her performance with her all-female choir, Little Queenie's Wahini Dakinis, and her string band, Mixed Knots. She was chosen Female Performer of the Year by *Gambit* magazine's readers. Her most popular recording to date is her musical interpretation of Ron Cuccia's poem "My Darlin' New Orleans." She has performed throughout the United States, including New York's Central Park and Town Hall, as well as in Europe, the Caribbean, and Japan. Recently, Leigh has also composed and recorded music for films and television, including HBO's *Treme*.

Having lost much (including recordings planned for release) to the federal flood-wall failures, Leigh now lives in North Carolina, where she continues to compose, produce, record, and perform her singular music with artists there and nationwide, including, of course, her darlin' New Orleans. (Eliot Kamenitz.)

Will Bunn Matthews III

In 1966, T.H. Harris Junior High ninth-grader Will Bunn Matthews III was told by the principal that he could either cut his Beatles mop-top hair or wear a bow in it for his yearbook photograph. He opted for the bow. Growing up in Airline Park, he went on to East Jefferson High, where, in 1967, his first big-time interview with Mark Lindsay of Paul Revere and the Raiders was printed in the school paper, where he was a writer, cartoonist, and editor.

After a stint at LSUNO, he began writing for *Figaro*, the predecessor of *Gambit* news, where his cartoons were first published professionally under the title "F'sure!: Actual Dialogue Heard on the Streets of New Orleans." "I would go out and eavesdrop on people's conversations, so I'd hear stuff, like, at Schwegmann's, and that would be the cartoon," he said. This would lead him to an interest in local dialect, culminating in the creation of *Vic and Nat'ly*, a comic strip about a Ninth Ward couple who owned a neighborhood bar and restaurant frequented by local characters, roaches, and a chihuahua. They premiered on January 3, 1982, in the Dixie Roto section of the *Times-Picayune* (Matthews was paid $75 per cartoon) with Nat'ly handing a bowl of used king cake babies to Vic, instructing him to "Wrench dem off in da' zinc." Vic and Nat'ly became so popular that "they" eventually opened an actual restaurant in Covington.

The kid from Metairie who was voted "most intelligent" by his classmates in 1964 has also published music reviews and cartoons in *Offbeat*, was the *Times-Picayune*'s music critic during the early 1980s, and came to know and befriend Professor Longhair, James Booker, and the Neville brothers. He taught art at St. Scholastica, was in league with the creators of Tipitina's (he's also a musician), and drew promotional posters for the venue as well as for The Warehouse. His artwork was featured at the 1984 Louisiana World's Exposition and is included in the Audubon Institute Insectarium, the Historic New Orleans Collection, the Louisiana State Museum, and the Ogden Museum of Southern Art. (Aaron S. Duplantier.)

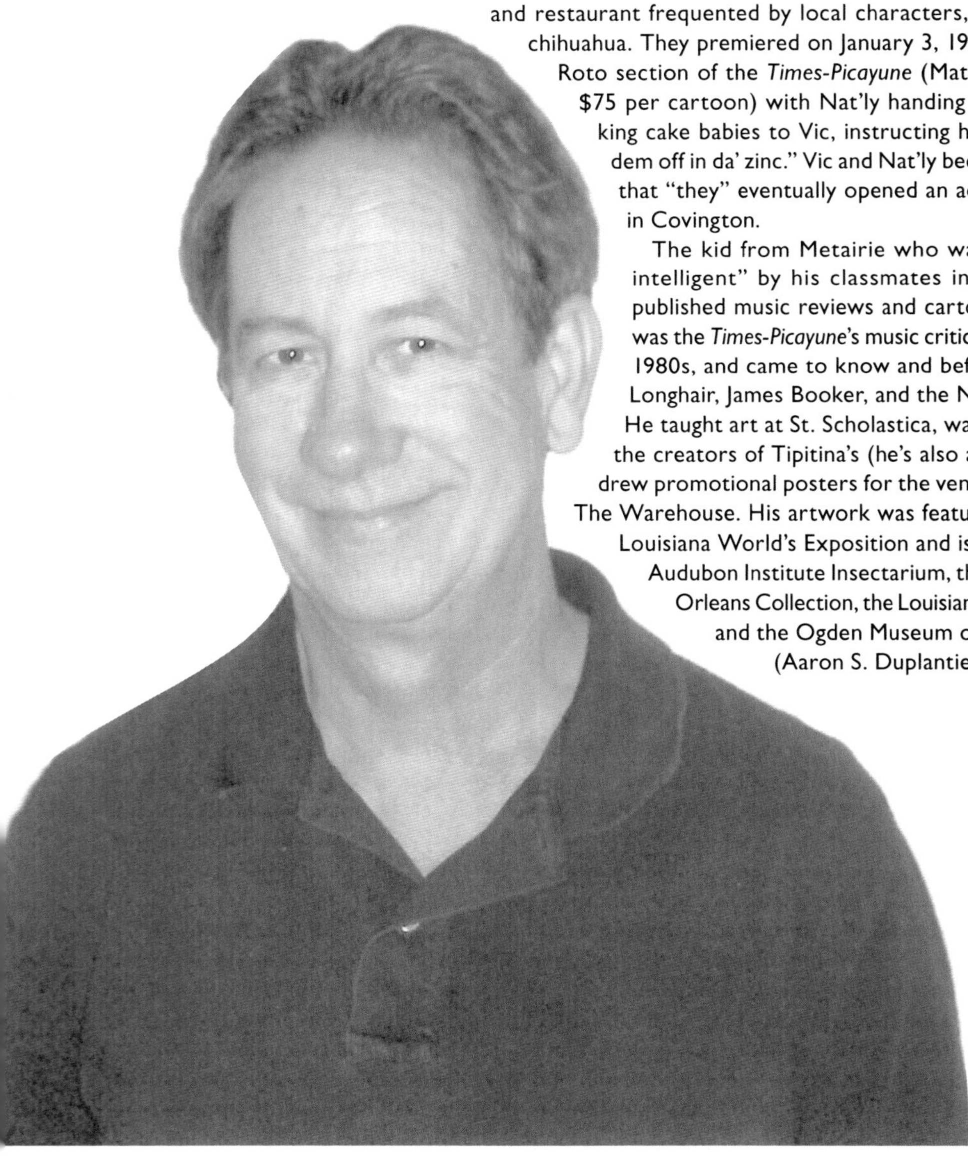

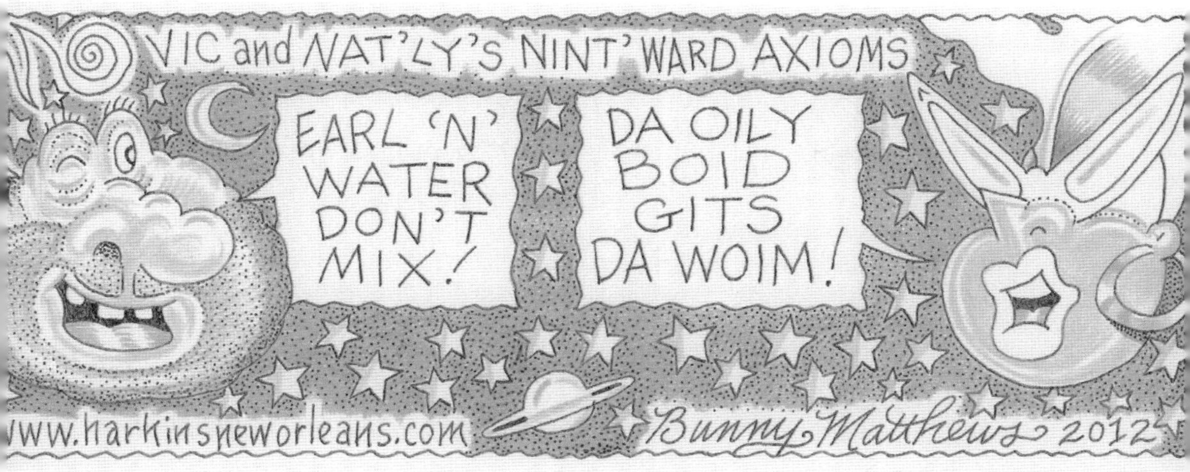

Vic and Nat'ly

Matthews has said that he modeled Vic on former mayor Victor Schiro—as regular a guy as anyone could meet. Nat'ly first appeared sloppy and obese but "became a bombshell . . . because I thought, if I have to draw this picture for the rest of my life, I want it to be attractive and good looking." They appear here in a 2012 drawing done for Harkins the Florist on Magazine Street.

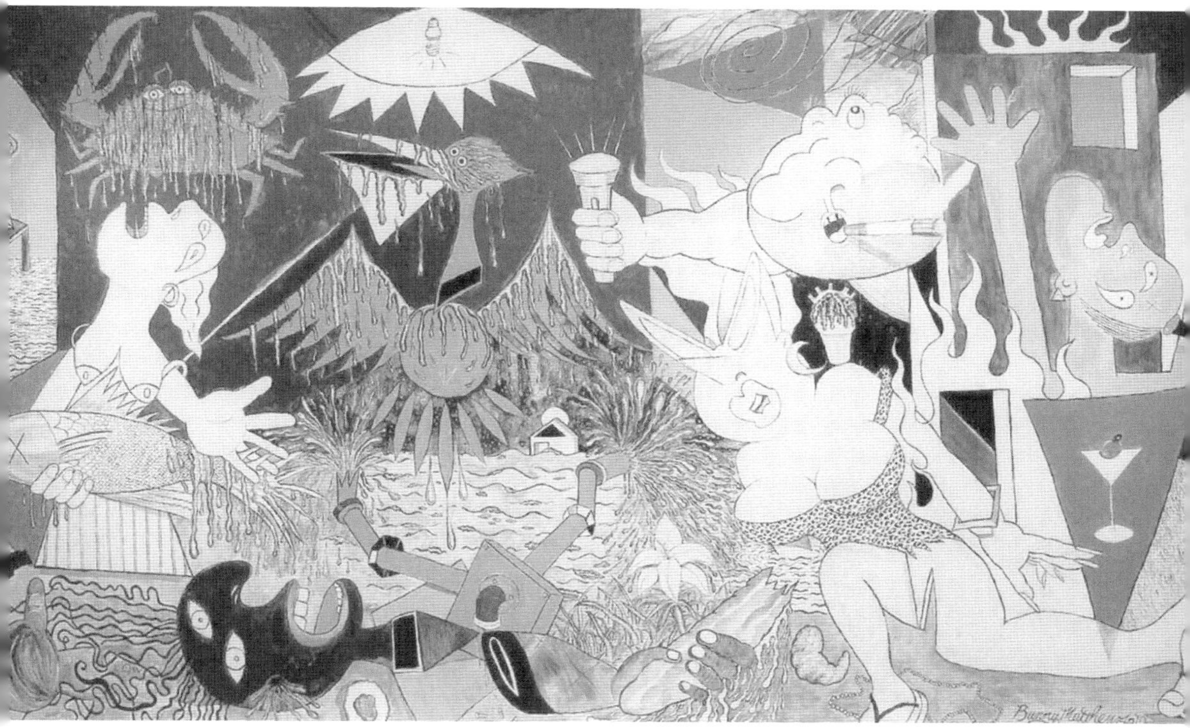

Nin't Wardica

One of Matthews's most recent works is the huge *Nin't Wardica*, modeled after Picasso's *Guernica*. It is his response to the tragedies resulting from the Deepwater Horizon oil disaster, the aftermath of Hurricane Katrina, and life in the Ninth Ward. It was featured at the Arthur Roger Gallery in the 2010 exhibit Black and White, along with other Matthews paintings and drawings (including Vic and Nat'ly).

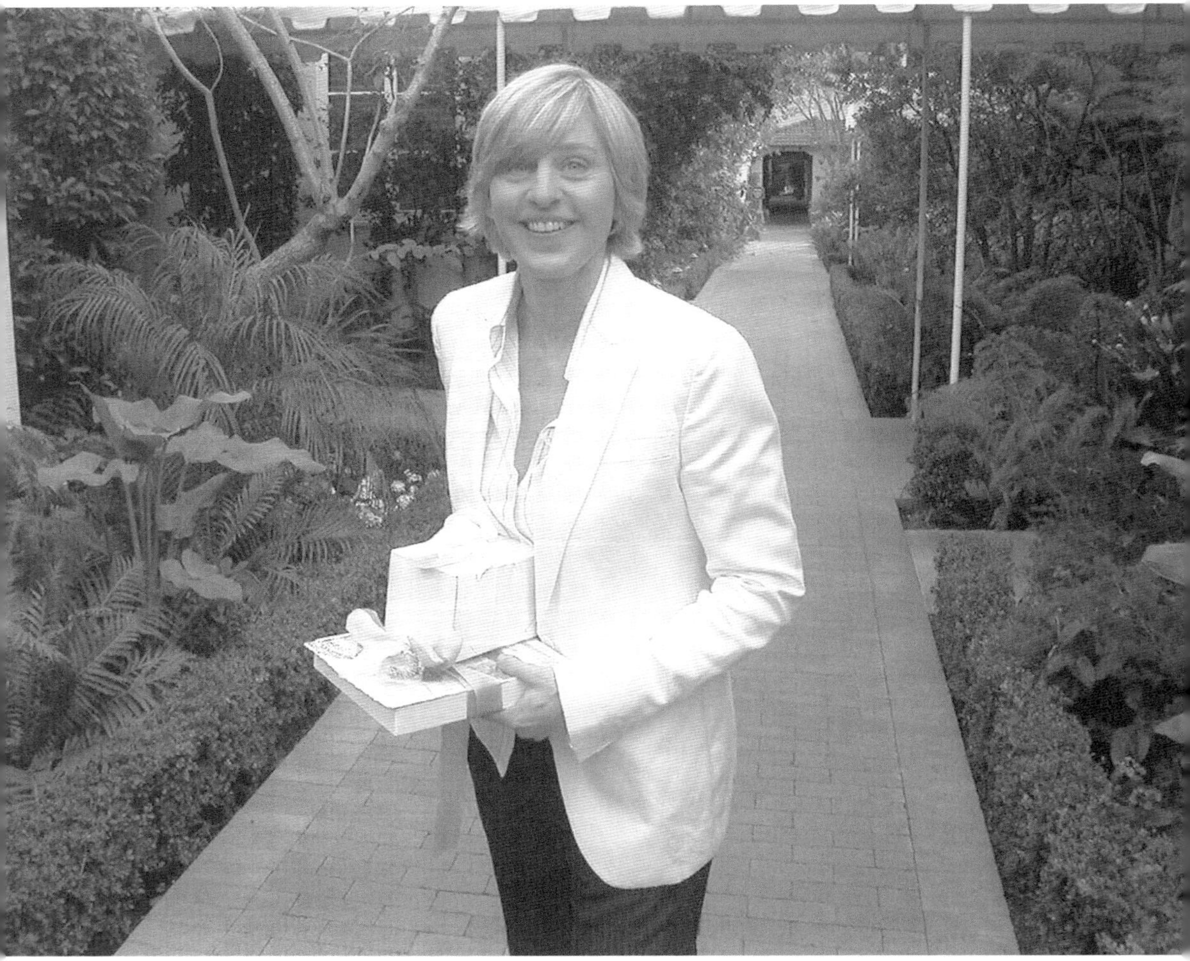

Our Ellen

Ellen's name appeared often in the local newspaper beginning in the 1980s when she was performing at local comedy clubs. When her face also appeared in a 1981 article, the 23-year-old Metairie native had been on stage for less than a year. Joan Kent wrote, "Her routines are exaggerations of real life situations . . . she comes off fresh with no four letter words." The same can be said today.

Before this article was written, Ellen had worked "79 odd jobs" including as a singer and songwriter. Her comedy writing was honed from observances of everyday people—at Walgreens, Woolworth's, and on city buses. "You can find humor in anything," she said. Degeneres reported that when performing she would choose a particular audience member: "The other night there was a woman in here just looking at me like I was the most funny person in the world. I realized maybe I could be."

Ellen Degeneres told the reporter that her ambition was to go to California and make a career of comedy. That she certainly did, and so much more. (Alan Light.)

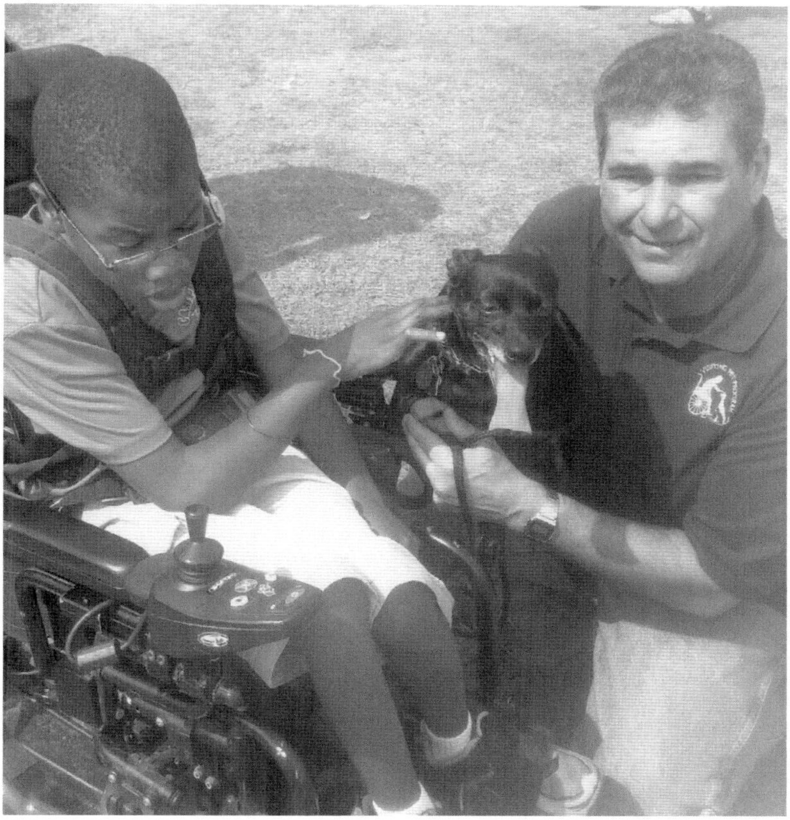

Nathan Burise, Mike Azzarello, and Olive Oyl the Therapy Dog
Olive's long tongue was made for happily licking those she encounters. She is pictured here with Nathan Burise at LSU Medical School's Camp Tiger summer program. Her owner, Mike Azzarello, is one of over 100 volunteer handlers who dedicate their time to bringing their pets to visit more than 20 area nursing homes, hospitals, rehabilitation facilities, and special facilities for children as members of the Visiting Pet Program. Created in 1987, this nonprofit organization is the only animal assistance/therapy program in the greater New Orleans area. Animal therapists include mixed and purebred dogs, cats, guinea pigs, and rabbits. Facilities visited in Metairie include St. Anthony's Nursing Home, Colonial Oaks Living Center, and East Jefferson General Hospital.

Visiting Pet Program dogs also visit the East Jefferson Regional Library as buddies to children who may be at risk of academic failure. The Reading for Rover component of the program helps children practice their oral reading skills in the company of gentle therapy pets in a relaxed, nonjudgmental, and comfortable atmosphere. Because docile dogs are so much less intimidating to most kids than adults, the program has been very successful.

Roxanne Varnelle, an LSU Medical School student, not only snapped this photograph but accompanied Nathan throughout the free, weeklong program designed for special-needs children. LSU's medical students raise over $100,000 each year to fund the camp, which features visits to local attractions throughout the New Orleans area, including the Audubon Zoo, Aquarium of the Americas, Children's Museum, the Global Wildlife Center, UNO's Saints experience, Adventure Quest Laser Tag, City Park's Storyland, and the outdoor carnival and banquet at Jesuit High, where this photograph was taken.

The community is blessed with these and so many others, pets and humans alike, who spend their time "Bringing Love and Leaving Smiles" (the motto of the Visiting Pet Program). They enhance the quality of other lives, and their own, by volunteering in countless ways in service to the community. (Roxanne Varnelle.)

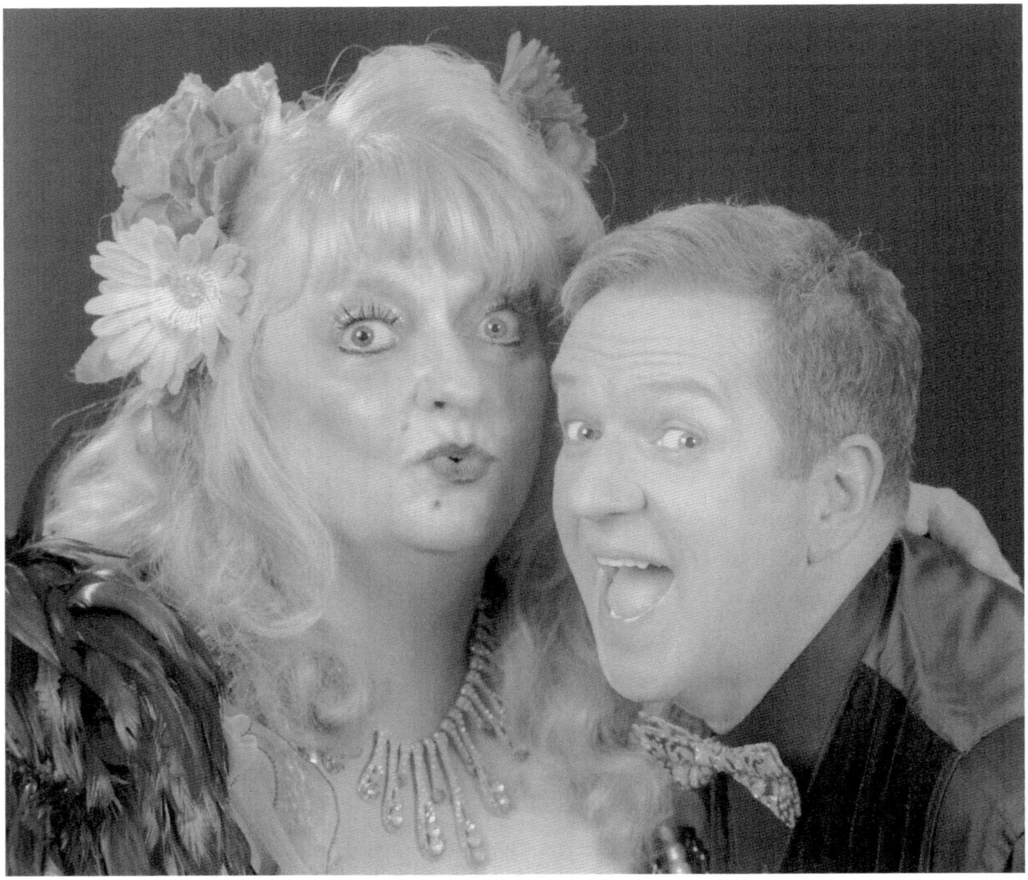

Becky Allen

Rebecca (Becky) Butzman grew up in Metairie Heights. From the time she could walk, she loved performing. At age five, she earned a second-place trophy as a junior baton twirler in a contest sponsored by NORD. At seven, Becky performed at Stage Night of the Children of Confederacy's state convention at the NOPSI Auditorium. She learned to play the trumpet and piano and took singing and modeling lessons. She was taught dance by Tony Bevinetto, performed at his nightclub at age 14, and performed on *C.C. Courtney Singing Set* on WWL TV. At 17, she was the second runner-up for the beauty title in the NOAC annual contest and a contestant in the Junior Miss New Orleans pageant at Pontchartrain Beach. She was lovely, statuesque (at five feet, nine inches) blond, and beautiful.

The daughter of Myrtis (a lively lady who died at age 97 at Harrah's Casino) and Jonas Butzman (a pitcher for the New Orleans Pelicans) captured the hearts of locals with her performances in *Where the Girls Where*, *And the Ball and All*, *New Orleans Ladies*, and many more plays. She captured their ears in the early 1980s along with Shirl Cieutat (who is from Pennsylvania) as the voices of "Rosemary" and "Anna Mae" who made Time Saver po-boys in local television commercials. Most people loved the "Yat" accents, but for those who did not, Allen said, "People who hate the commercials hate their heritage. They resent themselves." And she was quick to point out that "people in Metairie talk like that, too."

Pictured here are "Ricky Graham & Becky Allen, Together Again!" which is the title of the show they performed at Mid City Theater in 2012. Graham, a local native, playwright, and actor, and Allen have performed together often through the years and Graham has written many plays especially for her. A local columnist said of them, "Allen and Graham have worked together longer than many marriages have lasted." Speaking of marriage, Becky was once married "a long time ago" to the man whose name she still carries. (Mid City Theater)

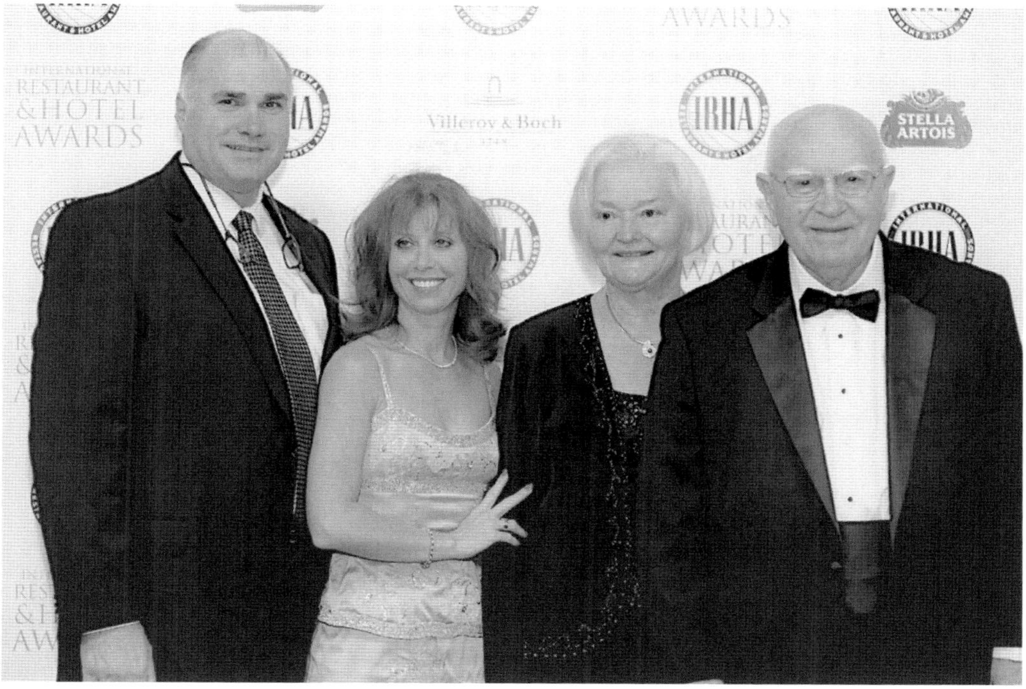

The Drago Family
Klara and Drago Cvitanovich opened their restaurant in 1969. Thirty-six years later, they opened their hearts to residents and rescue workers in the early days following Hurricane Katrina by feeding them. Tommy, Leanne, Klara, and Drago appear here as 2008 recipients of the International Restaurant and Hotel Association's Humanitarian Award for preparing, donating, and serving almost 80,000 meals. The family has been honored with many community service awards, including Tommy's cherished Times-Picayune Loving Cup. "My family and I have been blessed by the community, and we try to do the right thing by giving back," he said. (Courtesy of John Heller and Samantha Yanofsky.)

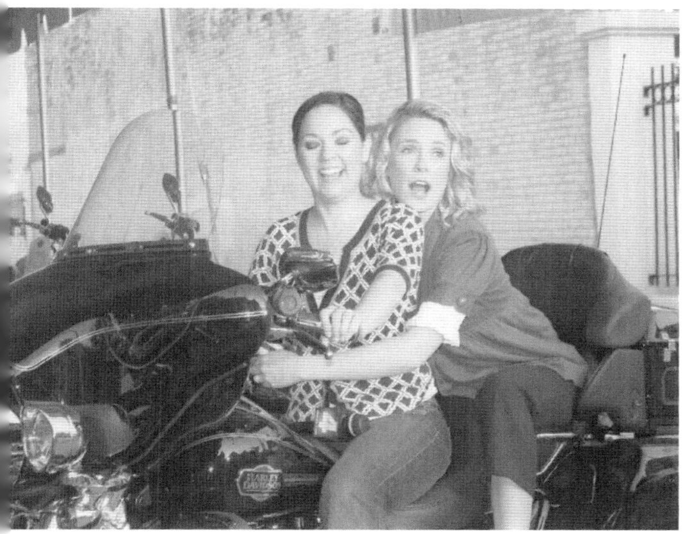

News Women
WWL television news and weather reporters Jill Hezeau (left) and Laura Buchtel clowned around at the 2010 New Orleans Bike Week rally/festival. Born and raised in Metairie, Laura joined the Channel 4 Weather Center in December 2005 and is the weekday meteorologist for the Eyewitness Morning News. Jill, a class of 1996 Chapelle graduate, joined the WWL staff in 2003 and earned, with the news team, a Peabody, Edward R. Murrow, and duPont-Columbia Award for Hurricane Katrina coverage. (bayoubikers.com.)

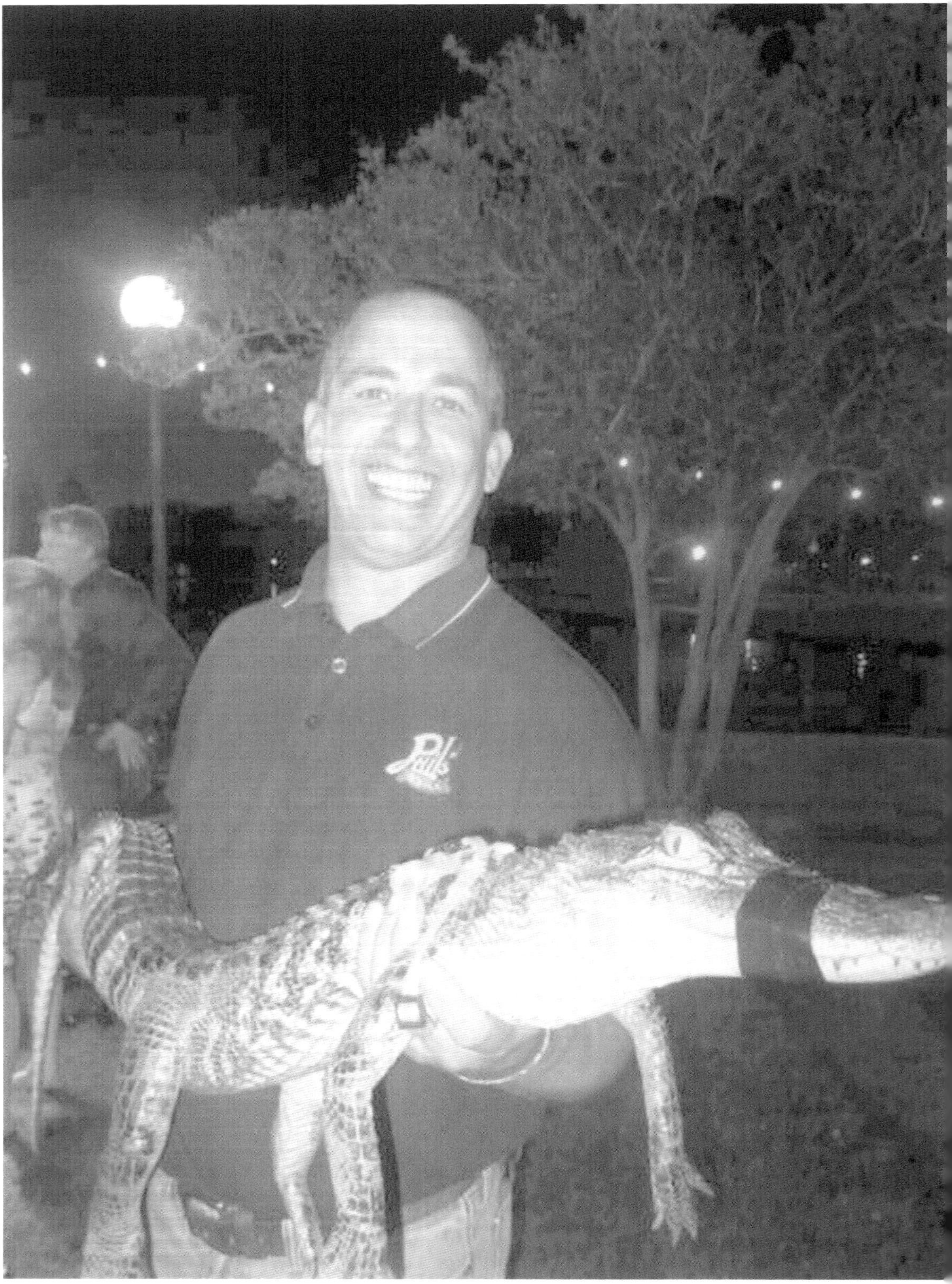

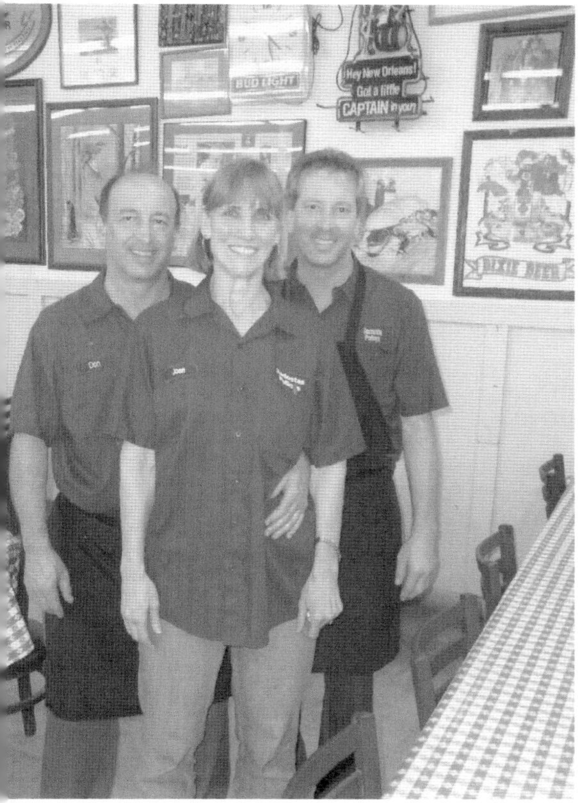

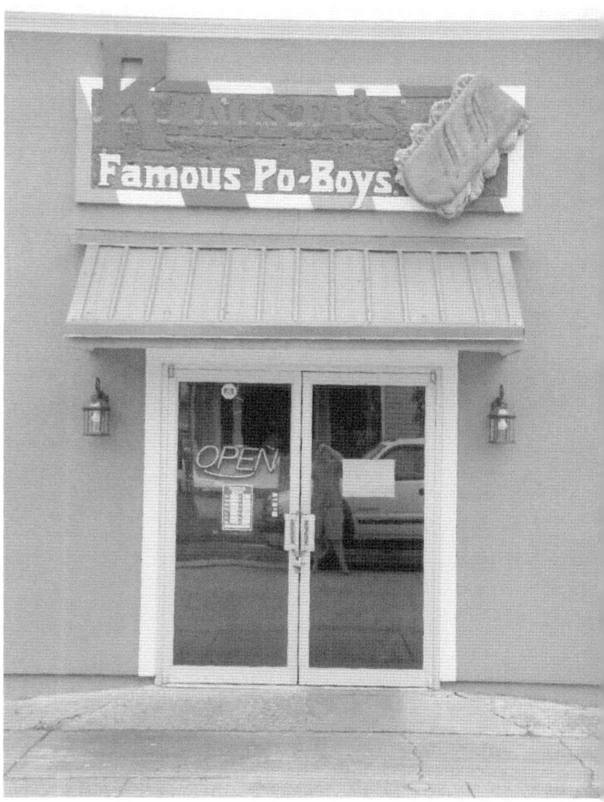

Radosta's

Don Radosta's family has been in the grocery business for four generations. Some 30 years ago, they moved to Aris Avenue and sold cold po-boys from the deli counter. Fifteen years later, they moved out most of the groceries and became a po-boy shop famous for hot roast beef. One of the few businesses opened six weeks after Katrina, they sold 100 Hubig's pies and some 200 po-boys per day—but that wasn't easy, because bread was scarce and Don drove to Denim Springs each day for ice to keep the meat fresh. Many new loyal customers were made at that time when so few other places were opened— longtime customers have always raved about Radosta's fine roast beef and homemade gravy.

Refusing offers to franchise the business, Don said, "We're fine right here." Joan added, "You really have to be devoted to it. You really have to love it." Pictured from left to right are Don, Joan, and Martin Radosta. (Beattie McNeal.)

Burgerpalooza and PHILanthropy (OPPOSITE PAGE)

Phil de Gruy offers alligator burgers at Phil's Grill. He is pictured here at his annual Burgerpalooza, which has benefited the Miracle League of Greater New Orleans each May during National Burger Month since 2008. De Gruy and his wife, Christina, have also supported the community year-round with donations to local churches, schools, and organizations in the form of gift certificates, gift baskets, sponsorships, and delicious food. They recently created PHILanthropy, which includes the Artworks program—a partnership with local artists whose works are displayed and sold, with 25 percent of the proceeds used to provide art supplies for local schools. Metairie beneficiaries of these endeavors have included Lutheran High School, East Jefferson Warrior Baseball, and the Wally Pontiff Jr. Foundation (see page 94).

In recognition of Phil and Christina's community support efforts, they have been awarded the Louisiana Restaurant Neighbor Award and were a finalist for the National Restaurant Association's Neighbor Award. (Phil's Grill.)

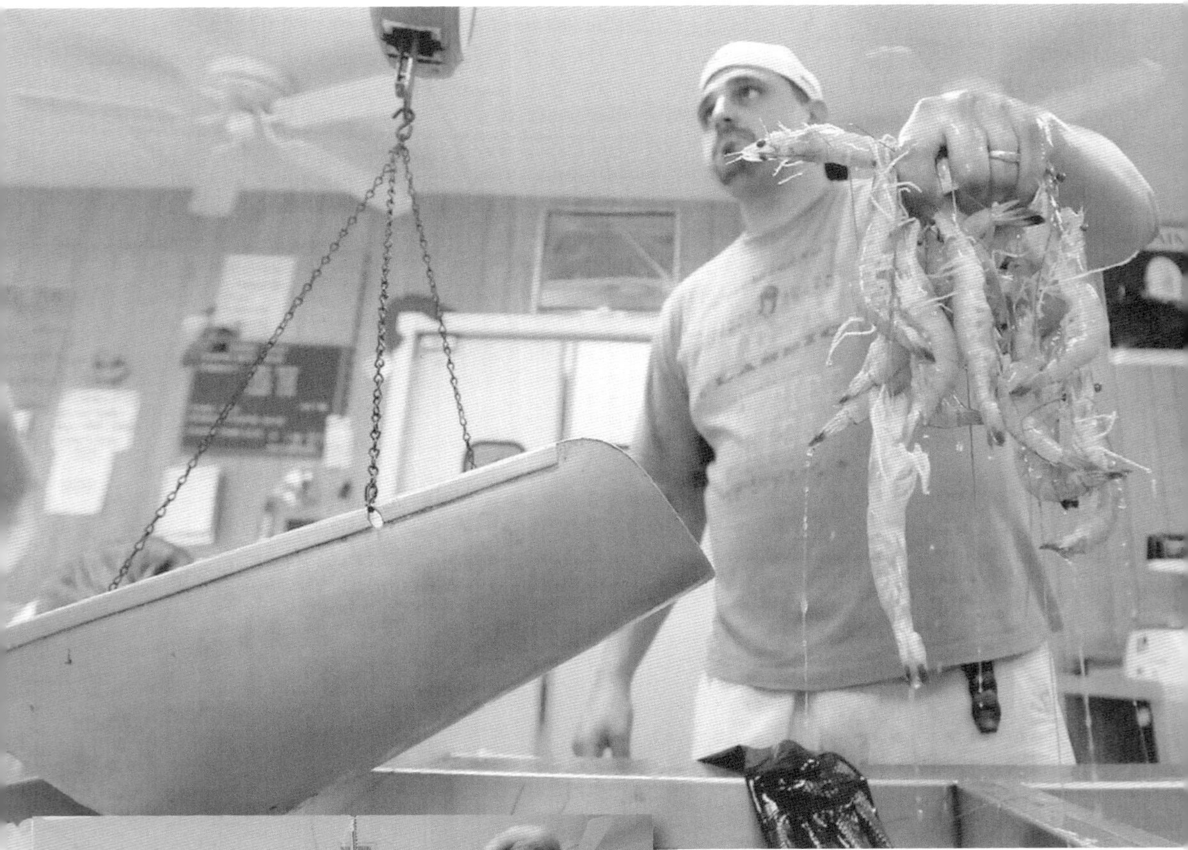

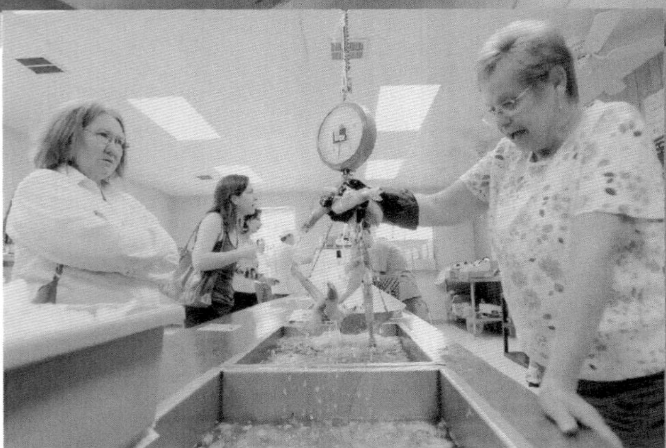

Schaefer & Rusich

"We don't mess with no imports," Merlin Schaefer told food writer Brett Anderson in 2008. True to his word, in 2010, while the Deepwater Horizon gushed oil into the gulf, he drove 10 hours a day to and from Texas to keep his business going by buying seafood there to bring back home to sell in his Bucktown market.

Merlin is a third-generation owner, namesake, and grandson of Merlin Schaefer who, in 1969, opened the shop on Lake Avenue with Johnny Rusich. The men fished, crabbed, and trawled for shrimp in Lake Pontchartain. Merlin's grandmother sold their catch. The little Bucktown business has survived storms, economic downturn, drastic changes in the neighborhood, and the oil spill, thanks to Merlin and his wife, Tracie.

Above, J.T. Thonn displays fresh shrimp to a customer. Left, Amy Lanteigne places her order of 10–12 count shrimp with Rosie Burger. (Chris Graythen.)

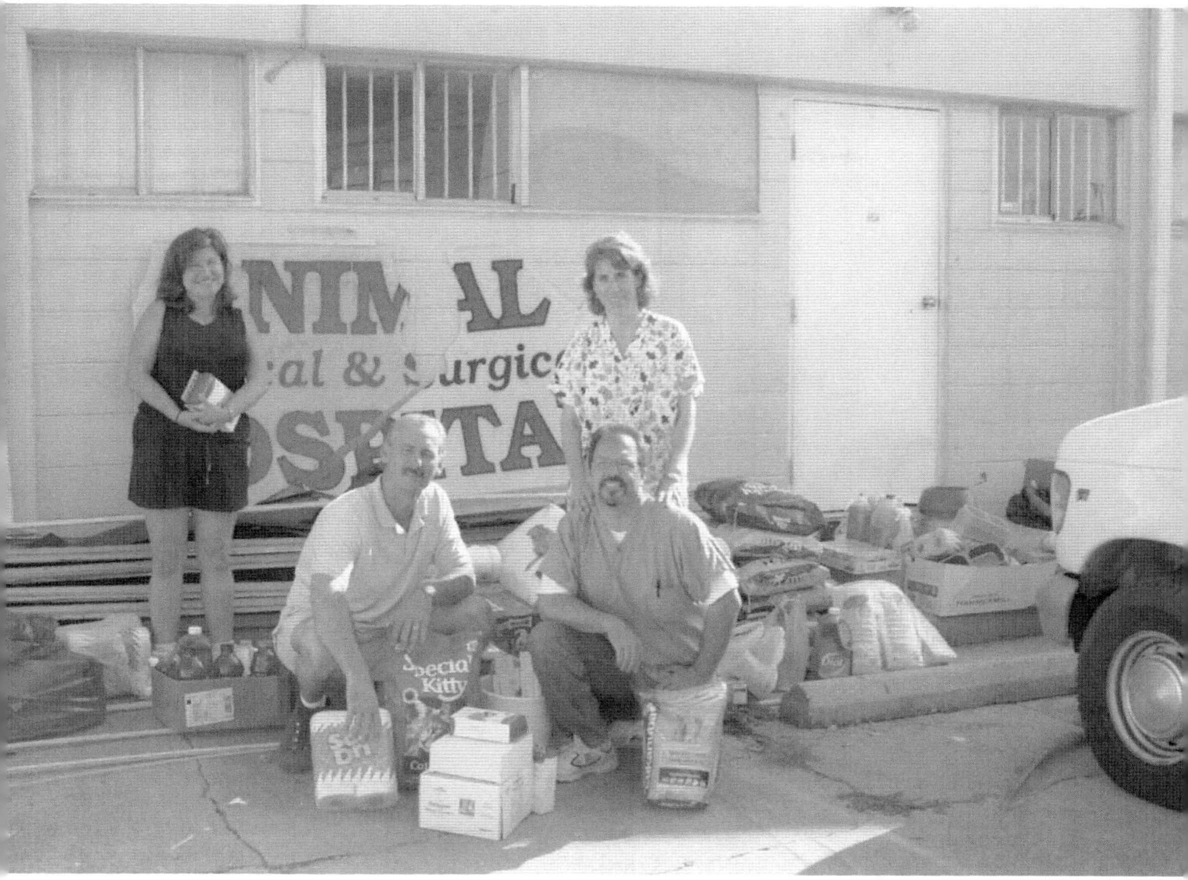

Above and Beyond

Veterinarian Patrick McSweeney was a longtime volunteer presenting weekly television segments on WDSU for the benefit of the Louisiana SPCA promotion of pet adoptions. Then Katrina came. He and his wife, Beverly, packed up their pets along with the many animals hospitalized and boarding at their Animal Medical & Surgical Hospital on Causeaway Boulevard and headed for higher, safer ground. Returning ten days later to a damaged facility (above) they began feeding and caring for other area animals who had been left behind by their owners. McSweeney's staff also took in the doctors and staff from Lakeview Veterinary Hospital, which had flooded completely, until they could repair and return to their original location. (Dr. McSweeney and Veterinary Relief Fun.)

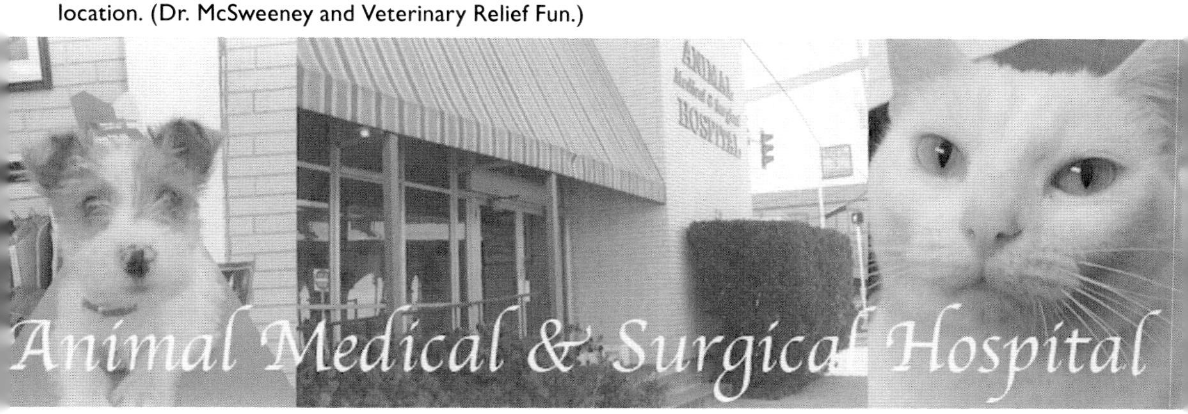

The Furniture Family

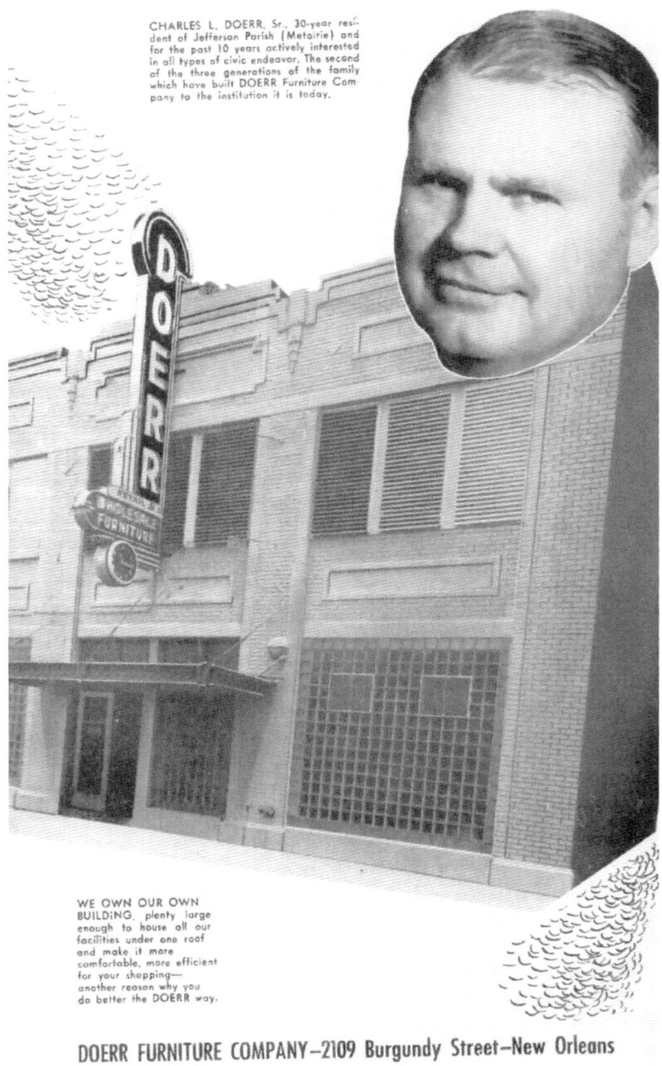

In 1932, carpenter George Michael Sturm built a cottage on Codifer Boulevard for his young daughter Elizabeth Gertrude, her husband Charles Louis Doerr, and their one-year-old daughter, Marilyn. In 1938, Charles founded Doerr Furniture at 914 Elysian Fields Avenue. He also dedicated much of his time to community efforts as founder of the Metairie Playground Association, chairman of the Metairie Youth Recreational Association (which raised the funds to light and build the football, track, and baseball fields at Metairie Playground in 1946), Community Chest chairman, director of the board of the Metairie Kiwanis Club, and president of the Lions Club of Metairie—all the while creating new business enterprises too numerous to name here, which included serving as a founding member of Metairie Bank and Trust Company (in 1947), where he served as chairman of the board as well as bank president and president of the Metairie Business Men's Association. He died at age 81 in 1990.

His daughter Marilyn married Julian "Lloyd" Mutter in 1949, and they settled into a home a few blocks away on Bonnabel Boulevard. Here were born sons Julian, Gary, David, and Randy. The Mutters moved to the house on Codifer in 1961. Daughter Melanie was born in the house her great-grandfather built.

Lloyd, who had worked for the furniture company since he was a teenager, became president and general manager. Marilyn was an active member and officer of the Beverly Knoll Garden Club, which often met in her home to plan community outreach projects. She also served as an officer of St. Catherine of Siena's Co-Op Club and the Charity Crib Auxiliary.

Third-generation Melanie and her husband, Manuel Giglio, bought the house next door to her parents in 1989. Her brother Randy (and his wife, Karen Macaluso, who grew up across the street) became the other next-door neighbor in 2006. All five siblings have worked at Doerr Furniture. Like their father, they started working there as teenagers and became officers and managers. They also formed Bedding Plus, and some of their children continue the tradition of working in the family business. The current generation also contributes to the community, most notably after Hurricane Katrina when the Mutters stored furnishings donated from across the United States by members of the Home Furnishings Independents Association. HFIA volunteers came to town to await company trucks delivering the much-needed goods and uncrated, unwrapped, and arranged them in rooms to make newly restored homes once again habitable. (LDL.)

The Sclafani Family

In a condescending summation of Metairie diners, a local food critic wrote, "The most famous dish at Sclafani's, though, was its stuffed shrimp hollandaise. Everybody ordered it. By the time I got there, however, something funny had happened. They decided that they'd make large batches of hollandaise in advance, refrigerate it, and scoop a ball of it on top of the hot shrimp when served. It would then melt like butter over the shrimp, completely broken. I never once had a proper hollandaise on this dish. This would be considered an atrocity these days, but they got away with it in Metairie."

Had Peter "Papa" Sclafani lived to read that, he would have laughed. Restaurant Sclafani opened in 1958 in a big red-brick building that was a landmark in Metairie. Suburban families with good taste celebrated weddings, bridal showers, business and club meetings, banquets, and special nights out at his large and successful business at 1301 Causeway Boulevard that employed 150 people and could seat 500 guests. Papa's sons Frank and Peter Jr. learned the trade there under their father's guidance.

Frank (pictured below with his father) became executive chef after Papa's death. Peter Jr. struck out on his own at Hayne Boulevard, where he owned and operated Sclafani's Restaurant and catering hall. After Restaurant Sclafani closed in 1985, Frank opened Sclafani Cooking School on Gennaro Place in Old Metairie, where he mentors future chefs.

Third-generation restaurateur Peter III, with former LSU linebacker Ruffin Rodrigue and T.J. Moran, opened Ruffino's in Baton Rouge in 1998. His dad helps out in many ways. In 2011, he was named Restaurateur of the Year by the Greater Baton Rouge Chapter of the Louisiana Restaurant Association. And so, the legacy of the landmark restaurant in Metairie continues. (Frank Sclafani.)

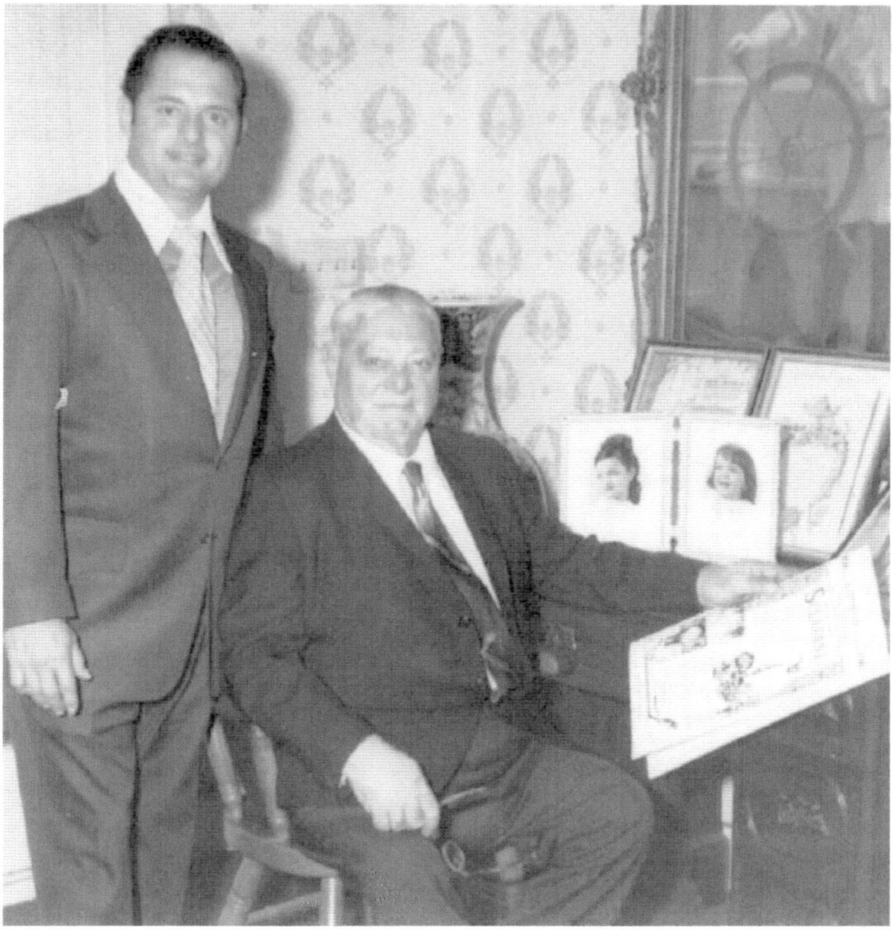

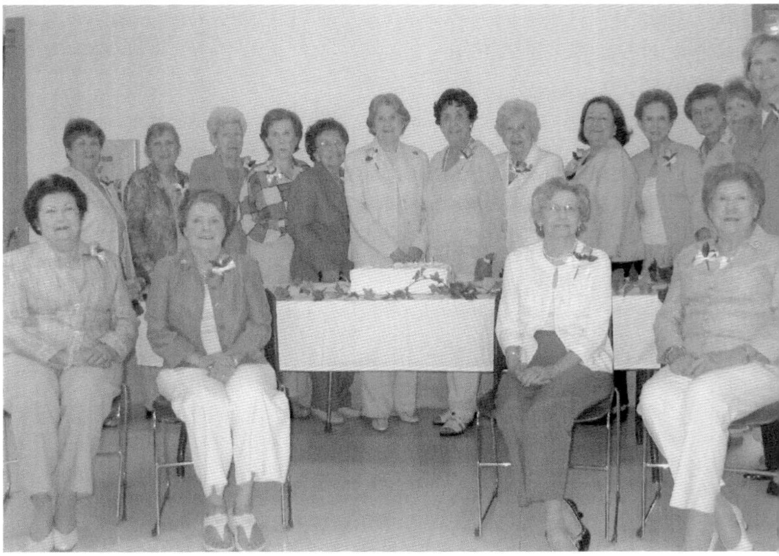

Metairie Woman's Club
In 1938, five women met in Irma Shepherd's home to discuss the need for a public library. From this cause sprung the Metairie Woman's Club, which has since supported levee improvements, a school for deaf children (Hilda Knoff was a member), and improvements at parks, playgrounds, and more. Pictured are the past presidents in 2010 during the club's 71st anniversary. (Courtesy of Metairie Woman's Club.)

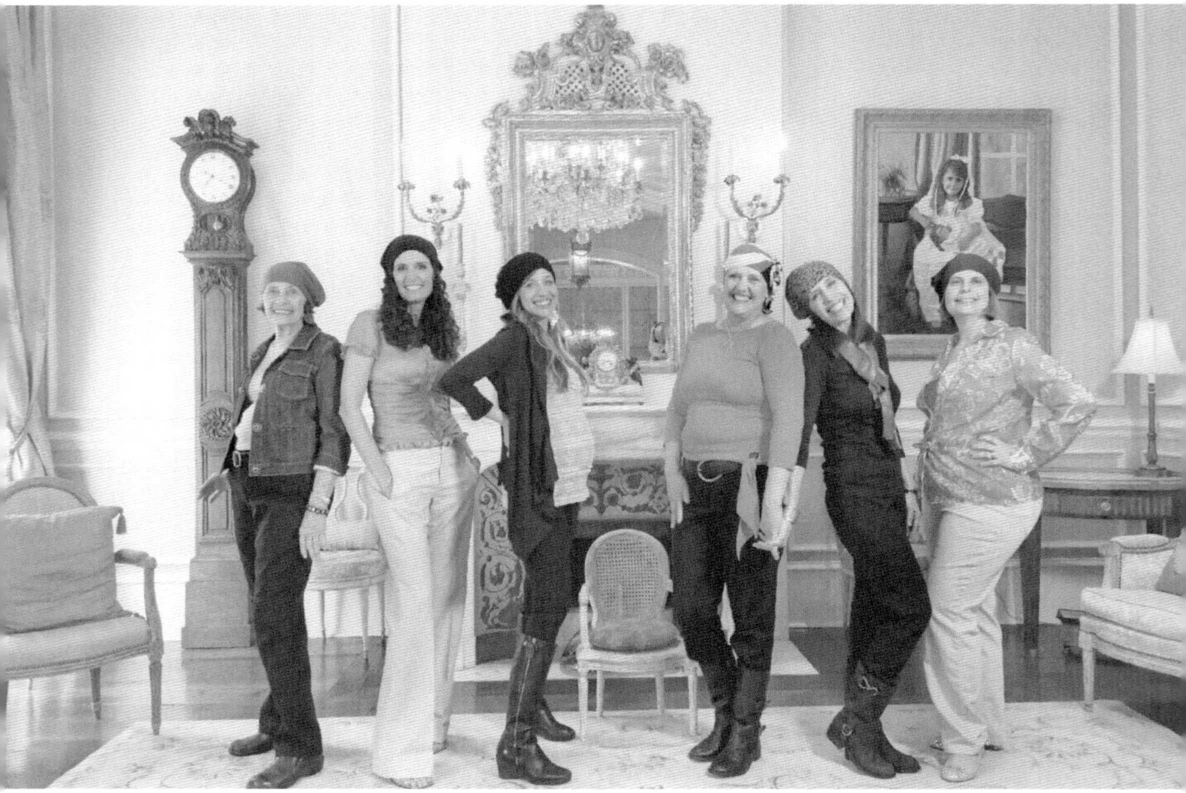

Chemo Beanies
A group of sisters came together in 2010 to support one of their own who was diagnosed with stage III breast cancer. Pictured left to right are Fournier family mother, daughters, and granddaughter Pat, Angelle, Adrienne, Danielle, Rochelle, and Michelle. Catholic schoolgirls once wore beanies, so it seemed natural that the St. Lawrence and Chapelle alumnae sisters would call their creation Chemo Beanies—stylish, comfortable headwear for chemotherapy patients. (Courtesy of Chemo Beanies.)

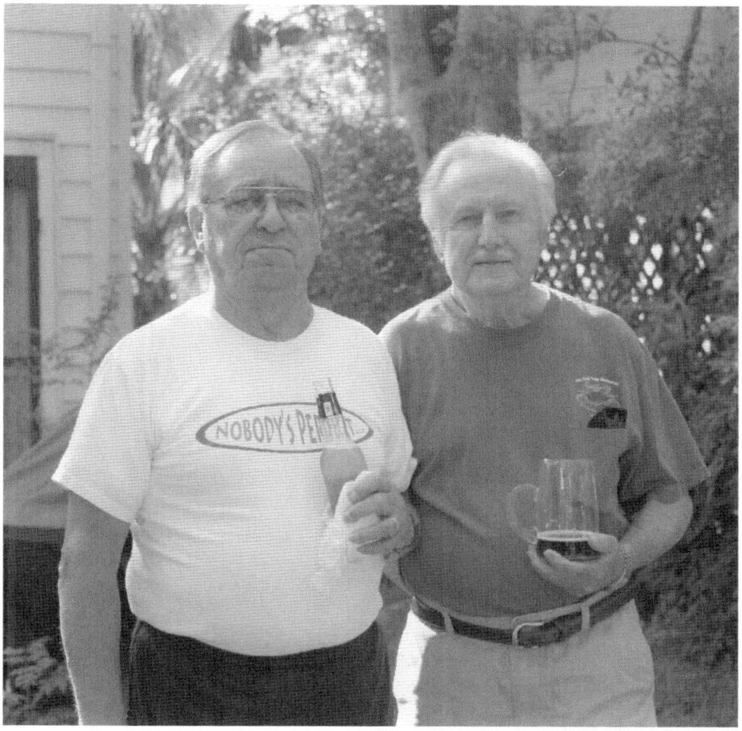

Silk and Satin

More than a half century ago, two men formed what would become a four-generation bond that remains strong today. Eddie Krass (left) and Vince Campanella epitomize the generation who, with their wives, moved their young families to Metairie when it was a bedroom community of New Orleans during the 1950s. "White Flight" had nothing to do with it. The suburbs offered affordable new homes on large lots with nearby schools and a built-in sense of community. Just about everyone who moved to Metairie then found friends or schoolmates from their old city neighborhoods living a few doors or a few blocks away.

True to form, their wives, Shirley Oubre and Meredith Knower, had known each other at "Third and Prytania" (the local lexicon for Redemptorist Girls High School, located at that uptown intersection). Vince was from downtown, and Eddie grew up in St. Roch. Shirley had lived in the St. Thomas housing project. Meredith spent much of her childhood in Carrollton. But, like so many other Metairie residents, their disconnected connections and common interests led to lifelong friendships.

They bowled in leagues at Paradise and Kenner Lanes. They joined the civic association (but were never bestowed Garden of the Month awards). They bought low-cost stock in the very modest Westgate Country Club so that their children could swim with neighborhood friends. They were active in support of their parish church and school, most notably for the annual fairs where they worked tirelessly for many years along with other families, including the Assenheimers, Ballases, Barbaras, Bensels, Brunes, Colemans, Connells, Dalimores, Davises, Delaunes, Eastmans, Hochhalters, Kennedys, Kropers, Lorias, Maras, Maronges, Mashons, McCarthys, McCoys, Meyns, Poches, Sauves, Stevens, Theriots, and Wiltzes.

The Krass and Campanella families celebrated births and mourned the losses of loved ones together. Along the way Vince and Eddie picked up the nicknames "Silk and Satin." Neighborhood friend Gary McCarthy first started calling Vince "Kid Silk" in the 1970s, and it was inevitable that Eddie would be known as "Satin." They may no longer be smooth operators, but they are beloved. Unsettled by Hurricane Katrina but settled into retirement, they have grandchildren and great-grandchildren nearby. And if you asked them now if they had a chance, way back when, to change their decision to move to Metairie, you know what their answers would be. (Julie Krass Kroper.)

INDEX